THE THIRD SHIFT

LaShana Spann & McKinley Horton

Publisher: PIAOTT Publishing LLC. Chicago, IL
The Third Shift
La Shana Spann and McKinley Horton Jr.
Printed in the United States of America
© 2013 All Rights Reserved by Shamack LLC.
ISBN: 978-0-692-73616-6

PIAOTT
PUBLISHING
A Limited Liability Company

TABLE OF CONTENTS

PREFACE

The Third Shift came about from a vision of God. Some would call it an epiphany.

La Shana Spann and McKinley Horton were going through dramatic times in their lives as we all do. While in North Carolina, something came to McKinley Horton like a vision, as La Shana was discussing her life and it's past. We all have one. God is talking to us all the time, but if we don't listen, we will miss it like the ESPN play of the week. McKinley was tuning in to God's air waves and said, La Shana we should do a book about your life and call it The Third Shift. The rest is history. La Shana Spann's life represents some of us all, whether good or bad, it's just that simple. The goal to life is to live it with faith, hope and power to never give up. The motivation of The Third Shift is to change lives starting with you. Pain can sometimes carry us like a marriage that is forever and propose on bended knee that it is okay to accept and understand. Sometimes, there is not a chance in finding a way of lifting pressure from the circumstances that we all go through.

La Shana Spann had been a victim of bad breaks. No way out exits are hard to take in this thing call life; instead she believes that it is our purpose to serve others as a vessel in honoring God. The Third Shift shows a path through life's journey of ups and downs and tight squeezes that we encounter every day. The Third Shift shows how life took La Shana Spann through tremendous pitfalls and broken dreams, which can be brutal, and lead her to new opportunities of love coming from the right places. The Third Shift shows the ability to merge through pain, sweat and tears with faith and hope being the reason to live, love and be happy. Everyone has a Third Shift in them, you may not recognize it. In understanding you, it can be the greatest love of all.

FIRST SHIFT

Mom & Dad

Don't worry because I am with you. Don't be afraid, because I am your God. I will make you strong and will help you; I will support you with the right hand of my righteousness. I am the Lord your God, who holds your right hand, tells you, "Don't be afraid. I will help you."

Isaiah 41:10,13

CHAPTER 1

Mom and Dad

I can't believe what I'm hearing while sitting here on Walnut Street. You know on a normal, clear day, just one of your old-fashioned summer times. My mother's name is Teresa Smiles. I go by the nickname "Scooty".

"Mom, where are you?" Was all we ever asked. I said, "Mom must have had a third schedule this week."

"Nah. Scooty she don't have no job!" My sister Heidi answered.

Of course, simply wanting to believe the things that were good, not things that weren't, Heidi went on and on about how my parents were truly messed up. As we called it, damaged goods.

"Don't talk about my mom like that!" I'd shout back.

Remembering that she was her mother too. Truth was, Teresa couldn't blame anyone else besides herself for the mistakes that she made in our lives. Her not being there erased the most important moments for us. Growing up in a natural environment. Nurturing us as young ladies.

One warm summer night down in the dirty, Teresa met Junior in South Carolina at one of them juke joints. He called her "a warm southern breeze". Junior later said that he saw something in her eyes. It was just how she smiled at him. Grandmother Amena gave me the 411 about them and what things were like when I was just a baby.

My mom and dad's marriage was a flop. They married for whatever reason and parted on some dumb shit. The whole thing only left me dangling. Maybe that's what truly helped build me to be as strong as I am today. It was God I know because they were both a mess.

As I heard, my father truly loved my mother. In the south back then it was all about racism, and it was enough to discourage any black, strong soul. But still, two people can get together with not a dime in their pockets, get married, and create a baby. My parents' relationship took a toll on me. To be perfectly honest, my father was whipped. Mom whipped him into a marriage proposal. My father had it bad, he was hooked! Wherever she went—he went, and I mean he followed. I have heard some men say punany is a drug most brothers, especially African American men, love to be intimate with. Particularly if it is an apple bottom. Teresa had just that. The only problem was that she wanted to sell it, so I hear!

What? Why is that? As Junior mentioned a few times, I just find it hard to believe because it's my mother. Junior said why when he supposedly caught my mother tricking on the block doing her thang. He claimed he had to look for her one evening. There was this guy named Dan, a real cool, old-head, who was always hanging around the way. You know one of those wanna-be-pimps who pick a small city to project his pimpology. You know the type looking for prey anywhere he could find some and don't you know, it was my crazy ass mom who fit the bill. Perfect prey for a town like Reading.

All that meant nothing to me, but I guess to my father it meant a disaster for his marriage. The first thing he asked, "T where is Scooty, and why aren't you watching her?"

Of course, my mother gave him some excuse. She was good at that. Another day Teresa approached Junior.

"Junior, I need some money!"

"What do you need it for?" Handing over a couple of dollars.

When she returned from the mall she dropped a few bags on her bed. "T try it on, you and I both know the truth."

Walking out of the bathroom he said, "You look like a damn hoochie. Teresa wasted no time in walking off into her very own spa-like retreat in the backyard. When Teresa decided that she had relieved some stress, she walked in the back door and discovered Junior and the kids all lying down asleep.

Teresa called one of her long-time girlfriends, Rose to pick her up. She quickly gathered some things, throwing everything into a bag. Rose arrived and they left for Rose's house. Teresa showered there, and they hit the streets once again.

"Rose I gotta make at least two stacks by tonight!"

"Why, what do you have to pay off?"

"Girlfriend I just need it!"

"Yeah okay, you need a'ight!"

Hours had passed and Junior awoke. He noticed that Teresa was gone and clothes were all over the place, so he knew what was up. It was three-thirty in the damn morning and Junior said, "What the hell is wrong with this woman?"

It was the first time she had done this. He saw a pair of panties lying by the door, knew that she had been home, and left out again. So, Junior did what he thought he would never have to do, he left Heidi and Scooty home alone just so he could go looking for his wife and bring her butt home from the damn streets. Junior was gone for about an hour and all he could think about was the kids.

"What if Scooty wakes up? Will Heidi hear her if she cries? Will she know what do for her?" Junior wondered aloud.

He was feeling guilty and worried, so he headed back toward the house. He never agreed with his wife's behavior. He could never seem to figure out why the streets were more important than her family to her. He knew something else would show up, it was only a matter of time. Junior was on his way home. He was tired as hell, funky and dirty from doing a sixteen-hour shift. As he pulled up, he saw Teresa getting out of a strange man's car. She did not realize that he was watching her the entire time. While Teresa was getting out of the car, the man kissed her on the cheek. She sat back down for a few minutes longer and they began talking. She kissed the strange man, and they laughed.

Junior waited. Teresa walked into the house, hit the kitchen up, and then headed to her room. Junior walked in right behind her. Teresa heard him and the feeling of guilt quickly enveloped her. She laid across her bed as if sleeping. The light came on and Junior paused.

"Teresa, you're not asleep. I just witnessed your little rendezvous outside."

Teresa glanced over at him. She was startled. Her eyes were already huge and now they appeared to be even bigger. Nervous, she said, "Oh that was just somebody giving me a ride." Teresa suddenly stopped talking because she knew she was caught in her own act. Junior said, "T, why don't you just come clean?"

Teresa hesitated. She didn't know what to say. Junior sat there looking and waiting for her to respond. Again, he asked, "T, so where have you been and what the hell are you wearing? Matter of fact… Who is this guy anyway, what's his name?"

Junior was clearly upset, his voice getting louder and he said, "I'm talking to you, Teresa!" But she refused to look at him because she was ashamed that her husband had witnessed it all. As Teresa sat on the floor she began to take the goods out of her purse. Junior began charming her to get an answer.

"Talk to me, baby!"

She met him halfway by standing up and stretching her arms out trying to hug him back. She knew the game of manipulation and went right along with it. Teresa immediately changed the subject, picked up a few outfits, and handed them over to her husband.

"Here baby, I got you a little something."

"This ain't gonna cut it! Teresa, tell me who the dude was outside?"

In the lowest voice that she could find Teresa said, "Junior, it was Mike. He's just someone I met a week ago."

"A week ago, huh?" His voice was getting loud again. "A week ago? Where at?"

"In the bar. That night Irene and I were with Rose."

"So, this is what you're out there doing while you're running the damn streets with them, huh?

"Go ahead and say it, you say it any other time, them hoochies. I'm a good one!"

"T, this has gotta stop, unless you're proud of what you're doing?"

"You're damn right I am! I gotta go get it some kind of way, especially now since I have a felony charge on my back."

"You have two beautiful daughters who need you here with them."

"Teresa you're their mother!"

"Yeah, I think I know that Junior."

"Do you hear me?"

"Yeah!"

"They need you! Think about your two beautiful daughters for a minute and ask yourself, how much do they really mean to you?"

Junior began yelling extremely loud. Then both started shouting back and forth.

"That's all I ever wanted to do was provide for my children. I took chances being out there, boosting day in and day out just to survive. I ended up getting caught having to go to jail for four months and of course, losing my job. All I really know how to do is boost! Yes, it obviously turned into a bad habit of mine, and now I'm faced with possibly having to do jail time again."

"I don't feel sorry for you at all Teresa. No, I don't because you, you, you hang out all night in them bars then decide to bring 'em into our, home," Junior said and paused with a disgruntled look on his face. "What do you mean them, it only happened once? That's all it takes is once Teresa! Ugh… What the hell is wrong with these women today? What are you thinking about sex? Are you saying our sex life isn't good anymore, that you have to go to a bar looking for it? Teresa is that all that really matters to you is sex?" Junior paused before continuing. "Whatever happened to you taking your ass back to school and getting your education? You know, like getting your diploma like you've been saying for the last couple of years. You dropped out in the tenth grade. Art and Eugene have been on your ass for the longest trying to get you to straighten your life out for the better. When are you finally going to grow up? You're a grown woman now with kids. Act like it! It's time to stand up for yourself!"

The expression on Junior's face was an indication that he had been dealing with a lot of stress. Teresa got started and didn't want to stop.

"I'm taking the kids over to my parents!"

"Instead of you always dropping the kids off, now that you're not working Junior, start spending some time with our kids!"

Suddenly Teresa got louder and her voice awakened the baby, who was only two months old.

"I'll make a bottle!"

Junior went to check on his Scoota-Boot, that's what he called me. As Teresa walked down the hallway she heard Junior softly singing. Junior gave the baby to Teresa and as she sat rocking me to sleep, Heidi awakened and asked Junior for something to drink.

"Why are you and mommy screaming? I can't sleep," Heidi said.

"Heidi do you like when mommy's home with you?" Junior asked.

"Yes!" Heidi answered.

"Well, that's what me and mommy are trying to discuss, we just got a little too loud. I'm sorry we woke you, kiss-kiss," Junior said in a soft tone.

Time passed gradually, and Teresa began to change. She started to stay home with the kids more. Whenever her girlfriend called, she would give her all kinds of excuses. Resse now began to wonder what was going on with the new personality change all of a sudden. One evening she decided to drop by unexpected. She rang the doorbell, and Junior answered.

"Hello Resse, how are you? Come on in," he said. "Looks like you and T enjoy wearing them tight, short-ass skirts."

Teresa said, "Junior don't even start, please."

"If you girls had any integrity about yourselves, you wouldn't be wearing that nasty looking stuff in public anyway. You both need a reality check, go get some damn education and stop letting sex define who you really are!" Junior said, walking off.

"Hey girl," Resse greeted.

"What's up, Resse?"

"Girl your man is tripping."

"Don't even go there. He's stressed! He can't help it!"

Junior was on his way upstairs to the bedroom and turned right back around. He said, "Whatever happened to the black women of today? I can remember when the women back in the day wore their own hair and stayed home being real housewives. Not out there running the damn streets with their girlfriends. It's so typical for an African-American woman to make a face whenever she's upset."

"What?" Resse said, cutting him off. "I don't sell it, sweetie. I dance in Philly at Oasis strip club every weekend, and I make a living doing it. Crazy loot, baby!" Resse said, nodding her head.

Teresa nodded at Resse and said, "Too-much-damn-info girl."

"Huh? No, let her finish!" Junior said. But Teresa nodded again, signaling for Resse to say nothing else.

"So, tell me Resse, what does T enjoy doing while you two are running them streets?" Junior asked.

"You will have to ask her, don't get me involved in that?" Resse answered him. Then she addressed Teresa. "Teresa, can I get a quick minute with you in private?"

"Let's go upstairs so we can have some privacy."

They began to walk and Resse lowered her voice and said, "Damn girl, what's been going on with you? I know you been avoiding me. Are you okay?"

"Yeah, I'm just chillin for a while, Resse. I have a family, and all I been doing is hanging out every weekend. Junior's been trailing me because I've been leaving him with the kids, too much!"

"He's the man of the house. Hmm, let him tell it!"

"He's been putting in long hours whereas I'm never home."

"Yeah, we're not as young as we use to be anymore, especially how we be running all the time. You have a lot of responsibilities, plus you're married. Damn, what were you thinking?"

"Resse, why are you saying anything when you have five kids with none of their dad's around?"

"But they're being well taken care of whether I'm there or not. They have bank accounts. Excuse me, that is what matters. I'm not out here grinding for nothing. It's about them damn kids having college tuitions, a damn future!" Resse said as they hugged! "Don't be a stranger, keep in touch."

Junior was plotting, trying to get Resse out of the house. So, he called Teresa because Heidi was up and spilled juice all over the floor. Both women came downstairs onto the patio. They saw Junior and wondered why he looked pissed off.

"Listen, Heidi spilled juice everywhere!" he announced.

"Damn, then clean it up then!" Teresa said.

"Goodnight Heidi," Resse said as she came out the kitchen. Resse bent down, planted a kiss on Heidi's forehead and said, "Goodnight baby. Don't let the bedbugs bite."

"I won't! Bye, Ms. Resse."

Junior could barely wait until Resse closed the door before starting. He said, "What the hell? T, you better say something. So, you have fun when you're out there doing what?"

"Can we please talk about this tomorrow?" Teresa asked before heading toward the steps. Then they all turned in for the night.

When you and your man have had the most heated arguments, the nightcap was good. There were plenty of "ooh's" and "ahh's" coming into play quick, and damn near for half the night. The next morning, they were cool only because they relieved a little stress.

Teresa was trying to make an effort in taking care of the family again. She had no choice. For the rest of the week, things were cool. It was now Sunday, Teresa decided to make a big dinner for the family, and surprisingly they ate early. Later that evening, Junior said, "Let's take the kids to your parents. They haven't seen them in a while."

"Cool," Teresa said.

She packed a bag and off we went to grandma and grandpa.

When we arrived, everybody was sitting back in the kitchen laughing and socializing. Eugene was the loudest one there. He was digging for his second plate of macaroni and cheese and lamb chops smothered in onions, mushrooms dipped in red wine. The food was usually very tasty! After the greeting was finished, Eugene spoke directly to Junior. "What took y'all so long to get here?"

"It was Duck and the kids. Your little sis cooked a big dinner and I laid on down after I ate," Junior said laughing. They both shared the joke, laughing louder. Junior continued speaking. "You know how it is when you eat a big meal."

"Yeah, you gotta curl up after you eat good. You gotta lay it on down!" Eugene said.

"You guys are crazy!" Teresa laughed.

Not too long after that, someone mentioned the word Monopoly. They played for hours before it finally ended. Teresa got up and took the kids upstairs to use the bathroom. She and Junior caught a glimpse of each other, reminiscing on last night, and how much they really loved one another.

"I got to get my act together. I truly do!" Teresa whispered.

"Teresa bring her over here so I can hold my baby," Mattie said. Heidi climbed up on her grandmother's lap and went to sleep. "Teresa how are you doing with the kids, since you act like you got some sense now. Is it that hard to stop running them streets?" Mattie asked.

The look on Teresa's face told the story. She regretted that she ever sat down at all. Her mother continued. "Teresa, how old do you think you are? You're not a teenager anymore. You surely need to know that you made this bed, so now you have to lie in it.

"You're right mom," Teresa finally said, giving her a hug. "I love you for this talk mother."

"Just do what you're supposed to by your family, and everything will work itself out, you hear! I love you too baby."

After a good, old-fashioned get together it was time for the guests to go. Four hours had slipped by, and everyone began to leave.

"Teresa are you and the girls ready yet?" Junior asked.

After gathering the kids' things, Teresa made her way into the kitchen. "This pie looks good, hmm. Ooh… Who made this?" Teresa asked. "Debbie."

"I have to ask her to make me one. Hmm…"

Willie put the kids' coats on and went outside to warm the car. "Teresa the car is out front, is there anything else to grab?" he asked. Everyone said goodbyes. Teresa was talking to her dad when he began to lecture her.

"Daddy, I'll be over tomorrow. I gotta go. Junior and the kids are in the car waiting on me," Teresa said, giving kisses. Then she left.

When she arrived home, Teresa was in the living room taking off the kids' coats and Junior spoke. "Baby, I had a nice time at your parents this evening,"

"Yeah, it was nice, wasn't it?"

"Baby, I just wanna say, it's sweet to have you back as my wife again and the mother of our kids."

If the story ended there, it would have been the perfect ending. But once Teresa got settled in, the phone rang. It was her longtime girlfriend, Pam, who she hasn't spoken to in years.

"Hey, Teresa!"

"Who's this?"

"It's Pam…"

"Get the hell out of here girl, it's really you? Where you been?"

"How you doing? How's the family?"

"Good, everybody's doing well! And you and your lovely family?"

"Teresa, how's Ethan doing, have you seen him lately?"

"Pam let's not even go there!"

"Teresa, I need a huge favor, I'm coming in town from Chicago tomorrow afternoon. I need for someone to pick me up at the train station."

"What train station?"

"The 30th street station in Philly."

"Why are you just now calling me?"

"Novella was supposed to be picking me up, but as usual something always comes up with her, you and I know that. Yeah! So, if you can, please be there by 1:00 o'clock pm because my train arrives at 1:30 in the afternoon."

"Okay, I will try my best to be on time."

"You're never on time, remember you were late for your own wedding."

"Alright, damn! Pam, you should of called me earlier, you owe me for this one."

"Yeah aight! I got you!"

"How long are you staying in town?"

"For about a week, maybe longer, who knows?"

"Pam, have a safe trip, I'll be there! Cool, see ya' then."

Junior turns over. "Teresa who was that on the phone?"

"Pam!"

"Pam who?"

"I know that wasn't Pam who moved to Chicago and all of a sudden forgot about you." "Why are you picking her up, where's Novella?" "Junior, please get some sleep." Still, Teresa knew something was up whenever Pam steps foot in town.

The next day was Friday. Teresa got up and prepared herself for the day. She called her mother making arrangements for the kids to stay over for the weekend not mentioning a word to Junior. Teresa was excited about seeing her longtime girlfriend. She knew they were about to get into something deep, but not really knowing, what it was exactly. Teresa often reminisced about the olden' days when they would hang out. She figured why not at least for the weekend. Teresa found herself again racing against time, rushing to prepare the girls and drop them off at her mother's.

Once she arrived, she talked briefly. "Thanks, mom I really appreciate it. I need some time to myself, and I have to go." Kisses and hugs and out the door she went into Philly. She was running a half an hour late. When Teresa finally arrived Pam's smiling all up in some man's face, as usual. It wouldn't be the Pam she knew if she wasn't chatting with a dude who had the benjis.

Meanwhile, Pam never noticed Teresa pulling up because she was driving a newer vehicle, a Range Rover. Teresa was glad someone else was occupying her time so she wouldn't have to hear Pam's mouth.

Teresa walks up behind her and says. "Hello, Pam and what do you think you're doing with this handsome man?" Pam excuses herself. These chicks are just as ghetto as they come, but let 'em get around a man and they have all the class in the world.

"Heyyyyyy!" They greet. What's going on girlfriend, both laughing loudly in the 30th Street Station? So, everything echoed, and everyone was looking at 'em like something was wrong. Teresa says, with an attitude, "What they looking at?"

The gentleman stood up trying to get their attention, "Hello my name is..." Pam stops and turns around. "Oh! Excuse me, Charlie, I'm so sorry, but we haven't seen or heard from each other in years. This is my longtime friend Teresa." Touching his face. "This is Charlie, we just met a few minutes ago. Wow, isn't he sexy!"

In her sexiest voice, she says, "Hello Charlie, how are you?" Teresa's eyes him up and down. "Damn and he smells good too. What scent is that your wearing?"

Pam turns to Teresa, "There you go hunting already. You just got here, damn!"

"Be quiet!"

Charlie asks Pam, "Do you mind if I grab your bags?"

"Sure!"

Walking back toward Teresa's truck, he said: "Don't you ladies just love the city of Brotherly Love?"

"I don't know about all that loving it, according to what the news has to say. Damn near every day of the week its pure craziness flashing across the screen, it's so sad!" Pam's loud. "No wonder why I didn't see you when you pulled up, you got a new ride. Scared of you! How many did you have to ride to get this one?"

Teresa crossed her big eyes at Pam telegraphing don't even start. Pam and Teresa began laughing wondering if Charlie caught on or was it over his head. Little did they know there wasn't too much that dude couldn't recognize now being in a big city, especially with men who call themselves kings.

There's nothing these women could ever hide from a Philly man. You wanna know why? Because they can take one look at you and tell if your trash or just one classy ass lady coming through. One thing is for sure and two things are for certain, they can definitely tell the difference. Hell, they teach 'em everything they know, especially how to get that paper and handle their business.

Pam asks Teresa, "You wanna go shopping just to see if the ole' head has some paper or is he just playing himself?

"Sure, whenever Charlie's ready!"

"Go ahead I'm ready! Where ever is fine with me."

"Let's go!" Teresa heads toward Saks Fifth Avenue and Lord & Taylor on City Line. Walking from store to store, spending dude's benjis, or at least that's what they thought. By now, it's been about three hours.

Pam asks, "Teresa what are you doing? He's spending his money. You ain't got to take them jeans!"

Teresa starts singing, "Give me the loot, give me the loot! What, give me the loot!"

Little did they know they would have to pay it all back, all $14,000.00 of it. The ladies left the store, "Thanks, Daddy. Thanks, Charlie!"

"Your welcome ladies!" Charlie's a ladies man. He knows what the game is all about. He's one of them ole' heads who created it. He went along with everything. He even caught onto the conversation they had in the car too. Now Charlie definitely knew just how to play these two so called chicks. He was not worried a little' bit about getting it all back. Charlie has a habit of always making sure that the ladies are well taken care of. Oh boy, the ladies love him for all that! Charlie witnessed that the game was all new for these two, but he let 'em play while thinking how to set a big date for that night. Charlie had them right where he wanted them.

"Are you ladies ready to check into your room because I have some business to attend to immediately? Listen, swing a left here and take me to my car."

"Charlie, where's the nearest hair dresser's around here?"

He laughs, "Teresa you're not back in Reading, hairdressers are all over Philly." Naming a few right around the corner from the hotel.

Pam says, "Oh, I forgot we're right around the corner from Katrina, I hope she's still there. We can go to Chaos!" Pam steps aside talking to Charlie while exchanging numbers, so they could hook up later at Buddahkans for dinner. "Awe, Charlie you're so sweet!"

This is my treat to the both of you."

Teresa says, "He's such a ladies man this place must be fabulous."

Charlie smiles when handing over his black credit card. "Pam guard this with your life, as soon as you check in call me, leave a voice mail, then I'll call you back." Pam kisses Charlie on the cheek, "Thanks, baby c-ya soon."

Before Pam and Teresa were off to their room, they grabbed a bite to eat. Once they finally arrive at the hotel, the bellman greets them. "Hello, welcome to the Ritz Carlton." Teresa didn't know too much about class, she was wondering why this strange man was opening her door. "Do you have any reservations?"

Pam answers, "We'll be checking in!" The bellman grabs their bags. After they checked in and ate their salads, Pam laid across the bed. "I'm so tired, I been running since early this morning.

Teresa says, "Shit I'm not, come on girl, get up, let's go. We gotta get our hair done for tonight!" Hands in the air and snapping her fingers, it wouldn't be Teresa if she wasn't dancing in the mirror as Ms. Happy Go Lucky. "Come on girl get up!"

Pam gets up sighing, "You don't know I've been up since three this morning catching the train, remember." "You know what, we have to get you an energy drink, or something because you have to wake up?" "Okay, let me jump in the shower and freshen up a little' first. I should be cool then," "Hurry up!" Exiting the bathroom, she says, "Alright, I'm up, I'm up! Hey, let's grab a Philadelphia guide so we can hit the streets."

As they're walking down South Broad Teresa notice's a lot of people on the streets. "What's going on, a convention or something?"

Pam says, "No Teresa, now you're in what we call society, where everyone has a real life." She goes on to say, "You're not back in the Glacier Mountains of Reading, where the human rats are running around doing nothing. LOL"

Teresa agrees, "You're definitely right about that!" Crossing the street, "Pam you know what, you're crazy! You just hooked up with this guy and got us out here in Philly, bubbling the entire weekend."

"You know that's right!"

"Girlfriend, you always been spontaneous, I just love it!" "Yeah, okay!" "I just hope dude's not expecting nothing in return from us."

"Teresa, I told you I had you!"

They arrive at Chaos and Pam asks for Katrina; she comes down. "Heyyy, it's been awhile. How you been?"

"Great, I moved to Chicago."

"To the Windy City, it's colder there. What were you thinking?"

"It's business, Hun! This is a good friend of mine, Teresa meet Katrina."

"Hello, Teresa, nice to meet you. What are you having done?"

Meanwhile, Pam never calls Charlie. She gets a phone call. "Hey, sweetie just calling to check on you two, how's are things going?"

"We're good. Right now, we're at the hairdressers on Chestnut Street."

"Nobody messed with you did they because we do have some real nuts out here on these streets of Philadelphia. They can spot newcomers from any angle."

"Nah, we're good Charlie, seriously!"

It's just in a Philly man to be overprotective of his loved ones, more on a natural level. Charlie says, "Oh, I know exactly where you are. Do you need me to come by and keep you company?"

"Yeah, why don't you do that?"

Minutes later Charlie walks in the door and Pam's face lights up, appearing not to be so tired anymore. "Katrina about how long?" He asks.

"Give us about an hour!"

"Okay, I'm going to run out so take care of my girl!"

"You already know I will."

Pam says, "Teresa, I'm going to make a run with Charlie. I'll be back in about an hour."

Teresa answers, "Charlie watch my girl out there and don't have me sitting here waiting for you!" Pam's been traveling to Philly for years and Teresa was nervous because she was so new to the game. Charlie and Pam rode through his hood, meaning allowing her to witness certain things. The only thing she would never do is snitch!

Charlie asks Pam, "Did you get everything that you wanted today?"

"Yes, I did", reaching over kissing him on his luscious lips. "Thanks again baby." Pam's intuition began to kick in. "Charlie, are you always this sweet to women you just meet?"

Charlie says, "A man is supposed to be a real man to all his women."

"Women!" What's that supposed to mean?"

Charlie responds, "Pam you're so sexy, I gotta have both of you, tonight! Your friend Teresa is too sexy!"

"I don't know about that Charlie! Listen let me ask you, is this why you did all of this today? Just so you can think, because that's about all you're gonna to be doing, is thinking?

"Cause no, I don't get down like that! Tell me what's up with that?"

"No baby, originally it wasn't that way. But when I heard how you two were talking in the truck, you two lead me there." Pam turns and looks him dead on, regretting what his next words would be. "I didn't think you two would mind pleasing me, together."

"Look, Charlie, it's never going to happen okay, so get over it! Alright! Alright! As a matter of fact, can you please get me back to the shop so I can catch up with Teresa? She should be ready by now, don't you think?" Looking over at Charlie, "I guess you were expecting for me to say yes, or for me to think that it was even cool? Man Charlie, who do you think I am? Damn what are these women really about here in this city? Hit it and quit it, just to make a quick buck? What if that's not my cup of tea, then what?"

"Look, I'm really sorry if I upset you in any way, I respect your wishes." Pam gives him a dirty look and nods off. "Yeah!" She refused to say anything else, pulling up in front of Choas.

"Sweetie would you like a ride back to the hotel?"

"Sure!" Teresa enters the car. "Hey, damn it took you long enough!" Teresa's upset of course.

Pam plays it all off. "Teresa your hair is sharp." She comes out with this look from the 60's. Real classy.

"Teresa, will you and Pam allow me to take you out for a drink?" Pam pauses, looking him dead on, then nods. "Okay, so let's head back to the hotel so you two can freshen up."

At the hotel heading toward the elevators, Charlie asks Pam, "Baby what room are we in? I'll meet you upstairs. I have to run out for a quick minute for some business that I have to finish up before the end of the day."

"Okay, room 713. I'll see you when you get back!"

"Give me about an hour."

Pam says, "Make it two, I just want to catch up on a nap. I'm tired. I had a long day." "Cool sweetie." He kisses her. "Your lips are so sweet. Oooo! What are you wearing, you smell edible?"

"Alright now! You might not be leaving if you keep that up."

Charlie checks in a room before he leaves and gives Pam the key, "I'll be back soon."

In the room, Pam gathers her things together. "Girlfriend there's been a slight change in plans." "What's going on?

"I'm going to be staying in Charlie's room for the weekend. So now you have your own privacy because you and I both know how you can get after you've had a few too many drinks in you. You can be buck wild."

"Sistah, that's cool with me, I actually was hoping that you would leave anyway."

Teresa knew where ever they were headed that night; she was due for a good time. They all met in the lobby and Charlie complimented the ladies on how sophisticated they looked.

"Thanks, not bad yourself!" Teresa says. "Where are we headed?"

"It's a surprise!" Charlie laughs. They pull up in front of Buddahkans. The valet opens the door. "Welcome to Buddahkans! Enjoy your meal!" While entering the building, Teresa is blown away by the ambiance of the place. "See Teresa, living in those damn mountains you don't experience much, huh!"

"Ha-ha Charlie, funny!"

The hostess asks how many so they could be seated. Looking at their menus, "Ladies are you ready to order?" the waitress asks. "Yes, in a minute, we just need to use the ladies' room." The ladies get back to the table to find a chilled bottle of Moet waiting. Charlie gets a hold of the waitress and the ladies put their orders in.

While they are waiting, they discuss the main events that were being held that weekend in Philly. Dinner arrives. Charlie says, "Raise your glasses for a toast to a wonderful evening, eating and drinking some of the best champ and food." Teresa asks Charlie, "What kind of business are you into?" "Technology, I love it." "That's wonderful!" "Last round ladies then we can go! So, ladies are we ready after that delicious meal?" "Yes, we are, it was delicious?"

They arrive at Vita's Bar over on Wingohocking Street. Vita happens to be having one of her illustrious private parties going on, balloons everywhere and people smiling. It was so crowded inside they could barely get in the front door. Vita had a bouncer checking everyone who came in. Pam and Teresa had to hold onto one another so they wouldn't get separated. As soon as Charlie walked in, people were yelling out his name. "Charlie how you doing man? Where you been brotha, traveling the world again?"

Charlie responds, "I was over in Dubai for a while taking care of some business."

"What are you getting into these days?"

"Yeah, trying to work on some new projects. But excuse me, I'm out with some friends right now. We'll talk later man!" As Charlie walks around toward the back of the bar, he runs into a woman coming in the back door. She's really excited to see him. Pam and Teresa look at each other wondering who this chick is because they already knew they were Sharp, Opulence, as they would call it, Chanel that is. Charlie and this woman hugged and started talking. Charlie excuses himself, Vita I want to introduce you to some new friends of mine from Reading. Pam and Teresa, this is my sister Vita."

Pam says, "Nice to meet you, Vita. You have a very nice place here. Charlie tells us that you love to host parties all the time."

"I'm guilty, it's true! I do private parties, B-day parties, and sometimes holiday parties." "Real nice!" Teresa responds.

Vita sat them in the private area upstairs. "What are you ladies drinking?" "Ummm...I'll take a Cosmo," Pam answers "And I'll take Disarno with Cranberry and Pineapple," Teresa adds. "And you Charlie?"

"Vita, you know my usual."

"Get comfortable ladies. Any friend of Charlie's is a friend of mine. I'll send a barmaid over with your drinks."

The atmosphere was lovely; sweet wood and vanilla scented the air. There were so many people approaching Charlie, men, and women, mainly women, though. "Charlie these women love you," Pam said.

"Nah, baby you're wrong about that. I'm just a popular dude who's hardly ever around anymore, that's all...You really don't know who I am, do you?"

Teresa looks at Pam as if to say, "Who the hell did you pick up from the train station?" "I don't know!"

"Well, you need to act like you wanna' know!"

"Let me go ask Vita," Pam says laughing. The waitress comes back with their drinks.

Pam returns with the information on Charlie; he's famous as all hell. "What?" Teresa was trying to figure him out. "Oh, that's why everybody was like... 'Yeah, now you getting it, damn!' "You know your butt is slow."

"Be quiet!" Pam laughs.

Pam and Teresa are bubbling after a few drinks. I think we all know how them drinks can sneak up on you after a while. Charlie also had his shots up until they all got ready to leave going to Blusettes and Swanky Bubbles for poetry night. They all were feeling quite nice.

Teresa's phone rings. She takes a look, it's her husband but she refuses to answer the call. She says, "The night is just beginning. I just got a call from Junior. Junior who?" Laughing, "Come on let's get out of here and go someplace else. I'm ready to party." Charlie and Pam stood up to leave, but when Teresa stands up she's just a little tipsy.

"Are you alright?" Pam asks.

"Don't I look okay, I'm cool!"

"Okay, just hold on to my arm." They begin walking toward the back door to leave; Charlie gets Vita's attention to say goodbye. "See you later sweetie, we're leaving."

"Okay!"

"Nice meeting you Vita, Charlie's taking us to poetry night at Swanky Bubbles," Pam says.

"You'll love it!"

"Really!"

"You two have a good night and come back again, anytime." Charlie and Rita hug.

They head toward Bluesettes, a hot and familiar spot in Old City. Charlie pulls up and parks on the street. There's a long line extending around the corner of Bluesettes. "Looks like it's crowded tonight, ladies. We can go to Swanky Bubbles; it's just down the street. As a matter of fact, we can walk if you don't mind. It's a lovely night to walk. Parking is not too good around here."

They agreed. As they are walking by, Teresa peeps inside the window of Bluesettes. "Charlie, you have a lot of class, you know that?"

"So, I hear!"

The air lingered of smoked turkey, BBQ, and fish. Charlie, the Mack that he thinks he is, decides to take the arms of both ladies strolling down the street of Old City. "Pam, would you mind joining me on a lovely trip to Paris?" Teresa says, "Oh I'm not invited, huh Charlie!" "Sure sexy, I mean Teresa," shaking his head. "Why not?" Pam says, "Excuse me, Charlie, can I give you my answer now?" "Sure baby, go ahead!" At that moment, some guy happens to walk by complimenting Charlie for being with two women at the same time. "You're a lucky dude!"

Teresa says, "Excuse me, but I'm actually alone tonight, dropping her arm from Charlie. "My name is Teresa." "My name is Lee," kissing her on the hand. "It's a pleasure!" Teresa's all smiles.

Charlie says, "Lee Johnson from Vernon Hill."

"Yeah, that's me, man!"

"I thought that was you, man how you doing?" "How's it going, I see you haven't changed, still loving all the beautiful ladies?"

"Ladies we go way back."

Lee says, "Where were you taking these gorgeous ladies on this beautiful night?"

"Yeah, I wanted to take them into the Marmont first."

"There's nothing going on tonight, I just came out of there."

"Okay then let's go around to Swanky Bubbles for poetry night. Lee, do you want to join us?" Teresa comments, "I'm hoping you will."

"I will darling. So, Teresa tell me, where are you from?"

"Reading, unfortunately."

"Why do you say it like that?

"I'm just so tired of that spot, I'm so ready to move from there."

" Then why don't you think about moving to Philly? So, you can be closer to me." He laughs and she smiles.

"Really! Nah, it's too damn crazy here for me!"

"You could move on the outskirts somewhere, something to think about."

"I really think I would rather move down south somewhere,

maybe Atlanta. I hear the weather is beautiful down there around February and March, while it's freezing up north.

"Now that's true."

"That happens to be great for me because I have been in the cold for too long, it's definitely time for a change. I would love to live some place where it stays warm all year round.

By the way, Teresa what brought you to Philly?

"I picked Pam up from the 30th Street Station this afternoon, where she happened to meet Charlie, then we decided to stay for the weekend.

"Damn you actually came down out of those coal miner ass mountains."

"You and Charlie need to stop tripping."

"It's true so admit it! If you don't mind my asking, what hotel are you two staying at?"

"I don't know if I should answer that, we just met."

Turning the corner, they walk into Swanky Bubbles. "It's not a bad crowd tonight,"

Charlie says. "It's usually more crowded than this. There must be a main event going on over at the Marriott or someplace else."

Ordering drinks, the ladies excuse themselves to use the powder room. While the ladies were gone the guys reminisced a little about old college days at Temple, the days they hung out in Philly. "Lee, whatever happened to those two fine ass girls we used to hang out together with who had a crush on you?"

"Who you talking about because you know how I do?"

"The one was fine as hell."

"Oh, you talking about Antonia or Mellania?"

"It was the sexy one."

"Hell, they were both sexy. Mellania, she's Brazilian, man I messed around and married her. I wasn't letting her get away. Mellania is a sweet lady, Intelligent, sexy and very classy.

"It sounds like you got lucky man."

"Yes, I am truly blessed. We share two beautiful little angels, Nevaeh is seven and Mia is four.

"How do you like being a father?"

"It makes me understand what my worth is each day, putting JESUS CHRIST 1st, and knowing that my family is great man, I really can't complain. What's up with you; did you ever get married?"

"Nah, I backed out from the relationship that I was in. She was so dishonest with me on things that were going on in her life. So, I cut her off. You know how it is man, I couldn't continue to be around someone that couldn't be honest with me, let alone herself."

"I feel you."

"I mean Sabrina, she was sweet too but.... I guess that puts me on the list of still searching. I'll get married one day when I meet the right person."

Charlie noticed the ladies walking back over to the table with this rouge all over their face like they just left some damn circus downstairs.

"As we were walking back over I noticed you two were in what looked like a deep conversation. Don't let us stop you," Pam says with much respect because they were real brothas.

After about an hour the ladies were ready to leave. By this time, it's about 2:45 in the morning and the ladies were beat from all the walking around they did yesterday and hardly any rest. Charlie asks, "Lee do you mind giving us a ride back to my car around at Blusettes." "Sure, let me go get the car."

Charlie comments, "Teresa I think you had a little too much to drink sweetie."

"I'm not drunk, I'm just tired as hell. I need to lay down, my feet are killing me and I gotta take these shoes off."

"Hold on, Lee's about to pull up any minute now."

Before they get out of Lee's car, he asks Teresa, "Do you mind riding with me?"

Pam says, "Follow us." "Okay," as Teresa leans the seat back. They all pull up to the Ritz Carlton together. In the lobby, Lee asks, "Teresa should I get my own room?" "That's simply up to you if you got it, then put the two hundred up. Lee just come on into the room. As long as you're a gentleman everything is everything. I don't think that I have to worry about you being disrespectful," as she reaches into her purse and pulls out her key for room 245.

"Damn baby! You definitely came prepared, didn't you? Shit, you scare me for real!"

"Nah, I don't play around when I leave town."

Pam begins whispering in Charlie's ear, as Teresa and Lee stand apart. "You're a naughty girl and I like that!" "I can be!" Charlie rushes her to their room.

Lee holds the door open to Teresa's room. "Please excuse my room, it's just been a long day." Teresa showers, Lee surfs the T.V. and falls off to sleep, snoring. Teresa lies down and looks under the covers. "Oh no, he didn't! He really thinks he's gonna get some punany or is he just the type who sleeps with no undies on. She turns over and gets comfortable falling right off to sleep.

The next morning, she slept in. As Lee is leaving, he jots down a few words. Teresa slowly wakes to a crazy hangover. She exits the bathroom and there the letter sits, it reads:

"Teresa, I just wanted to let you know your company was so pleasantly appreciated. I had such a lovely time with you, here's my cell #, call me. You are very a sweet lady...talk to you soon.

Yours truly, Lee."

She smiles. Teresa orders room service. By this time, it's about 5 pm. She calls Pam and doesn't get an answer. She then tried reaching her on her cell phone. "Hey, girl where you at?"

"Finally, you decide to come up for air, huh!"

"What?"

"Girl, we stopped by and knocked, no answer so we kept it movin'. Listen, we ran out real quick, he had to make a run! We're on our way back in about an hour."

"Pam do me a favor, grab me a bottle of Tylenol please."

"Girl, was I tipsy last night?"

"Your butt was tore up."

"Did I behave last night?"

"Yes, you did. I'll talk to you when I get back, feel better!"

"Please make sure you knock as soon as you get in."

"Ok!" They pull up to one his boy's house until bout 8:00 o'clock p.m. They then head to the drugstore. Pam's knocking on the door and calling Teresa's name, then finally she answers. "Here girl lay back down. Take some of this, you should feel better in a little while." Hours pass. Pam and Teresa are on the phone talking. Pam says, "You slept your ass off! Get dressed because we're going to grab something to eat." "Let me guess, a chicken salad." "You already know!" "I'll be dressed by the time you get back."

Meanwhile, Teresa's phone rings. She answers, hello! In Lee's softest voice, "Hi baby, how are you feeling, are you up?" "I'm just about to jump in the shower." "Okay, I will see you in a few." "Cool!" Teresa's cell phone rings. She checks the Caller I.D, it's her husband again and she doesn't answer. Twenty minutes later there's a knock on her door, it's Pam. Teresa asks Pam to quickly put something together so she could get dressed. "Hurry up girl, I'll be in my room. Call me when you're ready."

Minutes later, Lee puts his key in the door. "Teresa. What's up baby?" Lee stands in the doorway as Teresa greets him with a hug. He says, "Damn you smell good, what are you wearing?"

"Gucci."

"Mmmm! You shouldn't smell that good, just might have to pack you away and take you home with me."

"You could do that! I see I have to keep my eye on you."

Lee walks over and gives Teresa another hug, he's so tall he has to bend way down to kiss her. "I would ask to take you on a shopping spree, but it looks like somebody already beat me to it."

"Yeah it looks that way doesn't it, Charlie took us yesterday. Hey, what's up with you Philly guys?"

"What's up with your dialect?" Lee constantly teases her about her high pitch voice. "High pitched? What's up with you Philly guys?"

"Oh goodness, you sound so white."

"Well, I guess it comes from you hanging up in those damn mountains. You have to come to Philly more often, so you can get acquainted with your own culture, Sistah! You know what I mean?"

"Right!" Yeah, I might just do that. What's up with the fellas in Philly? The men here get off when they are capable of sending women on shopping sprees, huh?"

"Baby its a man's job to take care of his women."

"What are you really trying to tell me, the fella's up there in that lame ass spot don't cater to their women?"

"Nah, I don't know anything about that kind of treatment."

"Man, all they see is paying bills. I mean it's important to be sweet to your lady."

"What's that? Nah, all we see are suckers for dumb shit!"

"The hustlers don't even know the real hustle in Reading. In Philly, you see kids sitting at the gas stations waiting to pump gas just to make a fast buck, at an early hustle."

Teresa says, "Is this a way for the young men in the streets?"

Lee answers, "Yeah, for the ones who want it bad enough, ain't no hands being stuck out here in this city. Gotta get yours, baby! We make the youngin's here know what a dollar means early! Men damn near teach the woman here how to hustle too, you have to!"

Teresa says, "I envy that so much. You know what? When I really think about it, there's many women who don't know what having class and sophistication is."

"Damn, what's all up there, coal miners? What do you do up there?"

Teresa laughs and says, "You don't want to know it's not important. Let's just say that I'm a survivor that's all."

The mood in the room seems to change. You have some Luther Vandross playing in the background. Now picture yourself in the South of France on the beach with a warm summer breeze, Narcisco Rodriguez scents the air. Lee sits on a soft plush blanket, silk sheets and yellow rose petals falling from the sky, "Come here, baby." Teresa walks over allowing her robe to fall. "How you doing baby? You are looking sexy!" Reaching over kissing her on the neck. They shower, dress and go out for a bite to eat. As Teresa's leaving the hotel, she calls Pam in her room, realizing that they're obviously busy themselves.

So, they decide to stroll down Broad Street. Lee begins to show Teresa some of the amazing art that surrounds her in Philadelphia. "I feel so envious of you. You had all this growing up! Maybe it all depends on what you wanted out of life!" Teresa felt if she only had an opportunity like this living in Philly when she was coming up, her life probably would have been much different for her and some of her friends too.

"Teresa, it's never too late, though."

"I know," she says as she begins to elaborate on her family back in Reading. But Teresa never mentions her marriage. She figures that it was already over since she met Lee.

"Teresa do you have any kids?"

Yes, I have two girls."

"Me too!"

"So, are you still with their mother?"

"Who Melania? Nah! We've been separated for five years now. Every weekend I usually spend time with my girls. Melania took them to visit her parents in Atlanta this weekend."

"Oh, how sweet, this is my lucky weekend, huh?"

Lee holds Teresa tight as they kiss. "Yeah, sweetie that's just what it is, our lucky weekend together."

"Uhh huh I hear you!"

They kiss again. As they're on their way to Zanza Bar Blues for dinner, Teresa wants to know where the closest BCBG store is located.

"Sweetie do you mind if we grab a bite to eat first, aren't you hungry? Let's go after dinner."

"Cool!"

"Wow, this place is really nice and jazzy. Brunch is awesome too."

"Sweetie, I'm happy to know that you are enjoying yourself."

Once Teresa walked into the BCBG store it was like being in a candy factory. Everything was new and poppin' and she wanted it. Not too long after all that, they spent quite some time walking around Ritten House Square and Society Hill. Eventually, they headed back to the Ritz Carlton.

Teresa calls Pam. "Hey Pam, what's your plans looking like for this evening since it's only our last night in the city?"

"Well, we were thinking about driving down to Atlantic City. But I think we might just go someplace close since we're trying to leave in the morning, we don't know yet. Teresa, what were the fellas going to do?"

"Not sure, but we'll join you two if you don't mind."

"All right, we should be ready around 10:00."

"What time is it now?"

"It's early, it's only quarter 'till eight."

"Okay, talk to ya' later." Back up to the room, Lee falls asleep. Teresa surfs the T.V. for one of her shows. By this time, it's about a quarter after nine. Teresa showers and gets dressed then she wakes Lee. "Lee!" "Yeah! What time is it?" She pauses looking at the clock, "It's about 9:30 right now." He yawns and climbs out of the bed hitting the shower, dresses and is ready to go. The phone rings.... it's Pam, "Are you two ready? Hey, we're downstairs at the bar, so when you two love birds are done this is where we'll be." "We'll be right down."

As they arrive at the bar, Charlie asks, "Hey you two join us for a drink." "So where are we headed tonight?" Teresa briefly mentions something about Bluesetts since they didn't seem to make it last night. Charlie says, "Sounds good to me. It's a nice crowd on Saturday nights." Lee looks at Teresa, "Let's go see a movie at that new movie theater on Broad and Cecil B Moore." Pam disagrees, "Let's go another time." The timing was just right for Bluesettes that night, the line was already in the door and no one had to wait. It was crowded but spacious. The ambiance was vibrant, the lighting was a soft blue and the people were full of conversation, which absolutely set the mood.

Lee asks Teresa "Would you like to dance?"

She whispers in his ear, "You know I don't want to leave tomorrow."

"Really, so why don't you stay longer then?"

"I wish I could but remember I have my kids to tend to."

"Yeahhhhhh, so do I!"

"Did I mention how beautiful your body looks in that dress?"

The time is 1:50 am and the bartender is making the last call for drinks. Everyone is mingling and having a lovely time and it's about 2:45 a.m.

Lee pulls up to the hotel and the valet takes over the keys. While they are walking to get onto the elevator, Charlie and Pam are hurrying to get back to their room. All stepping off of the elevator walking toward their rooms, Pam says, "Damn slow down before you hurt something." Lee says, "Goodnight you two." "Goodnight!" Pam catches up to Teresa and grabs her arm as she's walking down the hall, for a little girl talk. "Don't do anything I wouldn't do!"

"What, he looks sexy as hell in that suit and he smells too good, hmm. I can't promise I won't give up the goodies tonight!" "You know what chick, you're just as crazy as you wanna be!" Walking off, "Goodnight!" Teresa couldn't wait to get back into the room. She had a surprise for Lee. Her surprise was strawberries and warm body oils. Hmmm. Let's just say it was a hot, sensual and steamy night.

It's morning and the sun is peeking through part of the curtains. Teresa gets up, orders brunch and heads to the Jacuzzi. She begins packing the majority of her things, dreading having to leave such a beautiful lifestyle. Once the food arrives, Lee awakes to the smell of coffee, crab cakes, grilled salmon, asparagus and more fresh fruit. "Lee, are you hungry?" While everything is still hot, she decides to feed him while lying in bed since he was the one who was so tired. She started out with some succulent strawberries and cantaloupe but he didn't seem to really want too much.

"Thank you, baby, that was very sweet of you to feed me." He gets up and walks into the bathroom and all you see were butt cheeks. Teresa laughs. Teresa didn't waste any time as she began chowing down. It was like her natural past-time when it came to eating salmon, crab cakes, and salad. She always maintained a healthy appetite and it showed. Teresa's body is absolutely a work of art, gorgeous and she knew it. She would do anything to show it off, in a respectful and classy way, though.

Steamy...Lee comes from the shower. "What's wrong?"

"What do you think Lee? I'll be leaving soon?" She walks over and hugs him. "I'm going to miss you, your scent... I just don't like that I have to leave you here in Philly to all these women."

Lee laughs. "Don't go back, stay here with me."

"Yeah right! I wish I could!" She reflects on back home and the treatment she gets from her husband. She just shakes her head.

Lee walks up behind her and says it's alright. "Look, let's just plan something now for next weekend. Can you do that now or do you have to wait and see because I know you have a family and all? Maybe I shouldn't even be asking you this."

"It's fine, my mother has them this weekend. I just don't want to make it a habit."

"Well, I can just come to Reading!"

"Nah, there's nothing like a nightlife there, like here. Seriously there's nothing to do up there at all? Why do you think we come to Philly all the time?" Right away she knew it would be the wrong move for him to even come near Reading. "We'll work something out one way or another." Holding each other for a while, Lee squeezed her as tight as he can then gave her a long drawn out kiss. "There, that's something for you to hold onto until we see each other again."

The phone rings, it's Pam. "What do you want chick?"

"Are you almost packed up and ready to go because I have to pick up something in Reading by 4:00 o'clock and I can't be late? I don't want to be stuck in this Philly traffic because it gets crazy around three. Alright, T, we have to be ready in a half an hour."

"Okay I'll be ready, my stuff is already packed and sitting by the door."

"Okay, okay I'll meet you downstairs in a half."

Teresa looks over at Lee. "So, Lee can I pack you up now because I'm about to go!"

"Awe darling, how sweet of you, you're serious too! So, what do you think about that, you wanna try it?"

"Ha! Ha! You're funny. It's about that time, are you ready to go downstairs?"

"Do you have everything?"

"Yes, I think so!"

"Are you sure?"

"Yes!"

Lee mentions, "Damn Charlie brought you a lot of stuff. You sure you really want to come back to see me and not him." He grins.

Teresa says as they are walking down the hallway, "You have to ask? It's all about you baby, you make me so happy."

Pam steps off the elevator and the bellman is loading the truck up with the bags. They all embrace saying their last goodbyes until next time. Teresa whispers in Lee's ear as he hugs her. "I really enjoyed myself last night!" "Ohhh me too! "Call me later!" "Okay!"

Teresa wasn't dumb. She knew no sooner than she got onto the turnpike, some other chick would smell her scent all over him. He wasn't fooling anybody but himself. Pam and Charlie locked lips for a few minutes and said their goodbyes.

The ladies were surprised, big time, at the fact that they actually met someone who truly knew how to treat a woman. Teresa mentions to Pam, "Girl, I have never met any man who has shown the integrity and class as those two men back there have shown us all weekend."

"You know what? It's because they are real ass men, that's why! They put the c in class."

"All the dudes you been messin' with all these years either didn't have a father figure to show 'em or they were just plain ass duds."

Pam laughs, "I hear you!"

"We learned a hell of a lesson, haven't we?"

Pam answers, "Never ever settle for anything less in a man as long as we live?"

"You know that's right, girly! I really enjoyed the weekend with you, you're so crazy!" So, tell me, how many other brothas you know like that?"

"I have quite a few friends in Chicago who treat me real well! They give me anything I want!"

"Why do I keep finding myself so damn envious?"

"Teresa because you're not aware of many things out here."

"I want to tell you something Pam and this normally would be hard for me to say. I've been envious of you for years."

"Why?"

"Pam, I mean you have a chance to get away, you have been traveling for years. You even get a chance to meet so many different and fun people."

"Well sweetie, that's only because I'm not married by choice and I don't have any Be-Be's kids running around, that's something that I just don't want right now. I love enjoying my life alone."

"Wow!!! Damn Pam, nice way of putting it. That made me feel better."

"It's the truth, isn't it?"

Their fun would be coming to an end in just a matter of minutes because now Teresa begins to feel guilty about her husband's ignored phone calls all weekend. She tries to get Pam to help her come up with something to say because she knew that Junior would badger her no sooner than when she walked in the door. They finally came up with something by the time they got in town.

Teresa was about five minutes away from picking up her kids so she called her mom to let her know that she was on her way. "Hello mother, how's everything going?" "Good!" "How were the kids for you, did they behave themselves?" "Teresa the girls were not a problem at all, my little angels kept us company. Junior called about three hours ago saying that he was going to come and pick up the kids." "Well, what happened? Why are they still there then?" "Listen I'm right around the corner. I'll be there shortly."

Teresa takes Pam over to her cousins, which was maybe two blocks away from her parents. Teresa pulls up helping Pam with all her bags. They hug and part, realizing at that moment just how much they really missed one another over the years.

Teresa has tears running down her face. As Pam walks away she turns around and says, "It's going to be okay. Call me later, I'll come over this evening after I meet up with Brian."

"Yeah, I hear you hooch!"

"You and I both know how things can get while you're here so if you don't end up coming by I understand."

"Seriously I do, just make sure you call me before you leave town and don't be a stranger, keep in touch. Thanks for everything Pam, I so needed that!"

Pam says, "I know you did! Hey, maybe we can do it again real soon, who knows."

"Yeah right, what are you trying to do, get me a black eye or something."

"No, I'm just playing."

"What, you better be."

"Don't I always seem to know the right time to come into town?"

Teresa looks at Pam as she walks back to her truck, "Yes you do! How coincidental is that?" Smiling and waving as if it would be their last time ever seeing one another again. Teresa pulls off yelling out the window, "I love you."

"Me too!"

Teresa arrives in front of her parent's house in no time, reaches in the back of the truck and pulls out her parent's gifts. As she's walking up to the front door, her mother meets her at the door. Teresa greets her with a big hug and kiss. "Hello mother, hey daddy," as she walks over and kisses him on his forehead. "How was your weekend, what did you two do with the little ones?"

"Not much, but we enjoyed having the kids over to visit, as always." "Oh okay!" She hands her mom her gift and as usual because it wasn't a holiday her mother asks, "What are the gifts for?" "I love you two very much, that's what." Her mother begins to tear up as she opens her gift. "Oh, Teresa it's so beautiful!" Teresa walks over to her father. He opens up his gift and says, "Nice, this is real nice. Thank you, T, give me a kiss." Their lovely gifts were matching pajama sets with matching robes. As the Wayan's dad once said, "They got to coordinate!"

Still to this day her mother loves silky pjs. Now her father he loves t-shirts and cargo shorts, relaxing on his front porch, even in spirit. "Teresa, you haven't left for a weekend like this in years." "I know mom and I so badly needed to get away for a while. It was just so relaxing. I'm back and we had a fabulous time! Teresa's dad asks, "So where did you go?" "We were down in Philly hanging out!" Teresa's well aware of what his next question would be, so she cut it short running off. "Thanks for watching the kids I must run. See you tomorrow."

As she walked off the porch to leave, her mother asks again, "So what did ya'll do for the weekend?" "Mom we'll talk to tomorrow, I'm a little beat. I just want to get the kids settled in."

"Okay, goodnight!"

She didn't fill her mother in on anything because her mother already thought what she was doing out there was already a sin, so she just left it alone.

Junior called his in-laws to see if she got back in town yet. Teresa's on her way home, getting more and more nervous about seeing the man she calls her husband who she happened to betray all weekend. Teresa pulls up. Junior meets her outside beside the truck. She sits there for a minute muttering aloud "Damn, what am I going to say to him about these bags?" She steps out and walks toward the back of the truck.

"Hello, T how was your long weekend with Pam?"

"Damn, Junior you scared me!" She looks at him trying to stay calm and says, "It was okay. How was yours, Junior?" Not realizing that she was setting herself up.

"It was long and lonely, no kids and no you." Junior didn't want to wait to talk about this in the house just in case they happen to get loud they would be away from the kids this time. "So where have you been hanging out with Pam? This is why I don't like when she

51

comes into town because the first thing you do is run off hitting every club in town. I keep telling you Teresa, you gotta' chill out. You have a family to take care of now." He stops her from grabbing bags, "And plus I love you, T."

She gives him a look as if to say yeah okay, that's not good enough anymore. Grabbing the rest of the bags she walks toward the front door. "Junior, can you close the door please?" Already she appears to be tired of his presence, the marriage, everything.

Teresa figures that she found a new man so altogether she's done with Junior. Junior grabs the door as she turns the knob to walk in the house. Heidi comes running up. "Mommy, mommy's home!" Teresa could barely drop the bags before Heidi was jumping up into her arms. Teresa stood there in a daze for a moment. The guilt had finally set in about leaving her girls behind too. Teresa washes her hands while reminiscing about her weekend with Lee, she's already thinking of a plan. She's just hoping it all falls into place right way.

"Junior, how's the baby doing?"

"Scoota-boot's good, she's actually taking a nap upstairs."

"Do you have the monitor down here?"

"Yeah, it's over there on the table!"

"Well, you have to turn it up so you can hear her. "Mommy has something for all of you." She goes into the bag and pulls out three outfits a piece for the girls. Heidi is so happy she has an outfit with a hat and a skirt; she takes off her pajamas so she can try it all on.

Junior asks, "Teresa where did you get all of these clothes?"

Right off the top of her head, she says, "Pam knew some guy that owed her so he gave her his credit card."

"Yeah okay, you expect me to believe, that right? Well, I don't!"

Teresa remains calm because Junior could read her every move. "I don't care if you don't believe me, it's what it is and that's the truth."

She helps her little girl with her clothes. "See baby girl you look so pretty!"

Junior says, "You look so pretty baby girl, try on the other one."

"Heidi, mommy wants to check on your little sister." She follows holding onto her skirt. Teresa intentionally waits until the next day to give Junior his gifts, to let him know that she still cared a little, but he stepped over the line by questioning anything she did for her family. At the same time, she's just so fed up with all of his nagging and complaining all the time.

Teresa turns on the lamp and sits on the bed looking at her babies realizing that she has two beautiful girls and one day soon she will become more responsible for them. She's seriously thinking about leaving Junior and moving to Philly to be with Lee. She leans over, "I missed you baby girl." She picks me up and gently squeezes me so tight. "Mommy love's you!" Heidi says, "I look pretty, mommy!" "Yes, baby girl you do look so pretty." She takes me back down to the living room.

"Listen, we have to have a serious talk whenever you can find the time." "Yeah okay Junior, tomorrow."

Junior asks, "What's wrong with this marriage, why is it turning for the worst?" As he walks off.

Teresa is busy trying to wake me up. "Hey pretty girl, wake up so I can see those pretty eyes. You smell good and she kisses my hands. In the kiddy voice, she mocks, "Mommy missed her girls so much." Teresa figures I must have had a long day, so she kisses my forehead and lays me down in my crib. As Teresa walks by the room Junior calls her to come in. She decides to stand in the doorway. "Yes."

"Hey baby, I missed you all weekend. Can I have a kiss?" She walks over and gives him a kiss on his cheek. "Oh, it's like that now! Who did you meet while you were away Teresa?" Junior could always seem to figure her out. They'd been together long enough that he just knew her ways. She sits down on the bed. Junior gets up and starts rubbing her back, "I missed you, baby!"

Teresa was not in the mood, plus she had just given up the goodies before she came home. "Look, Junior, I only came upstairs to lay the baby back down." She stands up and walks out of the room. By this time, she's really turned off. Giving Junior the cold shoulder, she tends to Heidi. There wasn't anything that Teresa wouldn't do to see her babies have something new on their backs. Hell, it was the least she could do for them, especially if she knew she wasn't going to be around for a few days.

As I hear, my cousin Abou Luv had to hustle too so his family could eat. You know that street hustle and Teresa was supposedly the chick who dated all his new customers first before any other chick got a hold of them. Hell, back in the day as I'm really seeing how it was put together, there were a lot of chicken heads running the streets of Reading and Teresa chose to be that chick. Hey, it's what she felt she had to do to get what she wanted; it wasn't what she needed by no means. Critics here we go again!

Teresa sits on the couch for a moment and begins to reminisce about her weekend. Moments later, "Heidi, mommy needs for you to pick up your things so you can get ready for bed." "Mommy, can I wear my skirt?" "Yes, baby tomorrow." "Okay!" Teresa grabs a drink from the kitchen, as she prepares a cereal bottle for me in about another hour. Then, turns out the lights and heads upstairs for the night. As she approaches the room she hears Junior snoring, so she checks in on Heidi making sure she's tucked in and that her night-light is on. Heidi jumps out of bed as Teresa's hanging up her clothes in her closet.

Heidi holding onto her mother's leg, "I wuv you mommy" "Aww

baby, I love you too! Give mommy kiss, okay get back in bed so you can go night-night." Teresa looks down at her trying to hold back her tears, all she could think about was how much she wanted the best for both her girls, knowing that she had to make some instant changes for things to work out.

"Good night baby girl, see you in the morning." Heidi has a special nursery rhyme that she repeats to everyone. She and Teresa say it together, "Goodnight, don't let the bedbugs bite." At the end, she always says, "I won't mommy."

Down the hallway, Teresa checks on me for the last time before she turns in. "Good night sweetie. Mommy will see you real soon, muah!" As she approaches the room she hears Junior still snoring.

She takes a long hot shower, gets out, ties her hair up and gets into bed surfing the channels. Nothing's on so she begins reading "Coldest Winter Ever." About two hours later I awake. Junior gets up and tends to me and brings me back into the bedroom. Teresa goes down to warm my bottle, excited Teresa hurries back upstairs. "Hey little one, I missed you. You finally opening your little eyes up. Were you a good girl for your grandparents while mommy was gone?" Smiling. Junior says, "She has really been smiling lately!" "That's Mommy's girl, yes, she is," and begins to feed me the bottle.

"T do you mind if we have our talk now?"

"Go ahead talk!"

"T you know I love you! I just want our marriage to work for the sake of the kids. There are quite a few things that we need to try and straighten out."

"What's that?"

"Do you realize that you have got to stop hanging out so much? You have two kids that need you!"

"Damn, Junior I'm working on it, anything else?"

"Yeah, when do you plan on giving me a hug. It's not like you to go somewhere and come back like this?"

"I'm just tired." He turns and looks at her as she feeds me trying to figure out what was going on with her. I finish my bottle and fall off to sleep, she picks me up and right away I burp and release some gas. "Wow, you should feel better." "I'll take her, and he sits her up in her chair. I don't like laying her right down after she eats because she's been spitting up a little lately.' Teresa lies down and continues to read. Meanwhile, Junior attends to me and I eventually drift off to sleep. Junior waits about a half an hour before he goes and lays me back down in my crib.

It's morning, Junior's up early making breakfast for the family. Heidi comes downstairs with her Hello Kitty pjs on. "Good morning baby girl, how did you sleep?" Heidi shakes her head, meaning good. Teresa wakes up to the aroma of turkey bacon and pancakes, goes into the bathroom and checks on me as they head downstairs. "Good morning and how did you sleep, baby girl?" Heidi walks over and kisses me on the hand then gives me a hug. Junior stands at the stove cooking as Teresa walks over and greets him with a hug and kiss. "Good morning Junior." He's shocked. Teresa realizes that she's home with her family and Junior doesn't deserve the harsh treatment; it was all her guilt and how much she was missing Lee.

"What were you doing young lady helping daddy set the table with napkins? You're a big girl." They all sit and eat breakfast. Junior cleans up the kitchen while Teresa gets the kids dressed. Heidi is happy about wearing her little skirt set. Teresa's cell phone rings, but she doesn't hear it because she's in the kids' bedroom. Junior and his nosy ass walks over and picks up her cell phone. Of course, not recognizing the number, he takes her the phone just to see what her response would be. He insisted on trying to give her the phone so she could check her missed calls. She turns and looks at him, "Damn Junior, it's Lee calling for Pam because her phone got wet so he called me so I could let her know that he called. What, it's not for me, it's for Pam! I can't help her phone got wet. Junior don't start your crap." She stops and looks down at Heidi. "Junior just stop please! The kids don't need to keep witnessing us arguing. Listen, we're going to my parent's house for a while."

She gathered snacks from the kitchen, milk and a few baby bottles and was out the door in no time. As soon as she pulled up in front of her parent's house, Junior pulled up along the side of her asking if she wouldn't mind taking a ride with him to Philly to take the kids to the zoo. She pauses trying to alter her anger. "Yeah, why not!" He parks, she gets out and says a quick hello to her parents. "We're on our way to Philly to take the kids to the zoo!" "Hi Junior, aww look how sweet they look sitting back there." "Ok, mother we'll see you when we get back. See ya, daddy!" "Have a nice time girls. Mom-mom and Pop-pop love's you, muah!"

Just as Teresa gets back in the car, they both apologize to one another, she reaches over and kisses him, and they pull off. It happens to be a beautiful day as they arrive at the zoo. Heidi becomes extremely excited because she always enjoys looking at the animals while eating funnel cake and taking pictures for hours. "Mommy, take a picture!" On their way out of the zoo, Heidi gets upset because she wants to see the tigers one last time. So, they ended up walking halfway around the park to get there.

"So, tell me where did you and Pam go for the weekend?" Junior asks. Teresa replies, "We ended up staying down here in Philly."

"Oh, so that meant somebody had some money. So, if I called

wherever you two stayed down here, they can verify that you and Pam stayed there alone?"

Teresa says, "Look, Junior I didn't come to Philly to be badgered about something I did a week ago, don't you think whatever I do is my business!"

He agrees and finishes by saying, "I just hope you didn't cheat on me!"

"Can we change the mood …PLEASE! Are you hungry, what do you feel like eating?"

"Something light."

"Okay good, there's a place that makes the best salads." Teresa gives Junior directions. Teresa ends up sharing a salad with Heidi because the salads are huge. I was content with my peas, peaches, and formula. "Heidi is it good." "Uh huh!" By this time, it's about 7:00 p.m. and we're on our way back home. Heidi and I are in the back seat knocked out. Teresa has her seat reclined enjoying the rest of her book.

Once we arrive home Teresa's phone rings again, it's Pam. She answers, "Hey, I'm just getting in the door. Let me call you back when I get the kids settled in." Pam quickly asks about Lee. "Okay, okay I get you, call ya back soon!" No sooner than the kids are settled in she goes out into her lovely seating area. "Hey Pam, listen I got a call from Lee." Pam asks, "Where's Junior at?" "Anyway, I told Junior that he was calling for you." Pam says, "Cool, I know what's up, don't worry 'bout that. Did you get a chance to talk to him yet?" "No, I can't seem to get a chance, Junior will not allow me to breathe. I tried to leave and go to my mother's house with the kids, so I could at least have a moment to use my phone, but he followed me over there too. Pam said, "Damn, girl it sounds like you got it bad. Junior is trying to block!" "Yeah, tell me about it, I miss Lee so much, he's such a sweet man to me." "I know because I been missing Charlie too, as a matter of fact, I'm going down there tomorrow night." "All damn, I think we might be going together!" "Come on you can ride." Teresa and Pam try to figure out how she can get away again for two days.

"Teresa!" Junior calls for her to come in the house. Teresa tells Pam, "Junior's calling for me, I'll call you later, but keep thinking of something." Teresa walks into the house, "What's wrong? You were calling my name like the house was on fire?" "What were you doing out there on the phone, huh?"

Teresa ignores him and makes it known because she looked right at him when he asked, she knew exactly what he was doing just to get her off the phone. So, she walks away and checks in on the kids. We were still asleep. Teresa grabs her jacket. "Junior I'll be right back." Teresa jumps in her truck pulling off not too far from the house. "Pam, did you come up with something yet?" "Yes, tell him that you're going to Baltimore to visit your niece Meka." "I guess that'll work." "Now you just have to get someone to watch the kids. You know what, I can ask my sister, she's off this weekend. Yeah, that's what I'll do!" "How is she with her kids?" "She's good with my niece and nephew, she knows that I don't even play around." "Is she clean?" "Yes, she's just like you, sickening!" "Does she have any animals?" "Alright, Teresa make up your mind by tonight because I'm leaving by 7:00 tomorrow night, so if you're going be ready. The phone beeps while she's on with Pam, she looks at it, excitedly she says, "Pam it's Lee, I gotta go. I'll call you back.

"Hello!" "Hello darling, what are you doing?"

"Waiting to hear from you. What are you going to be doing this weekend because I might be coming down tomorrow to see you?"

Lee disappoints her and says, "I'm not in Philly this weekend. I'm in L.A on business. I won't be back for another two weeks."

"Wow, baby I thought that I was going to have a chance to spend some time with you again, soon. I miss you!"

"I know, I miss you too! Well listen, we will have some time to make this up…I have to run, for now, I just wanted to hear your voice and say hello." Abruptly he says, "I gotta go, I gotta go. I'll call you again sometime tonight."

"All right, thanks for calling. Talk to you later. She blows him a long kiss on the phone. "Talk to you later sweetie!"

Later that evening while Teresa is taking a hot bubble bath she didn't realize she left her phone on her dresser. Junior hears the phone ringing so he checks the caller I.D., which happens to be the same number from the first time he noticed and this time he answers the call while he walks down stairs. "Yeah!"

"Hello, may I talk to Teresa?"

"Who's calling?"

"Lee!"

"This is Teresa's husband. How do you know my wife?"

Lee actually says, "I'm looking for her friend Pam, her phone got wet and…. is Teresa around?"

"No, and he hangs up."

Junior never gives Teresa the message, so she doesn't find out until she checks her phone an hour later. No missed calls, but she checked the last call, it was Lee. Now she becomes curious if it was Junior who had answered her phone. Right away she approaches him. "Junior, did you answer my phone when it rang?"

"Yes, it was that guy Lee looking for Pam again. I just want to say that I'm sorry that I didn't trust you, come here baby, can I have a kiss?"

"No!" Teresa flips out! "Why are you even answering my phone anyway?" Junior's now wondering why she's was getting so upset if the call is supposedly for Pam, he starts thinking and Teresa's wondering how Lee knew to handle the call. It had to be Pam! Teresa called Pam informing her of the hurtful news about Lee being in L.A. "Pam have fun and be safe while you're in Philly."

Teresa finally tells Junior, "Junior I'm going to Baltimore to visit my niece, Meka." Well, right away he wanted to know why so suddenly and only after she had received the last phone call. "Whatever, I'm leaving!"

"Teresa, are you taking the kids with you because I won't be here when you get back?" Tears begin to roll down his face, "I can't take this anymore. You're not even trying like you said you would."

"Go do what you have to do because I'm leaving to go out of town to go see my niece, I haven't seen her in a few years." Teresa's hoping that he wouldn't be there by the time she came back, she wanted to be with Lee anyway. Junior goes and starts packing up some of his clothes. Teresa comes in, "Where are you going?"

"I'm moving back to my parents in South Carolina." "Well good," and she walks away. She waits until he leaves the room so she could get some of her things packed up for her and the kids. Junior didn't say another word and neither did Teresa. She took her bags to the car, came back in. Junior was giving the kids a kiss and trying to hold back his tears. Teresa sat down and began to put the kid's jackets on and told Heidi to hurry up, she picked me up and walked out the door.

Junior was so upset because he tried talking to her time and time again. She left him no other alternative but to leave, she obviously didn't want the marriage anymore. He tried sucking it all up going and packing the rest of his stuff and putting everything in his car. Junior came to grips realizing that he had to let go, so he sat down and wrote Teresa a letter:

Dear T,

It really hurts to see that we had to end our marriage this way. I love and miss you and the kids already. So, what exactly is our next step, getting a divorce? This is something that you been wanting for a long time; I was the one holding on. I didn't want to leave, but you didn't want to change. The treatment that you continued to give was pushing me further and further away. You showed me that day in and day out.

How could you do this to our family T? Scooty is only a baby and Heidi is close in age to see the difference. Kids pick up on things, can't you see that! I just hope you tell them the truth, whenever you find the time when they're old enough to really understand. Please give them a big hug and kiss for me and always let the kids know that I love them very much. You had a responsibility while I was there, now reality will set in, once I'm gone. T… I left you something."

Love your husband, Junior.

Happy Anniversary xoxoxo.

Right after Junior wrote the letter, he walked through my room reminiscing about our family pictures, sobbing over his failed marriage, now finding himself having to move back to S.C. with his parents. Junior's a wreck, after all, he's been through with his wife, but yet he still finds himself in love with her. Before he hit 95 South, he grabbed a bottle of water from the fridge and some fruit from the counter.

Well, Teresa returns home after being away for two days to find a letter from Junior on the kitchen counter. She instantly became upset because she thought about him the whole time she was gone. Hesitant to read the letter, at that moment she felt so ashamed of what she's put her family through. Teresa began to cry, really feeling frustrated about the biggest mistake for her future. She sits thinking about her husband, debating if she should call his parents. She just couldn't grasp the nerve to pick up the phone. At that moment she stood up and opened the refrigerator to get something to drink and she ran across the gift that Junior left her, a beautiful two-carat diamond necklace, which Junior was waiting to surprise her with later that weekend on their wedding anniversary.

Every morning after Junior left, Teresa got up trying to adjust to a new life of loneliness. It wasn't until the next time she talked to Lee, "Hello Teresa, how are you doing darling, it's been awhile? "I'm doing good, I can't complain, I'm just trying to take good care of my family since my husband left!" "Your husband!" They discussed it and moved passed it. They continued to keep in contact whenever she went to Philly and he happens to go to Reading for a day to visit.

On more than one occasion, Lee said, "Man, what is there to do up here? Come on let's go back to the city where there is a nightlife, at least. We can have dinner, do whatever you want to do." No matter how bad Teresa may have seemed that she wanted to change, she always managed to keep leaving us kids behind for someone else to raise them. All the times that she neglected her kids, caused her relationship with Lee to fail. It's funny how certain things work out in a mysterious way.

The story ends up being Lee's also married to his lovely wife Mia for two years, a year into meeting his mistress, Teresa. He's often said how much he enjoys spending those special times with Teresa. Finally, it was something that slowed her down. Lee played her game up until the very end and just when she least expected it, the man that she thought she really loved, devastated her by being dishonest himself leaving her to ask the question, why did he do this to me? A beautiful man who was so kind, gentle and sweet, someone with so much to give. Huh, she never expected anyone of such character to show up and hurt her the way that he had. Men come in more ways than one, so beware! As I'm hearing now, all that Junior has shared about Teresa isn't so true... just as I figured!

"Lord even when I have trouble all around me. You will keep me alive. When my enemies are angry, you will reach down and save me by your power.

Psalm 138:7

CHAPTER 2

Growing Up Crazy

When you're growing up, nobody ever gives you an explanation for white imperialism or why you feel as though you have been locked up in your childhood. That's just what my black ass went through, a revolving door that has dealt me bits and pieces of racism almost daily. This racism was kind of surreal, but liken it to a deadly disease that wouldn't stop spreading. It was moving so fast, I was too young and naïve to recognize it. I felt strange knowing that this racism was alive and well and most of all, how it prevailed so silently. It was only being mentioned in certain places that you would never imagine. To think that something like this could take place in the north, a small town only sixty miles from the fifth-largest city in the country, Philadelphia. But it did, it happened in Reading, Pennsylvania where I grew up.

How many of us knew back in 1958 Caucasians held racial riot's all through Pennsylvania and actually lynched African Americans? Sad but very true! I recall my sister and I doing whatever we had to do, just to get through this madness. The only thing that made any sense to me was a saying that only my mother offered. She said, "Make the best of what you got, girl!" That's all I ever heard, make the best of what you have. But what did I have I wondered? I guess you get used to hearing that so much you just start believing it. My sister and I started to feel crazy, so I said, "Heidi there has to be a better way than this," which led me to probe into all my feelings.

Meanwhile, my sister Heidi was always involved in something she had no business being in, leaving me alone to fend for myself, but never hungry or dirty. The times that she and I spent together we played games to pass the time away. I remember challenging Heidi in a game called, "Ain't No Diva Better Than Me!" If we could have processed our dreams, it would have included cars, houses, clothes and anything we wanted such as Cadillacs, Lincolns, furs and diamonds because you know, diamonds are a girl's best friend.

Heidi said, "Cool! I like that anyway because I always get what I wanted. Scooty, you never know what you'll get until it happens." What was not forgotten was our biggest dream. I said, "I want to go shopping right now." "You sure are pushy. You ain't got no money and most of all, mom ain't got no money, so that makes us broke as shit, don't it?"

You see we lived in the outlet capital of Pennsylvania. The only thing that was missing was our dream car to go shopping in, a five hundred series Mercedes, in baby blue that is, Benz to whip in.

"I would say, "You don't even know what it will take to get all the stuff we want."

"How do you know? Heidi would answer.

"I don't know?"

"You're too young Scooty to know anything about stuff like that, you're only a kid."

"But I'm not stupid."

We would feud like crackheads over and over, but together we dreamed our dreams every day. There was one catch. Once in a while, I would glimpse peeping eyes staring through the cars as they flew through the block. I mean grown ass men. Some guy named Sammy from around the way used to look at me and say, "You're growing up girl, and you're getting big too. What grade are you in, now?" I would say, "Why don't you ask my mom; she would like to know how big you really think I am?" I would sometimes catch him sticking his tongue out at Heidi and me. Why? We were only babies, but that didn't seem to stop him. Sammy could care less about respecting females, if I can say so boldly, I'll never understand the reason for this. What could make Sammy seek jailbait? Well, I guess it's because we were so developed for our age and of course, Heidi being so damn fresh, that reflected on the both of us.

As I looked back I asked, "Mom are all men dogs?"

She said, "Scooty, as long as I can remember, older men would always view me like a Hollywood movie. They just couldn't help themselves, which makes me think the opposite sex is crazy."

But there was a paradox in all of this that in turn has a reverse effect, which made me so curious as to why men were always looking at me! I would say to myself, what do I possess? And Heidi would say, "It's your ass, girl!"

"Stop telling that girl that," my mom would say.

What did they know, that I didn't? One thing is for sure, it pushed me to grow up much faster than I ever expected. My mom would say, "Scooty, remember the movie 'Lady Sings the Blues'?"

"Yeah, I remember."

"Diana Ross played the role of Billie Holiday who was a simple girl trying to be a superstar, a classic film, that was staged in the 40's era. Billie Holiday was a jazz singer who had a bad habit that she couldn't seem to shake. It was called drugs and it took her life! Diana Ross sang with such grace in the film and her performance was absolutely amazing." My mom goes on to say, "You remember Scat Man playing the role of Big Ben in 'Lady Sings the Blues', when Big Ben said, 'You Fine Young Thang You?' Scooty, that's just how men, view women! I just want to put that bug in your ear."

"But all men aren't the same!" I insisted.

"Time passes. Again, when Alice Walker wrote 'The Color Purple'. Good Ol' Mister in 'The Color Purple' only wanted to get a piece of Miss Cicely's sister's punany. You remember?" Mom asks.

I said, "I don't remember that, but that's just how I felt growing up. It was so disgusting."

"I know!"

"But mom, I'm not you and that won't happen to me!"

It definitely did not stop us from dreaming anything as such because we sort of had a pit bull for a grandfather, who looked over and protected us. I'll never forget growing up hearing my grandfather say, "Don't let your fresh butt leave this porch!" Normally, when you're the young one who has an older sister, she normally drives the positive outlook for you. Following in my older sister's examples, I learned how to become curious at an early age. I took my fresh ass off the porch as my sister and I was thinking alike as one. God says that he didn't make me average. As I once explained to my sister God created me to excel, and he's given all of us the ability of insight, talent, wisdom and his supernatural power to do so.

So why did it miss my mother? She was so screwed up! At that time, she deliberately left the responsibility of raising us on our grandparents, Tot and Mom-Mom who lived at 146 Walnut Street in Reading. All we ever heard our mother say was, "I'll be back," never giving us any specific time when she would return, even when the adults would ask her. My darling and loving grandparents did the best they could for us. Food and shelter were the most important attributes they valued. They were old school, but that didn't stop them from striving each day.

It all began the day God answered their prayers. My grandparents were born in South Carolina living in poverty. They struggled to understand the challenges of everyday life as they dealt with the circumstance of what culturally the South had to offer. Never once did they use their feelings of despair of being torn away from education as an excuse to not work hard and make a good life for themselves. My grandparent's faith is strong and they have taught me to have that same strength in my faith. My people were the very poorest and as a result of this poverty decided to move many, many miles away to strive for a better way of life.

They both decided to move from the South aiming toward a much better life for their family in the North. A calm environment is where they wanted to settle and raise their children. As they traveled, they stopped in Philadelphia to visit Tot's brother, Evan, for a night. "Man! Isaac, how can you live here with all that shooting and screaming in the middle of the night like that?" Isaac, in his deep southern voice, said, "It doesn't bother me. Y'all act like ol' folk from back home who don't wanna change!"

They really couldn't get what the city's lifestyle was about so, they kept going until they ended up in Reading. A place they both agreed to live as a change from where they both had come from. Reading, Pennsylvania! To me anyplace else would have been much better than living in a small town called Reading. Let's just say, Jim Crow never left, he's still hanging around, as though he still doesn't get it. "Scat Man!" Some things never seem to change. Living like this, I mean really, it actually discouraged my elders and the next generation from searching out their black culture. I come to realize about 95 percent of black people don't know their true black African history which includes scholarly blacks too. We are doing and have done exactly what whites have wanted us to do, which is to distance ourselves from the past and to not look back so much. The more we do this, the less guilty they feel for all of the atrocities that have been done to us.

I have to question my past, why not Philly where the importance of African-Americans who recognize their black culture and really care in guiding their young ones? I mean the Unity of Black People actually having the power to run for Mayor, or even have their own family business which is a big thing to me, coming from a small town. New York City, where there is an international culture or even L.A. where there are beautiful flowers and palm trees to see, where the weather is always great year-round, and one has the option of choosing to live on or off a mountain. Plus, you never know who you'll see while being in L.A.

Getting back to Tot and Mom-Mom, as I think about it, what really mattered to them was finding a job to raise their chaps and live comfortably. An amazing day arriving in Reading Mom-Mom and Tot will never forget. It was like a miracle had surfaced, compared to where they had migrated from. As we got older they shared their hard luck stories with us. Tot's father, Jo, wanted to talk to him one day when he came in from school. In his deep southern drawl voice, "Tot, I need to talk to you. You gonna have to quit school and help us raise the family." "Why dad when all my brothers are older than me? I'm the youngest."

After dinner, Tot waited to speak with his mother. The next morning while grandmom Mary was warming up the dinner from the night before for breakfast, Tot questioned his mother about why he had to quit school. Grandmom Mary approached grandpop Jo, and in her soft-spoken southern drawl voice said, "Jo why you makin' Tot quit school?" "He's a man, he'll understand one day!"

Tot enjoyed every moment he had in getting his education.

Then that one day came when he was forced into doing what was necessary for becoming the young man of the house. Back then they couldn't think about having an ego. All his life, since the age of ten years old, Tot enjoyed giving back to his people.

Looking back at their past, it all makes perfect sense now as to how they thought they should raise us. Later in life, you hear stories of other families from the South, as it seems they all have suffered through some similar challenges and hardships in life. Some were even fortunate enough to go back to school; the hustlers in the family were like geniuses. Their family business was to clean banks and manicure the landscaping. Business is an opportunity. Social skills are a must as well as people who become investors.

My grandparents worked very hard with the jobs they were blessed with, which afforded them the opportunity to live as a middle-class family. Of course, we wanted all the finer things in life. The next time Tot went to Joseph's department store, I rode along so I could get some sneakers, but we only received what he thought we needed at the time. I was very thankful for my blessings early in life. Heidi and I both knew that things could have been much worse for us, like being caught up in foster care. I often asked, "Heidi did you ever think for a minute where we would be today without them?" Quite often a sistah wondered, but could you blame me given my dysfunctional history?

Our mother Teresa was never shy when it came to us, but could be very irresponsible. Responsibility was not in her vocabulary unless she made the time. Teresa just loved her freedom and got away every time she could, but reality set in sooner than she thought. Tot spoke to Teresa the very next time she happened to drop in one evening. "Teresa, I don't know what your plans may be, but Mom-Mom and I need to get custody of these kids. We refuse to have them in our presence and not have any legal papers on our grandkids. You and I both know that anything can happen and you'll have your ass out in them damn streets."

"Daddy you're right, we'll get this done."

"Alright Teresa, I don't want to have to say it again!"

You best believe in a matter of two days; those papers were signed with no questions asked. Bottom line is that our grandparents loved us so much, they became concerned about our stability.

It's tremendously important for children growing up to have a happy and healthy lifestyle. Because a child constantly thinks about what she had to experience while growing up as a young lady. Abuse, neglect and other negative things come to mind. Growing up with a suburban white rural world mentality was a challenge for me. But through it all, it was my God who gave me the guidance.

Saint James Chapel C.O.G.I.C is where I learned to fellowship with others just about every Sunday, while our mother would stray away. Trying to make a life, the church became like a distant family. She too would occasionally show up to church. There were certain things that appeared in our mother's presence and for some odd reason, she felt acquainted with them. See, sometimes the people we actually call our friends sometimes aren't our true friends. It sometimes leads us to do the wrong things in life. It was the drugs, then the booze. When she least expected it, imprisonment showed up at her front door on numerous occasions. The last time she served time was for four months. Believe it or not, those four months determined her future as to how responsible she would be to us as our dear and loving mother.

For weeks, we found ourselves being curious about our mother's whereabouts. Coincidently, one summer afternoon while visiting our great grandparents, Clint and Lizah Seriff on 4th Street, my mother exits an apartment building across the street from their home. The first thing I yelled was, "Mommy, Mommy!" When she turned around she was just as shocked to see me. I was glad to see her, even if it was only for just a moment. A month or so had passed and each day we felt more uncertain of her love.

Teresa always wanted us to have what we wanted despite her absence. But there was one problem; she could never find a decent way of getting it, so she boosted it. That meant taking me along with her like a family outing. It's crazy because here I thought we were going to the zoo or just maybe going to get some ice cream from Friendly's. Oh no! We were on our way to shop at John Wanamaker's, and little did I know I was the stakeout for my mother. A few times while she was boosting she would tell me to take the goods to the car and empty them out and return to the store so she could get more. Those experiences set the course for the rest of my life. I realized then just because I started my life out that way, that's not how it would end. My attention was directed to growing closer to God and developing a prosperous mindset.

It wasn't until about a few weeks later our mother peeped in on us at our grandparents' house in the wee hours of the morning. Believe it or not, she had her own key to get in, she chose to sneak in and out, just so she wouldn't have to face her own parents. We would hear our bedroom door close, which was only right down the hallway from our grandparents.

She would awaken us. "Shhh, don't talk so loud...Wow, you have Michael Jackson all over your walls." She always managed to bring us something by each time she stopped in to see us, but it never seemed to cross her mind that what I really wanted, was a Barbie Doll. Otherwise, that only meant I would have to go to my friend Denise's house to play with her Barbies and Barbie Doll dream house. I instantly become envious and as a result, was always seeking passion from others feeling like I had nowhere else to turn.

The majority of the mornings when our mother came by, I would be asleep and would wake to a note saying how much she missed and loved me. But that never seemed to take away the loneliness in my heart that was always left. Each time our mother came by, she brought more gifts; it was always about brand name items and leaving us a couple of dollars too. After all that, we still felt like something was missing. As we grew older, we realized material things could never add up to the love that she rarely showed us. I knew deep down inside that one day she would understand her mistakes and repent for her sins, as I often reminisced about the path my mother chose and wondered if anyone was there to guide her. I mean she had four brothers: Arthur, Eugene, Mark and Jimmy. It just didn't make any sense, to be blessed with so many brothers and not listen to any of their guidance. At least her brothers wanted something out of life; they all joined the service at different times, making my grandparents so proud.

However, Teresa eventually proved that she made crazy decisions. She gave birth to two children and dropped out of school to never return. Teresa too struggled to understand the basics of everyday life. I think this struggle must have started early in her life or was just too hard for her to comprehend overall. It hurts tremendously to have to admit that Teresa can be very vile.

I believe sometimes she may be bi-polar which may explain the reason for her unusual behavior. It's great to know there are mothers who set certain standards to educate their children showing that they care very deeply about their child's future.

There have been many reasons why I have chosen to go this route in writing a book searching for the truth. The person I am today realizes that my sister and I had a heavy-duty price to pay as a result of our mother's choices back then. There have been a lot of ups and downs, as well as comings and goings. For instance, Heidi knew of her biological father, I was the unfortunate one who wasn't so lucky. Teresa had taken this situation into her own hands, of course, twisting the truth. How can I say this? Well, there's no way of sugar coating it, my mother had several male friends. Actually, there were four men that I can remember her dating throughout my childhood years. There was Al, who was stationed in the service in North Carolina. We would sometimes travel back and forth by train from Reading to see him, whenever she wasn't driving. Kevin, David, and Jim were all from Reading. Can you imagine, three guys at once were bidding to be my mother's main interest. Number one had to be Kevin, who my mother claimed she was in love with. I guess he seemed to me to be the dude that my mother dated the most, although David walked around her as if he was that guy that made the Earth stop. Poor, poor Jim who I thought was my Dad, was there for a moment. I was told that he was my father and that turned out to be a lie also.

Now, what I will never seem to understand is why my mother would lie and look me in my face as a youngin and tell me that this man Jim was my biological father, knowing damn well that he wasn't and leading me to believe this for years. How could she do such a thing? Never feeling like she owed me any explanation! Plain and simple she hurt me deeply. A child needs to believe in everything that their mother tells them.

But in this situation, that was not to be. Plus, it got worst! She later realizes just who created me and now has to find a way to explain. The day I found out the truth at eleven years old, deep down inside it extremely tore me apart. The word on the block was that "Junior" is your dad!" Junior and I have yet to establish a father and daughter relationship. He chose to walk away after I was only here a few months on Earth. His decision to leave is a fact that really hurts as knowing the truth sometimes doesn't always feel like what's best!

Every year for about four to five years our grandparents would travel back to their hometowns, Manning and Alcolu, South Carolina for family gatherings. Every now and then I'd get lucky to spend a short time with Junior. Twice I had the pleasure to visit him. It was very rare that he even thought about coming to the hotel we all were staying at. When he refused to show up I would then request to seek him out. Someone would offer to take me to his house. Once I arrived, "Amena it's Scooty and them at the door." "Y'all come on in," greeting one another. "Scooty, you're getting so big you're gonna pass your mama in a minute." "Yeah, she's getting up there isn't she?" It felt kind of strange traveling 12 hours to Junior's hometown but it was something in me that wanted to get to know him. However, he showed me through his actions, that he could really care less about me.

After all of this, there was light at the end of the tunnel. It was God who had an awesome plan for me and it was all in his time. The day had finally come when I was blessed to meet the other half of my family. I just knew by looking at them I was like looking in the mirror. I felt such a relief come over me. In a way, knowing who and where they were, I didn't have to wonder anymore. I had to learn to accept the things that I have because everything that happens has a reason. There's a saying, "I know how to live when I am poor, and I know how to live when I have plenty."

The secret is being happy at any time, in everything that happens. I can do all things through Christ because he gives me strength.

Philippians 4:7 says "and the peace of God, which passed all understanding, shall keep your hearts and minds through Christ!" I needed to read that and keep it close in my heart. My grandmother gave me that verse when she said to me, "Scooty, God can heal." Mom-Mom always gave me things like that to remember, she kept me focused. I couldn't believe that this great woman was the mother of my mother. How could it be so?

I guess life sometimes can fool you, just when you think you really know someone you can meet a part of them that you don't know. Mom-mom would say, "Scooty, read your Bible and read, Isaiah 40:29, 31 'The Lord gives strength to those who are weary.' Even young people get tired, and then stumble and fall, but those who trust the Lord will find new strength. They will be strong like eagles soaring upward on wings; they will walk and run without getting tired."

The last few weeks of school were tough and final exams were approaching rapidly which meant we had to say goodbye to old friends, which was very hard to do. Summer vacation was finally upon us! The thought of a break and just knowing the excitement of going to all night skating parties, swimming, recreation and hoping to find my grandmother in a good mood was my idea of fun. "Mom-mom, my pal is having a dance for recreation day, can I go?" "How much is the dance and who's going with you?" "The dance is two dollars; Denise is going along with me." "You two be careful while you're down there." Kissing her on the cheek, "We will, thank you."

Little did my sister and I know what we were up against that evening, returning to the projects again. Hey, at least there's always something fun to do while we're there. Sometimes for the summer months, we would go spend some time with my mother's half-sister Jane and her three children, Rey, Nona and Misha. Misha and I were very close growing up, just a year apart. My thing was Double Dutch. We always made new friends anytime we jumped rope because every girl and even boys wanted to learn how to jump. Jacks were also a fun game to play, and riding bikes we went everywhere. There were days when we use to sit and listen to Jane's twelve-inch records of all the great legendary artists of today, such as Diana Ross, Marvin Gaye, Donny Hathaway, Harold Melvin and the Blue Notes, Smokey Robinson and many others.

There were always some funny looking boys liking us, but we played hard to get, which really meant in my book no interest at all. We didn't mind going to Jane's because we felt free. She was hardly ever home as she worked in town at a tavern. The parents of my friend Denise, Ms. Tina and Nat, owned a tavern named after her. Jane was a bartender at Denise's and she worked 1st and 2nd shift sometimes.

Remember those days when you wanted a certain kind of cereal for breakfast, but when the final decision came down, it all depended on the size of the family. You just had no choice, waking up to that big yellow box that read Honeycombs cereal, which was our daily requirement of three scoops of sugar. It's funny because after a while the phase didn't matter anymore. Days when Jane didn't have to work, she would make her infamous bang'n spaghetti and garlic bread which we couldn't wait to indulge our teeth into that sweet cheesy sauce. Eating was always good at Jane's.

It's early and Misha and I are almost done with our chores, washing and hanging up clothes on the line. Glenside had a summer program that handed out lunches and every day there were people lining up from one end of the projects to the other to eat sandwiches and fruit cups. It was something different about eating the same thing at home versus eating with your friends for lunch. This is one of those childhood moments, where kids are screaming and talking over one another and just having fun. No sooner than my entire group was finished, we were off and running again.

Suddenly, there was some disturbing news that was brought to us about our mother being in a serious car accident. As they say, she was out one night with a few of her friends and while they were coming down a steep hill, Rose, a close friend of Teresa's, lost control of the wheel. They ran head-on into a telephone pole. The car was instantly totaled and they all were hospitalized in very bad shape. It was days later when I happened to be out riding my bike. Upon my return back to the house is when I noticed someone sitting on the porch, on a lawn chair wrapped up in gauze. I hurried off the bike and ran onto the porch to find my mother lying there moaning. "Mommy, what happened to you?" She spoke slowly, "I was in a bad car accident baby. I'm hurting right now, but I'll be okay baby."

I felt bad for her during her traumatic experience. Her head was totally wrapped up in gauze; her doctor said there was a lot of glass that was left in her face that they couldn't remove. She also wore a cast on her right leg and a brace for her back for about a year. Today she still has back problems. Over the years she has had four surgeries on her back. It's a blessing for her to be here alive with us. Knowing that I hadn't seen her in such a long time, numbness suddenly came over me. I was overall extremely happy to see my mother and was glad to know that she was going to be all right in time.

The news kept coming; it was now time for us to pack some of our things due to the living arrangements at Jane's and move in with Ms. Bren, a friend of our mother, who lived just a half a block away from Jane's. Only this time we weren't too far from our mother. The timing never seemed to be quite right for us. We were so close but yet so far apart from our mother. It appeared that no matter where we settled in we were repeatedly packing up and moving from various locations. I always thought this day would never come to an end.

The next day couldn't come fast enough. Anticipating the moment of hugging my mother once again, all night we just laid there. "Scooty are you up?" "Yeah, I'm just laying here looking up at the ceiling thinking about mommy and how she's feeling right now. We'll see her in a few hours. What time is it anyway?" "It's 4:45 am!" No sooner than I stopped talking we both drifted off for a few hours. It's about 9:30 when Ms. Bren wakes us for breakfast. "Girls, are you ready to go see your mother?" "Yes, we are, thanks for breakfast." "You're welcome girls!" Before you knew it, we were off racing one another down the street trying to get there as fast as we could.

When we walked in that feeling of excitement came over me and my heart began to beat faster and faster. Like it was yesterday, humbly I asked, "Mom, are you okay?" "I'm very sore, but I'll be okay baby." Instantly, I felt a sigh of relief from her response. As days and weeks passed she gradually began to gain her strength back, thank God! Isn't it amazing when you have time on your hands versus taking advantage of it every day? You realize soon enough that you have been put in a position and sometimes you just have to wait it out.

"Hey, Heidi, wouldn't it be so nice if Mom could get a house out here in Glenside, so we wouldn't have to keep going back and forth because it's really starting to get on my nerves?"

"What nerves?"

"You are so damn grown!"

"No, I'm not, all I know is that I want to live with mommy."

Scooty sighs, "Yeah, that would be nice, wouldn't it?"

About a month or so later we received good news about moving in. I wondered if I had wished it into fruition. "Mommy, are we really going to be living with you for now on?" "Yes, baby you are!" Heidi was happy, but boy was my sister ecstatic about spending time with Mom Dukes! Ms. Bren lived in the same row as we did, maybe four houses away. "Heidi and Scooty you both know that you're more than welcome to come down and visit us anytime." "Okay, thank you!" Laughing, we both looked over at each other knowing that her son, Anthony, had a crush on me. I didn't like Anthony like that, nice kid, though. Little did I know my mom was setting me up and I wasn't even aware of it?

Mom Dukes approaches me and right away she says "Scooty, Kevin and I have plans for tonight, so you'll be staying down at Bren's tonight until morning."

"Awe, Mom, do I have to?"

"Yes, you do. Do you have anywhere else you can go?"

"No, I don't think so."

"So, get upstairs and pack a bag."

Wow, and you wouldn't believe Anthony just so happens to be one of those kids who urinates in his sleep. "Hello! Did ya'll hear me? "Dude peed on me! Unfreakin' believable!" Damn if it wasn't a big surprise to me being suddenly awakened in the middle of the night drenched in stinky urine. I tried my hardest to shake his little ass right out of his sleep. "Anthony wake up!" "Yeah!" "Yo, you just peed on me!" This brotha not only tried to ignore me by turning over to return to dream land but then says, "I always pee in my sleep as if there wasn't anything wrong with it. "Eww, now that's nasty!" It was crazy that night.

Anyway, I went home upset and wet. I stood at our back door knocking. When my mom finally answered the door, she said,

"Scooty what are you doing out here in the middle of the night?" "Anthony peed in the bed all on me, so I came home." "Go ahead into the bathroom, I'll grab you some clean pajamas." Minutes later she asks, "Scooty, are you asleep?" "No, I'm still up." Teresa walks in bends down and kisses me on the forehead. "I love you baby see you in the morning!" "Me too mommy."

Kevin, my mother's boyfriend for the past twelve years was a loving and caring guy but could be a bit irate at times. His parents were kind, caring and loving people who taught him about integrity, but he refused to show any respect toward my mother and other women.

The bottom line in this situation is Heidi may have known her biological father but Kevin filled the void for mine disappearing in the wind. He supported us when he really didn't have too. It was that summer Kevin and my mother began to work alongside his parents at the State Fairs in Michigan. We had some fun times while we were there with our mother, as she worked the bathrooms making tips we were off riding and playing games. I remember when Kevin won us these big stuffed St. Bernard dogs and that moment kind of stuck with me for years because it made me feel a sense of comfort whenever he wasn't around.

Simply, the love and quality time he spent with us will never be forgotten because that's all I ever knew. What little girl doesn't want to be a daddy's girl as she grows into a young lady? A father is a security blanket who guides you through life. Allowing you to explore the necessary basic things and definitely, perceptively to school dudes on what they're not going to do to his little girl. Hey, certain fathers have a code of ethics and simply there are some who don't. Sound familiar?

For whatever reason, Kevin and Teresa had been together damn near thirteen years with a relationship that was going nowhere. It was so bad that they could hardly get along anymore. We actually witnessed our mother time and time again experience mental and physical abuse. Put it this way, whatever it was that she had coming to her we had to deal with too. On a good day, Teresa would come by and pick us up for a few hours. Next thing we knew, these two would go into their world of drama. Whatever the drama was about, it left us sitting outside on the porch in the cold and all because he said so.

Hell! We could never figure out why she stayed in this relationship with him after all she'd been through. While we were coming up, we witnessed our mother fighting women over her old man in the streets and then during late nights, she would have to fight him for being a male whore in such a small town. Anyone who has walked in those shoes as a child can definitely relate to such circumstances. A woman dealing with her cheating man is never a good situation. Our mom was crazy. One thing she didn't mind was fighting. But in the end, her self- esteem became an issue.

There was one thing she often said, "If and when your man leaves the house and he's not doing what he originally said, then girrrl, you better wake up because the game has now changed."

Most of the time Heidi and I would have to be split up. We moved so much that it was very hard to keep track of the different places we stayed.

"Whose house are we going to this week mom?"

"I don't know Scooty, we'll have to see in a couple of days." I was about eight-years-old when we were going back and forth between mother's friend's homes and our grandparents' homes.

One late night, I discovered a beautiful movie that I always enjoy watching over and over again. "Lady Sings the Blues" is the semi-factual story of the late Billie Holiday who was an American jazz singer. I would literally stay up until 2 or 3 in the morning watching this movie. This would drive my grandmom crazy because she would repeatedly call me, "Scooty go to bed! You have school tomorrow, you need to go to bed!"

Man, this movie was so addictive, I just couldn't resist. The characters in the movie were awesome. Diana Ross and Billie Dee Williams' performances were incredible, which helped this film become a fantasy of mine. Each time we watched this intriguing couple play their rolls it made me feel as though I was actually living that classical moment.

Wow, Louis McKay and Billie Holiday were just so amazing in this movie. Imagine a sharp hustler, let's not forget handsome, who could have any woman of his choice but he chooses you. It showed me that a man could care and support his woman to the end, despite the trial and tribulations of drug abuse in one's life! It's real life. This sense exists now in certain places such as Las Vegas, which has many fabulous spots of such elegance and class. Berry Gordy, owner of Motown Productions, along with Paramount Pictures distributed "Lady Sings the Blues", a film that received five nominations for the coveted Oscar. The accompanying soundtrack became a number one album in 1973 on the Billboard Charts. It is still recognized as a great work of art forty years later. Can you believe that?

Time has passed, and we were beginning to notice the stability that our mother was now providing for us. Some light had begun to shine on our situation. Scooty says, "Mom since we're all together, do you think we can do something special?" Teresa says, "Yeah Scooty, like what?" "Go to Disney World." She says, "We'll have to see about that." We could never seem to understand what reality was truly about because every time we turned around we were being tossed like salads.

"Heidi, as long as we have to keep moving around, please know that we have each another."

"Okay as she stretched her arms out to give me a hug."

"I love you!"

"Me too!" At that moment we didn't know what the future would hold for us while spending time with our mother.

As more time began to pass things became more hectic. Days grew into weeks and sometimes even a month at a time where we wouldn't see our mother. After crying many nights from just going through all the turmoil for years, God answered our prayers. When my mother had finally surfaced, we were convinced that she was done running around and ready to become loving and committed to us. "Heidi, mommy's home!" "Yeah for how long, though?" She turns and looks at me. Mom turned her life over to the Lord and certain things began to change for the better.

After thirteen years Teresa finally decided to leave Willie. She decided to move on with her life without the man they called Scooty's dad, a man who took on his own thoughts, not giving a damn.

The last time they spoke, Junior claims that he was going to Reading to see his baby girl. Dude ran game, hurting her in the end. All Scooty ever wanted was to truly have a chance of knowing and loving her pop. It wasn't until that damn roller coaster ride, which left a sistah' feeling real messed up between Junior and his respect, let's not forget his integrity too!

Phone conversations weren't too often as you would already guess. The love never stretched any further than he wanted it too! As it seems, Junior may have had some serious problems going on within himself, but it will take time for him to realize the truth.

Uhmm, hello! Well, as it turns out, Junior wasn't as sincere as he pretended to be. After all, the father-daughter relationship we were supposed to establish never happened. Have faith! I faithfully believed as long as I have God in my life, The Heavenly Father will guide and protect me, and the blessings will flow.

Teresa eventually married her high school sweetheart, Benny. Take a minute and think back to your childhood and remember that nosy neighbor who watched over the block and would scold anyone at any time. Many a late night, a lot of us would be caught hanging out on the corner with the dudes from the block and around the way. Many nights Heidi would get scolded behind the night watcher snitching on her. You know, the lady that lives across the street who is always watching everybody. And would tell their parents and grandparents what was going on the night before. Well, my grandfather was damn near eight feet, 320 pounds easy. There would be days my sister would ask me, "Come on, you wanna go out with me, you wanna go out?" It would be late and we had to be in the house. So, I would tell her, "Nah that's okay, most the of the time I just stayed in and listened from the window...for real, though!"

No matter which way I came, I just couldn't seem to get through to Heidi. She wanted to do whatever she wanted to do. When you're wrong you're wrong. Not sure if the butt whoopings even helped, which became boring after a while, I guess. My grandfather in his deep southern voice yells, "Heidi, where have you been? When I say stay around the house, I mean it damn it!" "Pop-Pop I was right across the street at Drai's." Tot becomes excited and he goes on and on. "Heidi, I been looking for you, you always got your rump someplace else that you don't have no business. Coming in the house with liquor all on your breath. Where you think you at?" She walks away rolling her big eyes. He says, "Keep crossing them big eyes if you want to, one day they gonna pop out, you hear!" There was never a time that our grandfather wasn't trying to be funny in his own little way. He will always be our big, gentle, giant. We love you Pop-Pop.

This is a very serious time in my life, the beginning of soul-searching, trying to find out who I am. By no means did it come easy in trying to figure it all out alone. Next thing you know, my grades begin to fluctuate through all the moving around which we had to do. Many times, during this shift in my life I asked myself, "Who Am I?"

Each day was a drudge. At the same time, it was rough trying to stay focused on my homework. Suddenly, my strength showed up and grabbed my attention; it was a higher beam shining down on me. Not truly understanding who the creator was, but I felt great knowing that something was there watching over me.

As time moved on, I was surrounded by God and a graceful moment appeared. Let's just say a moment that one day you want to experience. It's an experience of complete humbleness. Wow, that pretty much describes it in a word!

How could I ever forget the day in 3rd grade when my mother heard I was failing a subject? She decided to take it upon herself to hold me back a grade. Instead of letting me proceed to the fourth grade, my mom felt I should repeat the 3rd grade. Even after my teacher explained to her that if I went to summer school, I could possibly pass to the fourth grade. The load was very heavy, but yet I refused to put it down. You know what I mean!

All I've ever felt growing up was let down from all of my mother's bad decision makings. Here it's one of the biggest moments of my early life in third grade and she now comes into the situation, not even thinking before speaking and gives the wrong answer. Wow, what am I to do? Throughout our moves in and out of different homes, academically I simply lost the struggle. There's no other way of saying it, we had to get through it the best way we knew how which for me was prayer!

I used to visit a friend named Sha who lived across the street from us. I always felt like it was my home as I slept, crapped, ate and got my hair straightened all in the same house. Unfortunately, Sha's mother, Kary was in a terrible fire that took her life. This hurt us all in a way that I will never forget. Sha's ordeal led her into faith and into writing a book, which gave me the inspiration to do so as well. Ms. Maden, her grandmother was a caring lady with integrity. She became a leader for the community and did whatever she could to keep the kids out of any trouble on the streets.

Ms. Maden would hate to see certain things go on. If she could handle it, she would. "Come here girl, I saw a blackhead in your ear. Let me squeeze it out." As she embraces me, between her legs, I'm already trying to talk my way out of it. It damn near hurt before she even touched my ear. I remember saying, "Ouch what are you doing?" "Hold still I'm almost done, I got it!" Ms. Maden was someone who everyone could go to on a regular basis for anything; she gave so much of herself to the kids in the neighborhood. She and a few other parents came together and formed a drill team for the young males and females. I tell you those were the good old days.

We all were proud about coming together and making it happen as the number one group in the history of Reading. "The Play Girls" were joyous moments that will never be forgotten. We won first place three times. We were proud of our performances because we knew just how hard we had worked to get there. Teresa and Sherry were our drill team leaders and boy they were tough; many days felt like we were in boot camp. We were ambitious, persistent, dedicated and strong with confidence all wrapped in one. This is why I'm where I am today. Mom, I just want to thank you because it was you along with others who instilled good principles in my life!

Trust me, if you messed up then you ran four laps without stopping and if you stopped then you ran an additional lap. It was rough, but it made us into strong young ladies. In order for me to understand that one day, we would all look back and say, "You made it out!"

Most of the time when I look at my life as a child, I often wonder where my head was at. Heidi always appeared to be ahead of her years, as we all wondered, was it best that "Heidi was too fast for her age?" As she got older, she began to take me along on bus rides out of town to meet her boyfriends. Heidi met a guy from Philly named Denim. They dated for a few months getting to know one another.

It wasn't until my mother found out that Heidi was pregnant at seventeen when she and Heidi began to get into major arguments. All along Heidi may have thought she was older, but my mom made it well known that she wasn't.

"Heidi you're not grown!"

That weekend my mom decided to go to Virginia and Heidi decided at the last minute that she wanted to stay home so my mother laid some rules on the table. "Heidi, I don't want anybody in the house while we're gone! You know my rules!" That statement obviously went in one ear and out the other. Repeatedly over the weekend, my mom tried calling the house and got no answer. My sister was nowhere to be found. No sooner than we got back, Teresa discovered all of Heidi's clothes gone from her closet. I guess Heidi called herself running away. Yeah! At seventeen and with Denim. Ha ha, figure that.

Teresa was not having it, she found out where Denim lived in a matter of minutes and before you know it, we were at his front door. "Heidi, what the hell is your problem?"

"What the hell is your problem! You call yourself running away to Philly, huh? Do you even know where you are?" "Mom!" "Shut up, I'm talking! When I tell you to talk then that's when you can open up your damn mouth. Until then I don't want to hear a word! Heidi, I guess I wasn't supposed to find out where you were?" "Mom we don't get along and that's why I left." "Well guess what, get over the thought of staying because you're going home now, so get your stuff!" I wonder why black women hold grudges forever?

It's November 2, 1989. Heidi's delivery date rolled around and we found ourselves sitting, standing and lounging waiting for her to drop her bundle of joy. Finally, the moment was here. Heidi says, "I gotta pushhhhh! "Scooty go get a nurse," she begins to strain as she speaks. "Get a nurse because I have to pushhhhh!" Running down the hallway, "Heidi needs a nurse, her baby is coming out." Nurses are running down to her room then check to see how far she is dilated and the baby's head is right there. She screams, "It's comingggg!" The nurses support the baby as he comes through. "It's a boy!" I am a proud auntie. "Oh, my goodness, look how light he is. He's so handsome!" "Oh, my goodness!" Heidi had shunned away her first-born son, a bundle of joy that we all fell in love with. The caring sister that I am, I step right in caring as an auntie should. And not to mention what my mother has also done for the new bundle of joy in our lives. Denim begins to see the patterns of my sister's lifestyle as a young mother and he becomes a responsible father by stepping up to the plate.

Wow, before you knew it, Heidi began to take us all for granted. Let the truth be told, the generation curse of being irresponsible was now set upon her. How would she handle it? The boy has been an extraordinary kid since I could remember. I feel bad for my nephew for many reasons.

Finally, the family has come together somewhat in making things work. I just believe when it comes to an innocent baby, no one should have to suffer, but never once did I ever think that after I graduated high school, this would be my life. It was a big surprise to me too. I mean think about, how many of us would stop living our younger life, our future, our life's lessons and dreams, to take on our sister's responsibilities in raising her child while she goes off to live her life by herself. Something sounds wrong with that picture, huh! Some may say I might have done the same thing and some might say I wouldn't have!

I often wondered what caused Heidi to take this route the way she did after giving birth, especially after knowing all that our mother put us through as kids. My mother and I took care of the baby, up until he was about five years old. Since then, his dad sought full custody of his son and did a wonderful job in raising him. My sister of course never changes a beat.

After her first born was here, she began having children like she's cashing in chips at the Arial Hotel in Las Vegas. Heidi's next son, Trey, was born by the time I was in the tenth grade. Two years pass and we're now welcoming a healthy chocolate baby girl into the world named Shan. Heidi ended up playing that same game my mother once played with me about one of her boyfriends. As time went on, Heidi became pregnant once again.

It's now four years later and my sister just so happens to bump into Steve and boom she's pregnant for the fourth time. Stay with me now. They marry and Heidi gives birth to her last healthy beautiful baby girl, named Kyah, on her oldest son's birthday,

November 2, 1996. How often does that happen?

A few months later I met a kid from Camden, New Jersey. It wasn't until he introduced me to karate when I later met his instructor, Washington. We spoke for a short while and he instantly had my interest. I gathered information and proudly took it home for mother to read.

Before you knew it, I was a big part of the Washington Academy of Martial Arts. It was wonderful because now I could believe in something positive about myself. I practiced every day! Eventually, I was able to do a full split, of course kicking very high, impressing myself. Excited about purchasing the protective gear, even Icy Hot to warm my muscles, I was now a part of a team and so ready to do just whatever was expected and more. I gained much confidence. Now, I thought I was ready to begin sparring with the instructor, fearing absolutely nothing by this time. Oh, and by the way, I gave the Instructor a run for his money. Washington seemed shocked at what I had learned so soon.

Mr. Washington became someone I could trust from a man's point of view considering what had transpired from my past with male relationships. It's simple, I now became open minded and a person who obviously was searching for prosperity. Just know when I fight, I fight hard! I have won a six-foot grand champion trophy in Ohio and a $50.00 savings bond. I gravitated toward self-empowerment but also had feelings of wanting to be a part of the karate team. We traveled to different cities and states for our karate tournaments. I lost the tournament in Lancaster, Pennsylvania. Mr. Washington believed in determination, hard workouts, confidence and building our stamina. Icy Hot helped too — can't forget that.

By the next tournament in Columbus, Ohio I was definitely ready. This was one of the biggest competitions our team had ever attended. We all were extremely excited about performing, especially me. This time around I was more focused than ever before. Mr. Washington was not only my instructor while growing up he was a mentor too. He truly cared about the community and brought such positive thinking into our lives teaching us to be focused. A few years later, I wanted to explore life more and quit karate.

I eventually started to date J, the Puerto Rican kid on our team who looked Caucasian. Hell, the black kids in my neighborhood were nothing but trouble! You could see them coming from a mile away. I had no interest in them. I figured at least J had an interest in something, karate. J was a close friend more than anything else.

Later as I found out, I liked him more than he liked me. He was a sweetheart, a respectful kid from New Jersey until we would find ourselves spending time together while we practiced karate. Later deciding to become friends, I found out that he was older than me which really only meant soon enough he would want a piece of that caramel toffee.

Southwest Junior High School is where many of us attended and as some may have called it, the school of fighters. Boy! Were they right! Because that's all I've ever been exposed to. I was strong willed if you can understand what I'm saying. Southwest Junior High School also had great teachers. Mrs. Williams was our only African American teacher (home economics); we had many fun days in her class. Mr. Mackle (wood shop) was definitely cool with us. He arranged for the eighth grade to attend Philadelphia to visit one of the great schools, Temple University. Mr. Fritz (electric shop) always was a disciplinary as he would say, "Scooty stop talking in line!" Awe Fritz you didn't have to call me out like that, dude!

Our teachers were too hip and we were fortunate because we never had to witness any of the racist stuff. The message of Dr.

Martin Luther King's dream stayed strong at our school. I'm glad that we're living The Dream, right here and right now, experiencing the second term with our 44th President of the United States and the first African-American President, Barack Obama. "Yay!" "Yes, we can!" Yes, politics have changed in American history! As Martin would say, "I've seen the promised land, I may not get there with you, but I want you to know that we the people will get to the promised land." What a strong message!

Imagine having to face the power of an imperialistic nation. Do you understand where I'm coming from? We the minorities were less fortunate, it was those certain teachers who took charge for immediate change as they believed in all fairness to us. What an experience we had! It was everything beyond expectations. But it gave a sense of direction and ambition to dream. A few weeks later we traveled to Washington, DC, which was another great trip. Monday morning came and everyone had on his or her rainbow-colored T-shirts that read Southwest Jr. High.

One day as I'm changing classes I run into some kid who has these gorgeous eyes and perfect smile. Of course, as I become more curious, I began to ask my girlfriends who he was because they all lived in the same projects. "Liz, who's that kid right there?" Liz shakes her head, "You don't even want to waste your time, girl that's Edgar." I turn and asks Marilyn "Tell me something about him." "Why you want to know him; he has a big ass nose." "So, he's cute, did you see his eyes?"

Marilyn says, "You should keep looking if you ask me!"

"For your information Hun, I wasn't looking. We just happen to continue running into each other, dang can't I be curious?"

"Yeah, but him? Ughhhh, not him!"

"Forget you, girl, I can't talk to you."

Iris started laughing, "You sure can't, not about Edgar!"

So finally, after learning very little about him, I approached him the very next time I saw him at a basketball game. Of course, one thing leads to another. Meanwhile, we grew to know one another and we became good friends in about two months. We introduced each other to our mothers. His mom, Lucia, has always been a sweet lady.

By this time, I'm fourteen. Heidi and I are finally reunited with our mother for a few years now before I go into high school. Finally, we made it while gathering wisdom along the way. I had to focus on having a healthy self-image but didn't know how to capture it. God made us in his image. Enjoying life is very important to me, it truly brings peace to my spirit.

Well, a hard head makes a soft ass watching Heidi all these years. It wasn't until the year of 1990 when I found myself knocked up. Yes, pregnant! No, I never married. My gorgeous son was cared for and loved by many family and friends, while his dad took a hike, walked off like a shift on a job.

However, many years later it caught up to him. Eventually, I joined a program called Teen Parenting. Teen Parenting is a class which supports young mothers by teaching them about motherhood. Services included baby daycare at the high school while the mother attended classes and vans that transported mother and child to the daycare at the high school daily. These services are very much needed when you are a teen mother. Trust me, I needed it. Because if I didn't have it, I don't know what I would have done.

Every day was a grind. I went to classes, determined to graduate from high school and go to college. My spirit was stronger than ever in meeting the goals of becoming a nurse. There was so much more I wanted to accomplish, but I was called to do something else, something that I actually enjoy although it may cause heartache. But faith keeps me grounded.

My God will use his riches in Christ Jesus to give everything you need.
Philippians 4:19

CHAPTER 3

"A Village Can Raise You"

"Hey, Denise?" As we pass each other in the hallways every day at Lauer's Park Elementary School. "Hey Scooty, ask if you can come over today after school!" I rushed through the door and quickly finished up my homework before asking Pop-Pop if I could go to my friend Denise's house for a while. In his broken English, he would say, "Where she live at?"

"Across the street from the school!"

"What time is it now?" "4:00 O' clock!"

"Okay, call me at 6:00 and I'll meet you at the corner!" I rush off and ring the doorbell.

"Hi is Denise here?"

"Yes, she is, come on in baby. What's your name?"

"Scooty!"

"Oh, you're Teresa and Willie's daughter!"

"Yes ma'am, what's your name?

"Ms. Tina to you darling." Scooty walks through the door.

I look around in amazement. "Wow, your house is nice! What kind of work do you do?"

"Well, I own my own business. That's enough for you to know young lady!"

"My mom says she's going to teach me how to handle our own business too."

"That's nice!"

Denise comes downstairs. 'Hi, Scooty! Do you want to see how many Barbies I have?"

"How many Barbies do you have? I don't have even one."

"Come on. I want to show you my new Barbie Doll Dream House!"

Denise was like a sister to me. I was fortunate to know her which later gave me the opportunity of knowing her mother. Ms. Tina was considered to be a "class act" within our community. To know her was to love her.

That evening Denise invited me to stay for dinner. Sitting at the table I noticed how neat everything was placed. Denise and I were always cleaning. Glasses weren't clean enough until they sparkled. I wondered because at home I could never seem to keep my own dresser clean, but everything else in the crib was neatly cleaned and put away. I asked if I could learn how to set the dining room table and for a half an hour, studied it. I was proud of my efforts because I was someone who wanted to learn something different than other teenage girls in the neighborhood, as Denise and I were being conscious of home etiquette. I began to realize that things were very different at Denise's house compared to how I was growing up just around the corner with my grandparents. Having a level of class in a row home took a couple dollars.

Denise says, "Come on I have some more stuff in my room." As we're sitting in her room on thick plush pink carpet, I say to her "You have everything, your carpet even feels special." She turns and smiles. "You like it!"

"Yeah, it's so soft, pretty and pink!"

"Do you like playing Barbies?"

"Yeah, my mom gets me everything that Barbie creates."

"Okay, Denise now you're rubbing it in!" I instantly became envious because the love my friend was receiving from her parents was truly hurtful to watch if you can understand what I'm saying?

Denise and I were very spontaneous girls, whether it was playing with Barbie's or making music with our Yamaha keyboards that we both received one year for Christmas. We tried our best at learning the keys although we never took lessons. We just wanted our independence on this one. Denise says, "I'm going to play the flute and I'm going to take up lessons." "Not me, I want to learn something else."

Ms. Tina was a beautiful lady, vibrant, loving and very outgoing. She was like a mother to me. This is hilarious and you are going to laugh. There's an episode that happened between Denise and me and all hell broke loose, just girls being girls. Denise got mad because I wouldn't stop teasing her dog. Denise said, "Scooty I'm gonna kick your butt if you don't leave Queen alone."

"You ain't gonna to do nothing. Denise, I'm not scared of you." Next thing I knew I was running home.

"Mom, Denise wants to fight me because I was teasing her dog."

"Scooty listen, I don't care who it is, make this your last time running home from anybody, you hear me! Now you take your butt outside and fight back!"

"Mom, are you serious?"

"Do I look serious? You damn right I'm serious. If you have to pick something up and handle your business then do that too!" Teresa didn't play around when she meant business. She was one to teach you early about them streets. I must have done something right because Denise didn't only walk home she ran home too!

Later that evening, Ms. Tina and Denise come around to the house. "Teresa, what's going on?"

My mom says, "Girls, what seems to be the problem?

"Scooty and me aren't getting along."

"Denise is a bully!" I blurt out.

"No, I'm not! Mom, she keeps teasing Queen and I don't like it, so I told her that I was going to beat her up if she didn't stop."

"Are you serious, is that what you two were fighting about?"

"Yes!"

"You two are friends and friends don't fight one another. You two need to apologize and make up."

We hugged each other and apologized. "I'm sorry." "Me too!"

"Girls will be girls," Denise says.

"Yes, we will!" Ms. Tina gives Denise this look and says, "Don't be a smart-ass, watch your mouth!"

The next day in school we were just as happy to see one another again like it was our first-day meeting as friends.

Time passes and Denise is sixteen and I'm turning seventeen. Both of us are excited about getting our driving permits. As soon as Denise had her driver's license Ms. Tina gave her the whip. I also gained more responsibility after getting my permit too. We were always busy going to dances, carnivals and looking at boys, of course.

I had other friends, Lisa and Lilly, who lived right across the street, where I always felt welcomed. Each time I would visit I made myself known by grabbing the hairbrush like a microphone singing, "Love on a Two-Way Street" by Stacey Lattisaw. Singing was my passion, as I thought. Many times, I dreamed of becoming a singer and traveling the world. Lilly would comment, "You can't sing girl," but I would never let anything stop me because I was persistent in learning.

Often times being home alone wasn't an option, so I would go to

Denise's house as a getaway spot for what seemed like a dream come true. Denise was an only child and spoiled beyond rotten. Denise had other friends who would often visit her too. We played Barbies, board games and dress up. We all couldn't wait to get together as we had so much fun. I became spoiled too and never wanted to go home. I said if Denise could have it then why couldn't I? "Denise, do you think that I can borrow your Barbie jet so I can show my mom?" "No!" "Why?" "My mom's not going to let me because she just brought it for me! "I wish I had one!" "What is it called again, so I can tell my mom to get me one?" "A Barbie Jet".

It all left me feeling kind of bad because my mother never seemed to budge even after I requested it more than once. "Mom, can you please get me a Barbie and the Barbie jet?" "We'll see baby!" To my mom, it went in one ear and out the other only because she had a daily grind of getting a lot of other things. I mean, she boosted everything she got us, even the clothes on our backs. After asking Teresa for the umpteenth time I began to feel let down.

Ms. Tina simply showed class and nothing less. Often times she would entertain her close friends and family. As you walked through her doors she would usually say, "Make yourself at home" and I always did feel right at home. There were many nights when Denise and some of her friends would stay up late playing games while the adults enjoyed themselves in a private setting. Ms. Tina was always the life of the party showing everyone a fabulous time. You see Ms. Tina was from Philadelphia. She just knew what the difference was in having class and not being ghetto. If you were ghetto, then you definitely tried to change up your game whenever you came into her presence. When it came to partying however, that's a whole other subject.

Ms. Tina absolutely loved kids and would do anything to show us a joyous time. "Scooty how's your mother doing?" "She's doing okay." "How about your grandparents?" "They're doing okay too." It just wouldn't be Ms. Tina if she didn't care for others as she did. Wow, I cherish and appreciate all the moments we could share together. I'm so honored to have known her for who she was, a great mother, friend and an angel sent from our maker.

I remember the times when Ms. Tina would get a few of Denise's closest friends together taking us all to the circus or to one of the Reading Phillies baseball games. These were such memorable times.

Ms. Tina even went so far as putting a girl's dance group together for us so we could have something to do during our weekends. It consisted of six young ladies. We never practiced so hard in our lives? The best was all she ever expected from us. Practice, practice, practice in the living room, basement and even at her tavern.

One time or another, Denise invited me along for the weekend to visit her family in Philadelphia. She gave me my first real hoagie while going to one of Michael Jackson's concerts, which we happened to miss and cried like babies. "I wanted to see Michael Jackson," cried Denise. "So, did I." Ms. Tina explained, "Girls, it's not the end of the world, there will be another concert." "Mom not like this one." "Denise I'm sure all the concerts are the same."

Each time Ms. Tina took me along she left a great impression of a mother's love. It was then I said to myself: God, I know you didn't intend for me to go through life being miserable, depressed, lonely, sick and defeated. God, I realize I have been beaten down by the struggles in my life. But lately, God I have grown accustomed to being discouraged and sad. Perhaps the devil has deceived me into accepting a life that's far less than my best.

The image that God wanted me to have of myself has been distorted by me. The mirrors in which I have placed in front of myself have reflected the words, actions, and opinions of my loved ones, my peers, and people who have hurt me. And in letting them do so, I have allowed those warped images of myself resulting in feelings of depression, poverty, and despair. But fear not through it all, I am tremendously blessed.

There were times when Heidi and I would have to split up and go into different homes, sometimes people we didn't even know. We had to learn to trust people again and again, but when I least expected it, there was one of my mom's friends who lent a hand while mom took off once again.

Ms. Joyce was an old school friend I guess. At least that's what the relationship appeared to be. "Scooty these are my two daughters, Monique and Dana." "Hi! Hello, you can sleep in my room," Monique said. "Monique, can you please put Scooty's bags upstairs in the bedroom?" "Thank you!" "You're welcome baby, I'll call you when dinner is ready."

Are you listening? Teresa would drop me off like a bad habit and disappear; it was something more than rough. Standing outside trying to get a breath of fresh air, I'd hear: "Scooty, get in here. If your mother knew you were outside after dark she would kill me." "It's hot in your house! "You need air conditioning, Ms. Joyce." "Well, if it's too hot for you, then find your mother and tell her to cool you off, Missy Ann." I would say to myself, lady you just don't know how I wish that I could!

It's been hard adapting to someone else's rules each time we had to change homes. Missing our mother was extremely worrisome and draining to our little spirits. Meanwhile, my sister was at her Godmother's house going through the same agony. Reaching deep down inside, I searched and searched for the strength to keep me grounded in faith more than I ever thought I would have to.

Many times, I would ask, "Why is our mother putting us through all this?" I would often say, I thought I was a princess, not Cinderella. It was bad enough I was already hanging with Denise, someone who had everything like a princess, while I had rags. I mean not that bad but bad enough. Plus, I didn't even have a castle to call my own. But there was one thing I did have, and that was a lot of tears. Tears were shed while falling asleep many nights. These tears would run down my face like water in a stream with no end. Striving to live through trials and tribulations each day was so bad I put my feelings away. I still have the lines between my eyes today that express all the pain that I held onto and pushed away.

"Scooty, what's wrong baby?"

"I'm okay!"

"Are you sure?"

"Yeah, I mean yes."

That was the stock answer I gave everyone who cared enough to ask about me. In some kind of way, I found the determination to get through all this madness. I asked God to put some fire in my spirit so I wouldn't get out there and deal with any bad situations. As time went on, I prayed and prayed, asking God every night "to bring my mother home and to please take care of her and my sister while they were apart. Let them be safe and make sure that mom hadn't lost her way because she sometimes would forget to come back and get us. And God, if there's a Barbie jet in heaven that you don't want I'll take that too, if that's ok with you and for anyone else, I may have missed, Amen."

Every night I prayed that prayer and as I stood up off my knees I would remember that dreams do come true, regardless of what they are. Early in life, I felt that God had a specific purpose for my life, so I refused to give up. Here it is another day that Teresa was off and running again doing her thing. It was the day before she was leaving and here we were already missing her.

"Mommy where are you going this time? "I'm going to work at the State Fair in Michigan." "But mom you just got here and I wanted to ask you something." "Scooty can it wait?" Walking away whispering, "I just wanted to ask if Heidi and I would ever go with you one day." Teresa rushes off. Each day she was gone seemed like an eternity, anxiously waiting and waiting for her return. Believe it or not, it was only about a week later when Ms. Joyce surprised me one evening after dinner. "Scooty your mom will be coming to pick you up soon." I threw my hands up in the air and started dancing around. "Yes, she's coming, she's coming!"

Minutes later the doorbell rang. "Who is it?" "It's Teresa." Teresa walks through the door with a big bag in her hand, hugging me tightly. "Mommy you're back!" "Awe baby did you miss me?" "Yes, I did!" "Hello, girls I have something for you." "Monique this is for you and Dana this is for you." "Thank you, Ms. Teresa." "Your welcome babies." "Well, I gotta run," Teresa reaches out to hug Joyce, "Thanks for taking care of Scooty" handing her something too. "Scooty where's your bag?" "I got it, I'm ready!" "Say thank you to the girls and Ms. Joyce for their nice hospitality." "Thank you!" "Sure baby!"

By this time, I was so used to going from one place to the next I never took it for granted. All the time that Heidi and I were ever apart, we never spoke on the phone making us miss one another's love even more. "Mommy are we going to pick up Heidi?" "Yes in a few minutes." "Scooty I might have to go back to work in two weeks, but I'm going to be taking you and Heidi with me." "For real mommy, for real, for real!" "Yes, for real!" Teresa pulls up to pick up Heidi and no sooner than Scooty sees her, she gives her a big hug and kiss. Teresa gets into the car. "Scooty, did you tell your sister the good news", she starts crying because she's so happy and excited too. "Mom is this true are we really going with you?"

"Yes, wow you girls are really excited, I tell you!" Heidi says, "We miss you a lot mommy when you're gone."

"I know baby when I'm gone it's all for you and your sister, though!"

"Uh huh, in a couple of weeks, we'll be staying for half the summer in Michigan."

Heidi and I were smiling and cheering because we couldn't believe what we were hearing. When you think about what we really had to go through, never really having any stability early, it left us always looking and wondering where we were going to end up each day.

At the fair, our mother hooked us up while she worked. We rode all the rides for free until we tired ourselves out. Kevin, my mom's boyfriend, made up as a father figure to me. He cared enough to join us on days winning us lots of different stuffed animals while mom worked. Kevin and Heidi were playing games as I walked off to go look for my mom in the ladies' room. Not knowing which direction to go, I somehow found my way there. I couldn't believe how close I was to my mother.

Opening the door to the ladies' room. "Hi, mom" giving her a hug and kiss on the cheek. "Are you done yet? Mommy, I want you to take a break so you can ride with us."

"Where are Kevin and Heidi at now?"

"Around the corner playing games," if I only knew the truth. I didn't really know their whereabouts so I lied and really didn't care. Come to find out they were on the other side of the park.

"Scooty, I'll come and play some games with you in a little bit let me finish up, okay Missy Ann."

"Alright, mom!" She made me sit still on a bench right outside the bathroom door.

"Are you ready young lady. Oh, girl, you're a complete mess, let's get you cleaned up. Then what do you want to play and where is Heidi?" Luckily as we were walking toward the game room closer to the ladies' room, they were coming out looking for me. When Kevin saw me, he picked me up and whispered into my ear in such a tone. "The next time you go walking off young lady, he pauses you better say something. Do it again and I'm gonna teach you a lesson, I'm going to beat your butt!" "Okay!"

Right away my mother kisses Heidi, "Hi baby."

"Mwah, hi mom!"

"What games did you play?"

"All of 'em."

"Kevin, Scooty wants me to play with her so badly she came looking for me."

"Yeah, I know!"

"Kevin, how many tokens do you have left?"

"All I have are these."

"Here do me a favor because we are going to need some more!"

"Mom do you like cleaning the bathrooms?"

"Scooty I'm doing the best I can for right now. I'm just making sure you and your sister have what you need to survive while we're out here. Aren't you happy to be here with me?"

"Yeah, mom!"

"What did I tell you, it's not yeah, it's yes and I'm not going to tell you no more."

"I love you, mommy!" Tears ran down her face, "Love you too baby!"

"Mom it looks like you really enjoyed yourself." She laughs, "I really did!"

No sooner than they got home, Teresa goes shopping for their school clothes, packing their bags and making arrangements for them to be picked up from her girlfriend's house. Next thing they knew she was gone handling her business, once again.

Today is Friday and school starts in three days. I'm nervous because I didn't have any money so what was I going to eat for lunch every day. I moved into my Aunt Tooty and Uncle Bubb's house where I had cousins up the ying yang running around playing games. "Aunt Tooty, please don't forget to tell Uncle Bubb that I'm gonna miss his sweet potatoes that he made for us," giving her a kiss.

"I'll make sure to tell him, baby."

"Your fried chicken is the best."

"Oh, you do enjoy it, huh that's good!"

"Baby we all enjoyed having you, come back soon you hear."
"Okay, I Aunt Tooty I will!" I felt lucky to have her as my Godmother as she lived just a block away from my grandparents. I visit as often as I can and even sit next to her at church. Unfortunately, Dupont relocated to California when I was still young. Wow! What a drastic change from living in Reading.

My mom invites me along to a wedding reception where I finally have the chance of meeting my Godfather Dupont. What a fabulous person he was. Dupont was a beautiful person inside and out. Anyone who knew him knew just that. My Godmother Barbara was there too, so it worked out perfect enough to get a snapshot of all of us together for once. Fabulous!!!!! It was finalized, we were all a family now.

While in elementary school, I stayed in touch with Barbara. She was always concerned with how things were going for me in school.

Barbara had already been aware of my situation and that my mother was always away. Barbara always made sure that I received good hospitality while visiting her family. After a few times of having chicken noodle soup and crackers, I was hooked. There were many times when I was dead tired from playing all day with my friends and after eating all my soup I would watch TV and eventually drift off to sleep.

"Scooty are you sleeping?"

"No Godmother I'm watching TV."

"It looks like the TV is watching you, baby, come on sweetie lay down on my bed upstairs," covering me up and kissing me on the forehead. "I love you, sweetie."

A few hours later I awaken to the bedroom door screeching. It's my God sister Bonnie checking in on me. "Are you okay?" Stretching and yawning, "Yes." "Are you ready to come downstairs now?" "Uh huh, gotta go to the bathroom. But Bonnie, I'm gonna go home because it's getting dark and I'm getting hungry." Looking back those were special times that were shared with Barbara.

My mom's girlfriend, Sher, was sort of out of the ordinary. Her house was like my house. "Scooty, what's up girl? How are you?"

I give a stock answer, "Fine."

Right then her mask would change again into another character that would seemingly chase her back and forth in her head, putting out the last energy that she had to give.

"Aunt Sher, do you have any jokes to tell?"

"Scooty, you know J.B. is the comedian around here."

"Are you gonna do my hair the way you did it last time?"

"Yes, your mother said to keep it simple."

"Simple? I want my hair like yours."

"Okay let's see what we can do here. I hope your mom doesn't kill me for this?"

"How can she kill you when she's not here? It doesn't even matter if she finds out."

"You don't know your mother like I do."

"I wish I did!"

We would tell jokes, play games or watch TV. It was routine because we all lived on the same block. When summertime rolled around a lot of us would be hanging out. Never really having anything else to do besides to play store with a homemade desk that we pretended was a cash register. After a while, I became bored with that and curious. So, I found myself sitting and looking out the window. All you could hear were the girls down on the corner laughing with the guys while they were busting on each other and beating on the mailbox singing Rick James and someone else beatboxing.

My mom had certain people she trusted to watch over Heidi and me while she was gone. Ms. Yannie was a childhood friend who loved mangos so that made it much more comfortable to be around. Yannie and Teresa were always out shopping and bringing goodies home for us kids: Miki, Jaine, Heidi and me. Here we found ourselves back and forth to the corner store buying up mangos like we were in the Virgin Islands picking them off the trees.

"Jaine my mango is sweet."

"Mine is too."

We would take long walks to City Park meeting up with friends. We were always busy doing something fun. Miki and I were around the same age so we became good friends. Jaine was a few years younger than us, so this meant whenever we went someplace Jaine couldn't go along and that kind of felt good, quickly remembering when I was in those same shoes with my sister and her friends.

Teresa says, "Scooty, I'm going to be leaving you with Ms. Joyce again until I get back from Michigan."

"Mom, where is Heidi going?"

"She'll be going to her Godmother's again."

"Why can't we just go with you?"

"Scooty because you two have to go to school. I'll be back real soon." She kisses me and says, "I love you baby, have a good day tomorrow in school."

"I will. I love you too, mommy."

This time, while staying at Ms. Joyce's house, her daughter Monique's coat catches fire from the electric heater in her room. "Mommy, mommy there's a fire in my room."

"What? Oh, my goodness, somebody hurry up and get the fire extinguisher in the kitchen!" Joyce enters the room putting out the fire. "Is everyone ok?"

"Yes! Now that was scary Monique."

"Yeah, I know."

"I wish my mom was here."

"She is."

"Where?"

"She's in you."

Along the way, there came another friend and you know what that meant for Heidi and me. Only, this time, we're together at Ms. Brena's house. Ms. Brena is a sweetheart, especially after getting to really know her. Often times she would go to town to run errands and visit her family. For us, it was convenient because our grandparents lived around the corner from her family. Although she enjoyed the time she spent with her and her son Anthony, he became annoying after a while because he insisted that I be his girlfriend at eight-years-old. "Anthony will you please leave me alone. Anthony, stop!" "Okay, okay!"

Aunt Dee lived with her parents, my great-grandparent's Clint and Lizah Seriff, who resided on North Fourth Street. Their home was such a warm and welcoming nest for family and friends who would often stop by every day to check in on them and say hello. It was one of those homes that you just couldn't forget about because we all practically grew up there.

There was enough family to go around. It's a large family, with children, grandchildren, great-grandchildren and many friends who helped out in the kitchen with cooking and cleaning. Those were beautiful times. It's so sad for those who take times like these for granted.

Think about your past for a second. What's changed for the worse in your family? You know when our loved ones had respect, integrity, and morals with each other so children of today learn the same. It's so important.

The loved ones who have paved the way for us today, even after what they had to endure coming up themselves. Rough times, but they all persevered. Some are bitter, some still try to be humble. With, of course, a lot less than what we have to this very day, and yet they're grateful for just crumbs.

Along my way, I've gathered some wisdom and realize that no one can keep a good person down, continuing to strive and walk through life by putting Christ first, and always caring for others. My future lays before me, so why should I allow myself to be traumatized when I was given a second chance!

The lord will teach all you children, and they will have much peace.
Isaiah 54:13

CHAPTER 4

Betrayed

Where am I going to be this weekend? Well, it turns out that Heidi and I are going to be at Jane's again in the projects. It wasn't until that day when I was forced into having to play hide and seek. Teresa ran here and there doing whatever it was that she did, never really communicating too much with her kids. Put it this way, I was on my own in the beginning even with loved ones lending a hand. I felt this way because my mother was never around, which built anger inside of my precious little body.

"Jane when did my mom say she was coming back to pick us up?"

"She said in a few days"

"What day?"

"I believe she said Wednesday, but who knows it could be later than that. You know your mom." Ok, my mother called saying that she was coming to see us, yet she pulled another fast episode. No clothes for the entire weekend, which meant I would have to wear my cousin Misha's clothes, at least the ones that I could fit into. She was much skinnier.

Tomorrow is Sunday. Jane calls for me to inform me of the news. No clothes again! Ughhh! "This time you have to stay home with Rey while we go to church."

"Jane, can you buy me something to wear to church?"

"Do you have any money young lady?"

"No, then it looks like you're gonna be staying right here."

"This isn't fair, I wanna go to church."

Once again for the umpteenth time feeling dragged through the mud, because Jane knows how much I enjoy going to church. Misha and I eat breakfast, then run upstairs to get dressed. "Misha I wish I could go with you, try and find something for me to wear."

"Scooty, you know all my clothes are too small for you."

"I know, I was just hoping there was something for me to wear around here!"

Once they leave, I sit there hoping my mom would still show up at any minute. Rey calls me into his mom's bedroom to see if I wanted to play him in a game of Pac-Man. "Yeah, why not I'm gonna beat you anyway!"

That was the only thing that seemed to cheer me up, determined to win a game against the kid who thought he was a pro. Revved up, I actually wanted to finally beat him at his own game. Rey was always undefeated with everyone else, so I walk around to the other side of the bed where Rey was sitting. "You know I'm going to win so get ready, buddy!"

"Naw, I'm the pro! Are you ready? Go!"

He started the game for two players and we played for about an hour. He won two games and I defeated him in the last round. I was excited that I won the last game. "You know that was pure luck that you won that last game, right?"

"Yeah, uh huh!"

Rey turns and gives me this weird look, slowly reaching over trying to touch my legs and pushing me down on the bed. "Rey, what are you doing? Stop!" Rey says, "You know you want it!" I scream, "Get off of me! Stop!" Realizing at that moment no one else was around or even home to help me. Rey forcefully tries to pull my shorts down at the same time I could feel my panties coming down too. I fought and I fought and I fought back as much as I could. "Get off of me!" I still fought my hardest to push him off of me, remember he's seven years older and much stronger than my little body. Eventually, I became very weak, but in my mind, I refused to give up the tussle with him. Screaming and crying. "Stop, Get off me!" Suddenly Rey ripped my panties off, forcing himself onto me.

I felt so scared and extremely violated, all I could do was cry. When he finally stopped he looked me straight in my eyes as though he did nothing wrong, with a smirk on his face. As he goes limp I'm finally able to push him off.

While getting off the bed, I quickly discovered blood all down my legs, everywhere. In shock I run into the bathroom locking the door, climb into the tub and begin to cry frantically with my head down on my knees. At some time or another, I try to get up the nerve to clean myself, confused at nine years old. What was I really going through? Was I traumatized for life? I didn't know what to do; it left me so violated and alone. Now I'm left wondering if and when I decide to come out of the bathroom would Rey try and attack me again. Besides all that, I hadn't received my menstrual just yet. When I saw all the blood everywhere, I panicked.

While sitting there in the bathroom this torment replayed over and over in my head. I scream out, "Where's my mom, why did this have to happen to me?" How could he do this to me? I'm just a little girl."

The minute I opened that bathroom door I wanted to run outside, but I panicked and ran into my cousin's room hiding in the closet next to a tall green trash bag full of clothes, hoping that he wouldn't see nor hear me. I worry if he could hear me moving around as I try to disappear. The bathroom door opens and seconds later I suddenly feel someone standing over me. He was so cold he just stood there. All I could do was curl up into a fetal position, as I heard his voice.

Rey says, "Why are you hiding in the closet?"

It was such a weird feeling because nothing had seemed to affect him at all. My world would never be the same; it had changed from that moment on. So much for trusting the wrong ones, but I never thought in a million years Rey would hurt me. "You took advantage of me! Now you must answer to God!"

Hours later, Jane and the girls arrived home. Now feeling safer, I wipe my tears away. Jane asks, "What's wrong with you?" Instantly feeling ashamed, thinking that Jane wouldn't believe me if I told the truth, I said that Rey hit me. "He did what? Rey, bring your ass downstairs, right now! What do you call yourself doing hitting on Scooty? You don't hit girls." Rey was speechless and surprised. "Rey, you owe Scooty an apology." I regret so much holding the information in which actually damaged my spirit for many years in the worst way possible.

Looking back, I was more upset at myself. It's as real as it get's because whatever hides in the dark, will always come to light. The truth be told, Rey Decoy raped me when I was nine years old and that's what set the course for a very long time in my life.

As he turns looking at me, I turn away in such shame. In a soft voice, he plays the victim. "I'm sorry Scooty." Then he walks away.

Days pass. Me, Nona, Misha, Heidi and Mark all decide to play some of our favorite games, like Monopoly and Uno, for hours. Time pressed on and it got late. Us girls went upstairs to change and eventually we all turned in for the night. I don't quite remember when I fell asleep, but I definitely remember being awakened by Rey laying right there next to me. He lifts the covers and once again is trying to touch my legs. "What are you doing?" I quickly jump up and lay down next to Nona waking her. Nona says, "Rey will you please leave her alone so she can go to sleep?" She turns and drifts back off.

I try my hardest to stay up for as long as my little eyelids could stand it and eventually drift off to praying that he wouldn't bother me anymore.

The next morning I made sure that I was safe in someone else's presence at all times just so he wouldn't try anything. Of course, Rey plays it to no end, as if nothing ever happened which became very scary. He knew to chill out because his mother didn't play around, she's the beast of the family. I say, "I see why now."

One evening Heidi and I sat talking about the past and certain things began to surface. Shocking things! Heidi says, "I remember when we all used to go to Jane's for Christmas and she would cook everything you could name in a cookbook. And I might have to add mom's good ol baked macaroni and cheese with the sharp cheese. We'd all be cramped up in that little ass bright orange living room."

"Uhh, huh I remember. Did you know that Rey raped me?" Heidi looks at me with hurt in her eyes, "You too?"

"Wait a minute! This is crazy all these years, you mean we shared the same secret and nobody knew?"

Heidi says, "There was something else that Rey did to me one time." She laughs, "It's really not funny…. Rey made a hole in his pants pocket. He asks for me to stick my hand inside the pocket leading me to think that he was playing some kind of joke and when I put my hand in his pocket, here his penis was sticking out. I realized what it was and quickly pulled my hand out. 'Your nasty!'" Now, this goes as far as saying that Rey's a disgrace to his own family. Iniquitous! Rey now resides in California. Whenever the time came and Scooty knew he was going to be coming into Reading from California, she tried her best to stay away from his presence.

It's summer of 2003, a few of us were visiting our grandparents while sitting on the porch enjoying the weather when I noticed Jane and what I thought were her and her two daughters and kids pulling up to park. Everyone's greeting one another and I catch eye contact with Rey... my skin crawls and heart begins to beat faster. Wow, I damn near run off, but decide to stand there and deal with it head on.

For some reason, his conscience wouldn't allow for him to stand tall enough to approach me. Good! The entire time he was there I felt very uncomfortable because he made himself known, I was afraid as an adult to leave the porch. It wasn't until Jane and her kids were walking down the street ready to leave when Rey hung back while I sat there next to my grandmom not realizing at first that my feet were hanging through the banister. While talking to grandmother, he touches my feet, gives me a look and says, "Bye".

Mom-Mom says, "Rey they gonna leave you!" He looks at her, "I wanted to give you a hug and kiss." I pull my feet back and give him the nastiest look. That feeling quickly resurfaced even after all these years; my grandmother even noticed that something was wrong. "What's wrong Scooty?" Whenever I think about it, it makes me sick. As he walks away, I fill my grandmother in on what I've been holding in all these years. I had never felt so uplifted and so relieved to get this off my chest.

Mom-Mom, Rey raped me when I was just a kid."

"He did what?" shocked as all hell. "Scooty, as long as he has breath in his body he will walk around with a guilty conscience and one day he will have to answer to God for what he's done to you."

Again, feeling ashamed. "Oh yes, he will!" Feeling so relieved after all the time had passed, I figured if that day ever came and I would decide to share the biggest secret of my life, why not share it with the one I loved most, my grandmother Mattie Wilson.

Honestly, I have often tried to block it all out, but somehow it always seems to resurface, watching the news and hearing about innocent kids getting raped was never a good look for me. These crazy pedophiles out there today who violate kids is enough to upset anyone, let alone how I really feel. So disgusted.

My mother is steadily trying to make a way for herself. She's actually going away again. Mom makes arrangements for me to stay at Ms. Bren 's house for the weekend. The very next day Ms. Bren happens to go into town to visit my family. When they arrived at our family's home everyone's gathering in the kitchen eating and socializing. Ms. Bren's brother Curt DeBoise walks in. He's someone I don't know. We're introduced. "Scooty do you know how to play any of the newest video games?"

I was naïve and answered "yes." I've always been anxious and competitive to learn how to play new games, so we leave the kitchen where all the adults were and head toward the sitting room upstairs. Once we arrived upstairs, something came over me, not realizing what it was right away. Maybe I was just excited about learning how to play some new video games. Curt started pulling out a variety of new games asking her to pick out a few to play. Right away he began to show her different moves in ways to play in order to win.

"Scooty do you have a boyfriend?"

"How can I have a boyfriend, I am only nine years old?" While focusing on the game she began to play, ignoring him, he stood up from the floor and walked over closing the door.

"They're making too much noise downstairs."

Instantly I became scared and very nervous. I said, "I have to leave the room." As he walked back toward her, he took out his penis, "I want you to suck my penis or you can't leave the room." Realizing at that moment that I had to get away, fast. All I could say to myself was how did I get into this situation again just by wanting to learn how to play a damn video game.

When I tried to get up to leave he grabbed my arm and forced me to perform oral sex on him. I jumped up and ran down the steps and out the front door. I never turned around until I reached my grandparents' house just minutes away around the corner. Once I got there no one was home. I said to myself as long as I could sit there, I would feel safe, sitting there for hours in rage. Crying asking myself, "Why me? Where's my mom? Where's my dad? Why me?"

Ms. Bren pulls up in front of the house. I was in a procrastinating state of mind afraid to tell her the truth, again feeling blamed, but it's all I could think about. "Scooty come here, why did you leave my parents house without saying a word? I was worried. I didn't know where you were." At that moment I wanted to blurt out the truth, instead, I froze not knowing what to say, making up another lie. I asked myself who in a million years would ever think that this would happen to me again and again. Feeling alone, hurt and even ripped to pieces in my spirit. When does this stop? It doesn't. My life gets worse.

Come to find out years later Curt, you know the kid who made me perform oral sex on him, well his karma followed him right into the hands of the law sending him to jail for many years. Huh, see when it comes to God's work, he always has a plan and we may not even know what's next for us especially when we choose to do wrong to others.

Learning through all of my trials and tribulations, the way I experienced love and security meant everything while growing up. Unfortunately, I'm lacking big time when it comes to love and trust because my dysfunctional past has placed me in very unhealthy relationships. Since then some things have changed.

I asked myself many, many times, "Why was I raped and forced to do the unimaginable things? I mean how was I going to deal with the pain at such a young age?" Could you ever imagine yourself living in a shell and being left to find out what and how your adult challenges would really be at such a young age? Truly I'm referring to my parents not being around to protect me when I truly needed them most, getting raped, forced to perform oral sex and constantly moving around into different homes was simply enough for me to be sitting in a crazy house somewhere today. But no! I'm blessed by God!

My soul was in turmoil for many years, deep down inside I knew that I had to forgive and move forward with my life one day. My story is just so traumatic. But again, I asked God to help me find my way out of all the darkness.

I send this message to Rey he knows exactly who I'm talking too, "I forgive you, but I'll never forget, Christ lives within me. I can only tell you this because of my faith in God which makes me know and understand what miracles really are."

For God so loved the world that he gave his one and only Son, that whoever believes in him shall not perish but have eternal life.

John 3:16

CHAPTER 5
DNA

Could you imagine at a very young age wanting to have a closer relationship with the woman you call mother? But at the same time in doing so, you felt that there's something missing. Most daughters want a close relationship with their mothers, one that a daughter would cherish and embrace. This nurturing relationship is supposed to teach one how to have a love for children in the event of having them. Kids need to love being kids, they don't know anything else and they expect to be loved and nurtured so they can feel secure. Playing dress up, Jacks, Double Dutch and going to the parks to meet up with friends.

Someone once said, "Remember, when you're down to nothing, God is always up to something! I think it's just amazing that I made it through my childhood. Life is full of surprises and let downs, but God is truly awesome. No sooner than I began to believe in Him, He rested his hands upon me.

That one day came when I was beginning to feel incomplete about who my father was. So, I asked my mom, "Who's my dad?" I remember asking numerous times, although Teresa never really gave me an honest answer, but what she did was take the truth and twist it quite a bit, leaving me to believe that it never really mattered. Still, I had yet to get the truth out of her. Teresa dated a few guys but that still didn't answer my question. Let's just say that I was very determined in finding out and I never gave up! I got older and I asked again, "Mom, who's my dad?" Teresa finally said, "Jim!" "When can

I meet him? "Tomorrow evening after he gets off of work, he'll be stopping by!"

Okay, I was excited and definitely anticipating the moment of actually meeting my dad for the first time. It wasn't until later that next evening me and my mother would walk outside to meet Jim sitting in his truck. As rude as it sounds, he never once adjusted himself to greeting his daughter in a proper way. I thought boy if he was my pop, he was a rude dude for sure. Then, Teresa introduced us, "Jim, meet your daughter, Scooty."

"Hello! How are you doing?" Of course, I was young and very shy and didn't quite know what to expect from him. "I'm fine!" So, I gave a two-liner each time we spoke while standing afar for just a few minutes, then quickly running off up the street somewhere with my friends. "Byyye! He says, "Cya later baby!"

Never quite understanding what was really going on, overall, I was happy to finally have met my dad for the first time, very strange, though. At least that's what I thought anyway. Teresa was dating and spending a lot of her time with Jim, who she manipulated me into believing he was my biological father. Now I'm not sure he is! After mom and Junior had their crazy rendezvous, them splitting and going their separate ways left a lot of things so unclear for me while growing up.

Get this... Jim was a married man who ended up having an affair on his wife with my mother. Jim would come by at least four times a week, but no matter what I was doing, Teresa would always manage to pull me away from playing just to come and say hello to this man who suddenly appeared in my life. I often wondered who this man really was that my mother always talked about. At the time I never really felt any sincerity, no real vibes coming from this man what so ever. I just believe that a mother and father are supposed to protect their child from being in any hurtful circumstances. Sometimes love ones can make wrong decisions, but when that child is left in the dark fending for herself in trying to figure things out mentally, then the parents look crazy in the whole situation. What it really shows is that neither one of the parents cared enough about that child's well-being because they were entirely too busy wrapped up in their own crazy lifestyle they were personally going through.

The father gets mad, moves away and turns his back completely neglecting his wife and his child. Now, where does that leave me standing with no father to turn to while growing up? What will the future outcome be for me mentally? How can two people become so selfish after falling in love and getting married for a short period of time! For one, I think that my mother's dishonesty has really hurt me. I feel pushed aside and let's not forget the truth about my dad, which is disastrous for me in so many ways. Really, in reality, it's just another hurtful circumstance that Teresa created. But, I really can't blame just my mom, I have to blame them both.

Hey, but as they say, no one is perfect. I'm not! It's obvious that I had no other alternative moves besides praying to my God. Repeatedly saying to myself, "There's no way, I'm going to continue destroying my self-image on the count of someone else's decision-making. Life isn't over!"

Truthfully, if it weren't for our family trips to Manning, S.C. I probably may not have ever known who my biological father is today by name. What does that really matter, though, I still haven't established a relationship with the man. For the short time that we met, I felt the bond of being a family; we were all a spitting image of one another. Sounds crazy right! I say, "Wow, I finally get the chance to meet you all." Tears roll down my face. "It's okay Scooty don't cry, we are all here now." Grandmom and grandpop you could never imagine what these two have put me through, all these years and now seeing him for the first time it felt like they wanted me to feel something out of this brief moment. Junior reaches out to hug me. "What's wrong?" Teresa stands afar. "Are you okay?"

"No, I'm not and I don't want to talk about it right now." Teresa gave into her guilt you could see it all over her face. I said, "Grandmom, when am I ever going to meet the other half of my family?"

"I was hoping soon baby."

Finally, the day came when I met three of my four uncles. I also had an aunt named N'vella who is now deceased. Often, I wondered how things could have been being raised around the other side of my family too. Laughing, I say, "I would have been country that's for sure." Many times, my grandmother Amena would remind me how much she favored her aunt N'vella. Wondering how beautiful it could have been to live the American Dream by having my mother and father love me unconditionally as their daughter, together, as one big happy family. Junior and Teresa never seem to get along, whatever their differences were, they refuse to let them go. "People get over it, I'm an adult now!"

Hey, it was very simple. They had no admiration, integrity or respect about themselves let alone their daughter. The kicker is that my parents allowed me to grow up outside of our family, instead of grasping me in their arms with love. Wow! It was then that I became a statistic. How much love can two people give in one family; although I was excited and very grateful for being able to spend some time with Junior and his parents for the summer.

Unfortunately, this was the last straw for me. I wanted to stay and Junior pretended as if he wanted to have a major part in my life… Yeah right! Don't believe that for one second. I barely saw him while being there seven weeks. "Grandmom, when is my dad coming by to see us?"

"I don't know baby, hopefully, today he'll stop by."

Every Sunday Amena and I would attend church service. After church, Amena cooked dinner and taught me how to set the table for dinner. My chores were to sometimes clean the kitchen and to take out the trash. The kitchen door opens and its Uncle George stopping by to see how everyone's doing... "George, this is your niece Scoota - boot, I mean Scooty."

"Hi, Uncle George!"

"Come here girl and give me a kiss! You're getting so big, how are you doing?"

"I'm good and yourself? Do you know where my dad is?"

"No baby, I'm not sure? You know what I'm gonna drive by his house and see if he's home, I'll be back in a few minutes." He walks into the kitchen, "Mom and dad I'm gonna run over to Junior's to see if he's around anywhere." Grandpop says, "Good!"

While I am there for the summer, I happen to meet a dear friend by the name of Lela. They called her Pinke. She lived directly behind her grandparents. "Scooty well I guess you'll see Pinke another day now since your dad came by," grandmom says. "Yes, another day because my daddy's here."

"Oh, then you two should have a real nice time together." Junior walks off asking his dad for a few dollars for gas. "Junior, you need to find a job?" "I know I went looking today."

"That's what you said two weeks ago!"

After an hour drive, we finally arrived at Santee Beach. "Dad this is nice, look at all the water, there's a lot of seashells out here." "Here's a rock for you Scoota - Boot. I'll paint it for you before you leave." "Okay, that will be nice!" As I would say today, "yeah something to remember you by. Hmm, exactly. It's the only thing that I can remember."

We had a great time together at the beach, then heading back to my grandparents. Then I stood outside under the carport while he cleaned and oiled the chain on the bike that I would be riding. I was so excited. Actually, it was one of his bikes he used to ride when he was younger. "Here you go Scoota-Boot!"

"Thank you but that's not my name!" He laughs. "Yeah, I know. It was my name back in the day. You're actually riding one of my old bikes." The door opens and it's Amena.

Amena was up early every morning preparing breakfast and listening to her gospel music. One morning she had to run some errands and bumped into an old friend of the family's. It was a coincidence, as they knew the same gentleman from Reading. "Hello, Mr. Hidge how are you doing?" They greet one another and chat for a few minutes. She asks, "When ya'll going back up north?"

"In a few days, we'll be leaving out. We're down visiting family."

"That's always nice. "Are you full going back?"

"No why?"

"I have my granddaughter Scooty down here for what was supposed to be for a few weeks. She gotta get back to school in two weeks."

"Oh, okay! Do you mind if my granddaughter rides back with you?"

"Sure, write your number down and I'll call you on Sunday."

The door opens and it's Amena. "Scoota-Boot come here I have some good news for you. Here grab this bag for grandmom. While I was out I happen to run into a mutual friend of the families, Mr. Hidge and his family came down from Reading to visit their family and he said that you could ride back with them on Sunday afternoon." Amena begins gathering some things to wash, placing her bag on the bed as she begins to pack Scooty's clothes. I'm happy to return home but very saddened by my dad's neglect.

It's Sunday. The phone rings. "Hello there, it's Hidge we'll be by in the next hour to pick up Scooty." The doorbell rings. "Ya'll come on in." William and Amena embrace and chat for a minute. "Well, I hate to have to drop in and leave so soon, but we have to get on the road." "Alright, now! Take care of yourself, baby call us when you get home." Tears roll down my face, "Thanks for everything, I love you guys. See you later!" "Okay, baby!"

Since that day Mr. Hidge has become an adopted Uncle to me. I was so appreciative of what he and his lovely wife had done for me. I frequently visited them. Little did I know, it was God working miracles back then. Instantly they became part of my family. The very next time I spoke to Junior was years later. He seriously expected me to understand one lie after the next. Let the truth be told Junior could care less about me and what my future holds. I often wondered did I ever exist in his eyes? Junior promised me so many things, so many times, but by the time I'd grown I was absolutely fed up with all the promises he's made. Ughhhhh!

He would often say, "I'm coming to Reading to see you as soon as I can" Years later my grandmother happens to speak to me about my parents and how they created a problem for me as a child, mentally and emotionally. "Instead of them sitting you down and discussing what actually happened, they left you wondering for years. Some would say they couldn't imagine how difficult it was for me and my sister to grow up that way! It wasn't fair to us!"

Recently, this time when I spoke to Junior it was the same old same old. He's always so nonchalant. Although this time, he told me something that I least expected to hear. Hell, only after asking for what seemed to be a damn eternity. Who really knows if Junior is telling the truth? I can only remind myself of all the lies he's told in the past.

He said, "Your mom's been creating a bad situation in our marriage by seeing another guy and it's caused for us to have a few run-ins." Junior went on to say, "One day we happen to be visiting my in-laws and Harold stopped by threatening me with a gun and I told him you would be less than a man to shoot me, while I'm holding my daughter." They exchanged words in front of his in-law's house. Just for the record, Junior has a past of not being honest with his daughter, so who's to say anything he says is really truthful.

Meanwhile, Teresa comes walking out of the house. Harold yells out of the window, "Come here hoe!" Junior supposedly said, "Don't you move?" Teresa felt guilty knowing what she put her family through, so she just stood there. Harold got upset and drove off pointing his gun at Junior. "This ain't over, I'll see you again!"

Weeks later, Junior went walking down Second Street as he noticed Harold and took off running through an alleyway. As the night was approaching Junior decided to go down to Abu's speakeasy, his cousin's spot on Third and Elm Street to have a couple of drinks. When he walked in the door, right away he noticed Harold sitting at the bar. He caught up with Boo and gave him the 411 on his cousin Teresa and the moves that Harold was trying to pull on him.

"Hey! Cuz, I'm having a bit of a problem with this guy. He refuses to show me any respect for my family and he threatened me with a gun the other day. It's time for him to be dealt with man." "Alright, I'll handle it!" So, Abu played it easy, Harold was unaware what was about to go down. Harold had no idea of Abu being kin to Junior and Teresa. Abu called Harold over and told him he needed to talk to him in his office. Once Harold got back in his office and he shut the door, they beat him down really bad. The only way Harold left the speakeasy that night was someone helping him up off the floor and carrying him to the emergency room.

Junior says, "Harold was real lucky to even be walking away with just some broken ribs and a disfigured face." Harold refused to show him any respect about his wife in the streets; it's too bad that he had to find out the hard way.

Out of my mother's womb, I was a very strong individual. As they say, I always love to smile, showing all my gums. I even had ribbons taped to my hair while I was in the nursery. Yeah, all that was beautiful, but the question still stood. "Who was I going to be one day? Would I ever have a chance to prove myself?"

My parents made their final decisions amongst themselves on what they thought would be best for them. Before I knew it, I was taking my first steps, weeks later I was walking with a single parent. Soon enough I was beginning head start at Lauer's Park Elementary School. Everything was exciting at that age. I met plenty of friends, but only two of us remained close. Gem and I became very close; we enjoyed finger painting, snacks, and drawing. We would learn our A, B, C's and 1, 2, 3's. We would have three-afternoon snacks, animal cookies, and milk, then we were dismissed for the day anxious to return the next day. When summer finally arrived, we made the best of it.

My first two years of school were fun. Once I moved to the third grade I met my favorite teacher, Mrs. Fiorini. "Mom, I can't believe that you are making me repeat the third grade." "You need it." "No, I don't, I could have gone to summer school and still passed, my teacher said. Why did you decide to do that?" She never even gave it any true thought, it's what she wanted and that's all that really mattered. But, it hurt me.

Mrs. Fiorini simply explained that it would benefit me in the long run and of course, still having the choice of putting me in summer school. It hurt emotionally. I said, "My mother doesn't understand or even care about what we are really going through while she's constantly away from us." It took some time to accept her wrongful decision. "Mom, if you were there helping me with my homework, I would of been more focused and I would be going to fourth grade." "Okay, Scooty there's nothing I can do about those times now can I. We can only try and change things for your future." "Mommy, I tried very hard. "I know baby!"

The day finally came when I realized that I was beginning to grow into a young lady. The day of my graduation, my mother showed up out of nowhere. Prior to that, I hadn't seen my mother in weeks. The moment I saw her I began to cry and my heart began to beat of excitement. "My mom's here, Mommy!"

Mrs. Fiorin calls me over and asks where is she standing? Mrs. Fiorini has been anticipating the moment of finally meeting her all year. Pointing her out, "She's over there in the cream suit! You see her!" Surprised, all she wanted to do was embrace her. After a few minutes, the audience began to applaud, and quickly I run up to her squeezing her as tight as I could. "Mommy, you made it to my graduation."

"Scooty, I wouldn't have missed it for anything in the world, I'm so proud of you baby."

"Where are you sitting at?"

"Over there. There's my teacher, she wants to meet you!"

"Hello, Mrs. Spann." "Hello!"

Of course, I was not just proud of myself, but also really proud that my mother was present, especially after knowing that I have struggled for many years through school. I say, "Wow we're going to the seventh grade." Mom asks, "What school are you going to?" "Northwest!" "Why?" "All you hear is that Southwest is about trouble." "Where did you hear that?" "Everyone says that." "It can't be that bad!"

As some grandparents often share, they were teenagers now and you couldn't tell them anything different. Half of them who were very close were now split up going to different junior high schools. Denise and Verene went to Northwest, and a few of them went to Southwest where it all seemed to take off. Seventh through ninth grades was challenging, but also learning experiences for me. Boys and their manipulating ways, trying to sweet talk us out of our goodies. All you ever heard was, "Come here, girl!" "I gotta get to class." "Can I see you later?" "No, I don't think so." Although Scooty knew what was expected of her to finish the ninth grade, this one boy's name kept resurfacing.

Recently while trying to reach out to Junior at my grandparents, I asked, "Have you talked to Junior at all?" "No, we haven't talked to him in years." "Tell me something. How was my dad as a child growing up?" "Junior was a good kid. He was rough at times, you know a typical boy." "Grandmom what really happened in their marriage?"

"Well baby, they split up so early after just being married." She sighs holding some things back. Let's just say there was so much that I didn't know and now I do. I definitely got it all now; they were married broke, selfish and incompetent young parents. Wow, what a hell of a twist. Several times I tried reaching out to Junior, but there was no luck. Many times, still giving Junior the benefit of the doubt, my grandmother would call me, and we would sit on the phone discussing how hurt I was behind his selfish ways. She was in my corner because she simply understood.

One day she called, but this time, she had excitement in her voice. "Scooty your dad's here, wait to hold on." As he began to speak he lowered his voice. When I heard his voice, I felt a little at ease, hoping that it would be the day for some kind of closure for both of them.

"Hello, how you doing Scooty?" "I'm good, but certain things could be better." Wow, what a surprise. "Yeah, I know." "So, tell me, Junior, what have you been up to?" "Well, I'm working now doing odds and ends jobs." "Like what?" "Handyman work!" "Oh, so you finally found something, good for you." "So where are you staying now?" I'm in Massachusetts with your brother, Bryce." "Oh Really!"

"Listen, all my life I never asked you for one dime, but I need for you to send me some money through the Western Union."

"Scooty unfortunately, right now I don't have it."

Can you believe this? After all these years, he's still telling me he doesn't have it. I had to pay Burt something towards the rent and a bill. I said, "Yeah, I see, look I gotta go I have something that I have to do too." He says, "I love you Scooty." I told him "Yeah, I bet you do Junior. Bye!"

Right now, I'm just so focused on the positive things around me. I just wanna say God bless my grandmother Amena, she was the only one who was generous enough to let me know that there was even a brother named Burt. You can just about guess that was the last time Junior and I spoke. Here I am thinking that I could solve those issues. But now I think it's all over and put it all into God's hands because he makes all things possible. Well as it looks, Junior, continues to embrace his lies within himself. Quality time means nothing to him, treating his parents the same way. Wow, he really doesn't know how to show compassion.

I can't fully blame him because I once read a book that stated with all that we endure in being adults, we carry it into our adulthood. So, I can't just fully blame him. He said his father never embraced him. As far as Teresa, I eventually realize the lost times between her and her girls being together and decide to make a change for the better. In her defense, Teresa gives me a surprise Sweet Sixteen Birthday Party. But not one Happy Birthday from Junior through the years of my life. With a host of family and friends, I pretended to be surprised; quickly learning of the party.

Everything was beautiful especially the five-tier cake. The guests were happy to be a part of something so nice; Teresa and her friend Brittany cooked all of the food. Teresa decided on a new start for her family and with her parents help she bought her first home. Heidi and I were damn near adults by this time, but better late than never at all, right!

People make plans in their minds, but only the Lord can make them come true. Depend on the Lord in whatever you do, and your plans will succeed.

Proverbs 16:1,3

CHAPTER 6

Hustling

There were days when a girl was just dead ass broke. I had to find a buck because every morning going to school meant chasing a dollar down from the night before. So, this means I had to ask my grandmother for $3.00. No sooner I'd be up for the day, I would hit up my favorite consignment shops spending all my cash for the day.

Just as soon as I would approach my grandmom I would sometimes ask her to talk to her husband CW. He was already relaxed in one of his lazy boy chairs, just after eating his morning salmon in those old fashion rolled back cans, grits and butter biscuits with jelly. Damn that salmon and grits don't sound bad right about now. I went and collected that $3.00 for lunch. Uncle Eugene and Aunt Darla happened to stop by and I asked them too for $ 3.00. Uncle Eugene said, "How's your report card for this marking period?"

"Good!"

"Do you still have your report card or did you return it yet?"
"Yes, I still have it, it's not due back until tomorrow."

"You did very well young lady, we are so proud of you, here's $6.00." Now my account is up to $9.00.

One of Tot's buddies, Isaac, drops by to see how everyone was doing. "Hello, Godfather."

"Hey, baby girl, how are you?"

"Guess what, I did really well on my report card this marking period."

"You did huh, hand it over." He takes a brief look at it and hands over a $5.00 bill. "Thank you. I am sooo happy. Everyone is so proud of me!" Showing him some love back. "Keep up the good work baby," kissing me on the forehead. When I finally counted it all up, my grand total came to $17.00. The money that I had received in just that short time made me realize I wanted to make my own money. Hell! A sistah had to get hers too!

Reading had many jobs for teenagers, either the mall or the outlets. Reading also had many stores where the public shopped for many years. On the weekends there used to be busloads of families traveling together from all over to get the best bargains they could find. At one time back in the 80's and early 90's there were outlets and more shops on Eighth and Ninth Street. Believe it or not, these are the same outlets that my mother and her associates boosted from, getting their hustle on to feed their families.

Over the years due to the town's economy and violence, many things have changed. There was a write-up in the newspaper about the rent going up on all the store properties. Designer's Place would eventually be moving to a new location next to Vanity Fair. Designer's Place became a hot spot to shop. You got more bang for your buck along with a classier look too. I decided to get my first job working at a shoe store at the Vanity Fair outlets. I made the best of it, a check for myself. Only wishing that family's business mindset was around me, that way I could have worked alongside my family instead of working for someone else's company. Nine months later the company began doing their layoffs for the season and I happened to be one of them. Hell! I had to look for something else.

The next day I was applying at the mall; I loved making my

own dollars. Don't laugh; I became a cashier working for Burger King. After being there for six months, I quit again. Only this time I wanted to make a higher salary, but something that wouldn't interfere with getting home much earlier. Many days, tired from school all day, then rushing to work for another four hours, no sooner I would be punching out. I constantly found myself running late for the next bus and by the time I would get to the front entrance most times, the bus would have already made the stop riding right by me. Now, I would have to do just what I have been trying to avoid, waiting for the nightline. Frustrated and tired, I had no other choices but having to wait forty minutes for the next bus.

"Damn, I missed it again. I'm tired of this!" Instead of just settling for that, I would make my way back down to the main entrance trying to catch a ride from anyone that I happen to know.

"Nicky!" She turns around to see who's calling her.

"Hey, girl!" "I need a ride, I just missed my bus!" "Come on girl I got you!"

"Thanks, girl!"

"It's been awhile, so what have you been up to?"

"School, my son, and working!"

"How's the family?"

"Everyone's cool."

"Give me a call sometimes, don't be a stranger."

"I know, I'm just grabbing as many hours that I can right now."

"I hear that."

"Thanks, take care!"

Finally arriving home, I could barely keep my eyes open, so I put my homework off until the next morning in homeroom. No matter what I was up against, I always managed to balance it out. Often times I would find myself thinking about how to find my niche.

It wasn't till I grew into a woman that certain things were just missing. But somehow I had to figure out how to gain it all back. There's one thing that I learned early, being open minded can take you many places and I definitely wanted in. A prayer was always near. God forgive me for what I do not know. Come into my heart and give me guidance and strength to know the difference. I love you Father God your works are amazing! Amen.

Meanwhile, Teresa and Ben were working in group homes with mentally challenged kids and adults. The requirements called for training and attending classes on administering meds, CPR and charting assistance to and from doctor appointments. Unfortunately, the day I go to put in an application, the secretary informed me that they weren't hiring right now, but there was another company that was. I went right over to put my application in the next day.

"Aren't you Teresa's daughter?"

"Yes! Yes, I am. Hi, are you Miss Joyce?"

"Yes, I'm Miss Joyce."

"Nice to meet you."

Instantly I got a called back for an interview. It's a rehabilitation workshop for M.H.M.R. mentally handicapped, mentally retarded, adult training, vocational and senior programs for the mentally handicapped. The majority of them goes to workshops during the day to earn a paycheck for themselves. Every home is set up according to the men and women who live in that particular home. I had the opportunity of working in three different homes. The first home was located way out in the boondocks. As they say, out in the woods.

There were three ladies who lived in this particular home. The oldest woman was elderly and bound to a wheelchair. I adopted her as my grandmother, a very sweet and dear woman. The second woman in her early forties was paralyzed from the waist down. The third woman was in her early thirties considered highly functional, and very capable of living on her own, which she eventually did.

I chose second shift, which meant the ladies had to be picked up. I would have to report to work by 3:00 pm, pick up the company van and head back towards the company by 4:00. By 5:00 o'clock at the latest they would all be walking in the door for the evening. The other staff members would already be there preparing dinner. After dinner, the ladies' meds would be administered and by the end of the shift, the women's charting would be done.

Eventually, I switched to another home. This house also had three ladies and all of them were in their mid-forties. They all were on a controlled substance, which could be a challenge. At any time when the residents would go to the doctors, their milligrams would be changed on their meds with no warning. One evening one of the ladies had to go out for one on one time. She was also known for having what they call "episodes" in public and sometimes with the staff members. That evening just before my shift ended, the woman had already showered and was in bed. Something sent her into a rage as she came downstairs furious.

"What's wrong, why are you out of bed, would you like something to drink?"

"No!"

"Do you need something else?"

"No!"

Heading towards the kitchen, she begins picking up glasses and whatever else she could get her hands on, throwing them at the staff. As the director taught us, always try to redirect to calm the residents down. When we attempted to get close to her she began screaming, reaching for a knife. By this time, she's not only a dangerous threat to herself, but she has also put staff members in harm's way. The staff walked out onto the front porch waiting for the supervisor to arrive who wasn't that far away.

As they say, sometimes it may take someone different to come into the picture in order to change the circumstances. In many cases, changing the circumstances can make the difference for the residents. In this case, picking up knives and chasing staff down was not what she intended. As they later found out the resident had an appointment two days prior to this incident and the doctor had changed her dosage on a few of her medications, which played a major role in her behavior.

Every two weeks the grocery shopping was done and the petty cash was counted each evening. Later requesting overtime at a third house, I only worked a part time shift at that particular house. Steven was in his early thirties. Jake was twenty-two and Dan was thirty-two.

Thinking about it over time, I decided to move in the direction of using my two-year scholarship from Teen Parenting by attending Reading Area Community College for computers but really wanted to take up being a director of films.

There was one problem, the struggle of my confidence level, which I believe caused me to withdraw only after being there two semesters. If only I could turn back the hands of time for all the wrong decisions I'd made in my life. I couldn't tell you how many times I felt as though I've been in a whirlwind, which really amounted to stealing my joy from right under my nose, weird as this may sound.

Finally, realizing later in life just how important it was to maintain my focus on whatever it was that I was truly after. As they say, "Better late than never, than not at all. Right!" Through it all, I gained wisdom. After withdrawing early from R.A.C.C for computers and tussling with it in my head, it wasn't until later I decided to go back to school for nursing.

Over the years, I knew of a couple through her family and church I attended at the time named Charles and Bee. They happened to be running a temporary agency at the time. "Yo, did you hear about Carpenter Technology having openings for internships for nine months?"

"Yes, I did, and I'm headed there in the morning bright and early."

"Me too!" Carpenter Technology has a model they stand strongly by, safety. Safety glasses, hard hats, long sleeved shirts, jeans and steel tip boots are required every day as you enter each building. It was mandatory that the staff gave us training courses in order for us to drive their equipment.

A tour of the ten buildings in which we all would be working in was also a requirement. There was one plant that I remembered most, the "melting plant." The steel is loaded down into a huge melting pot then it becomes an unbelievable temperature of one-thousand degrees. The pot itself weighed at least four-thousand pounds. There were twelve in the group who attended the training classes. Heidi also attended.

The first job I started at was at 5:00 a.m., which was feeding the wires through a machine. After about a week I eventually came off that job due to safety issues. They didn't have to tell me twice about not feeling safe. I was out! I later switched to a different department, dyeing coils. On this job I drove a boom truck, gathering up ten bundles of coils at once from the outside, then transferring them back inside where I would dye and deliver them to their different departments.

The whole trick to it was how you picked up the coils up off the floor with the boom truck. It took me a day or so before I finally caught on. Some days I stayed in working on the floor, using the hand crane dipping and dyeing the coils and tagging them for the next pick up. What seemed like every two weeks I continued to fill in on different jobs.

If things weren't already crazy enough my mother was being prepared for her fourth surgery, a herniated disk in her lower back. Prior to this, she had three surgeries. This time, she made the decision of getting the surgery done through her stomach even after her cousin, Doctor Bobby, warned her of possible complications. Only time would tell.

Faith is the belief that God is real and that God is good… It is a choice to believe that the one who made it all hasn't left it all and that he still sends light into his shadows and responds to gestures of faith. Faith is the belief that God will do what is right.

Hebrews 11:1,3,6

CHAPTER 7
Scooty Gets Popped

W here did the name Scooty originate from? Some say that my grandmother and beloved grandfather in South Carolina gave it to me. What were they thinking? The name Scoota-Boot changed to Scooty in a matter of weeks. What does the name Scooty mean? Scootymack Inc. since 2004… In the dictionary, Scooty means an Indian brand of Scooters designed for a woman.

It was my southern family who started all the name calling. Last time I checked I thought my name was La Shana A. Spann, born to Teresa and her then husband Junior.

Guess what, this is where I got Scooty to jump off! It's another one of those days having to get my hair done so I could be pressed for school the next day.

"Ouch. Damn. Heidi, take it easy, what are you trying to do, pull my brains out?" Heidi says, "Just hold still so I can get done because you are getting on my last nerves!" I started frowning, "Just hurry up!"

Heidi always managed to make me look crazy and she was the one braiding my hair as tight as a rope. You couldn't imagine what I had to experience with her heavy hands, dreading it each time too. It got so bad I wanted to look for my own hairdresser at only nine years old.

It's now the next day, and boy was I excited about attending Southwest Junior High School and all my new friends were going out for basketball. I chose volleyball instead. "Come on Scooty just play basketball, so we can see how tough you really are?"

"Excuse me, I don't need to play nobody's basketball to be tested, sweetie!" Liz tried to talk me out of it, but my mind was already made up.

One of my girlfriends named Liz invited me to stay over for the weekend and from there, our friendship grew. Next thing you knew I found myself hanging out in the Oak Brooke Projects and this time by choice. I met Liz's mother Maria, a sweet lady. All their crew met up at the park there where people were playing Chinese hockey, some were balling and the girls were double dutching. Guess who was on the court? Edgar, you guessed it.

Edgar and I would catch each other's eyes glancing, while he was playing ball with his boys. I'd smile. He already thought he was a stud, he glances over and smiles back. My girls and I eventually drifted off into another direction. "All right who's got winners? Who got the ends? Come on let's go, let's go!" Kary and Venice on the ends, Bria and Bossy jumping rope. I didn't know Bossy could jump Double Dutch like that. Spectators walking by stop and watch him. "Get it, Boss!" He enters the ropes and the damn rope gets caught. He's excited! "Come on let's do it again!" The ropes begin to turn again and he jumps in, he's jumping for a few minutes and just when Bossy thought he could jump, one of his boys walk over and stops the rope, he says, "That's for girls, Bossy." Well, why did he have to go and say that? Now they were competing against one another and jumping for long periods of time together. They had everyone out there for hours...

Fun times. Miss you dude!

There was another group of girls that I hung out with who moved here from Brooklyn. They loved Double Dutch, they were always trying new moves. The girls were into competitions and they were really good. After knowing them for a while she ended up taking a trip with them back to Bed-Stuy. It was so crazy, brothas down the street were shooting it up, while they dove underneath cars, trying to avoid from getting shot. First time going to Brooklyn was a bad experience. Wow!

We all stayed awhile at the park until it began to get dark, then we headed back to Liz's where my mom would swing through to pick me up after work. Just as we arrived in front of the house Teresa was there talking to Maria. Next day after school, I had an unexpected visitor stop by. The doorbell rings. I answer it saying, "How dare you just show up at my front door, who do you think you are?" I sounded serious, but was really joking! "No, I'm just kidding! How did you find out where I even lived anyway?"

"I just asked around!"

"What did you say?"

"Does anyone know where Scooty lives? I saw Dawn and them up the street."

"Edgar you're crazy for riding your bike all the way in town." I didn't want to stick around my mother, so I suggested that we go down to the park for a while where the guys were playing ball. He agreed! "You wanna ride or sit? I give him a weird look. Edgar says, "No seriously, I don't mean it like that...." I say, "Yeah right, I'll ride on the back thank you!" Hell, I was always adventurous anyway, why not?

Edgar says, "Hold on and don't let go, no matter what stunts I do!" I said, "Are you serious? Are you really that good?" He said, "They say I'm pretty good with my stunts." He laughs!

We take the ride down to the park. He runs into Paul. "Hey, Edgar what's up? You came all the way in town to see your girl, wow! You really love this girl? You playin b-ball or what?" Paul excuses himself. Out of nowhere, Edgar asks a question that stuns me. "You know I'm one of those Benny Blonco types of brotha's. Yo, did you ever have sex yet?" I looked at him like he was crazy for even asking me something like that. "What, nooo! And I'm not ready for that yet, so don't even think about asking again. Edgar you know we're too young to even be thinking about sex! Don't you think?" He looks as if to say that he had definitely asked the wrong question. "Damn girl, chill out! It's alright, it's cool. It's not that serious."

"You chill out with all the questions." She tells him. He says, "Sorry, but my past follows me everywhere I go!"

"There are other things we could be talking about, you know!" He continues, trying his hardest to lure her in, "Man at 13 and 14 my hormones began to go crazy." By me pushing him away each time he tried to kiss me, only left me more curious than I really should have been from the get go.

Time passed and before we knew it Liz and I became the best of friends. Just about every other weekend, Liz asked me to stay over, it gave me something else to do. Liz enjoyed dancing in the mirror and I always thought I could be Diana Ross. We danced and sang so much we worked up a thirst. Liz says, "I'm gonna get us something to drink. Girl, you are too much." Minutes later, "Scooty, somebody's at the door for you."

"What, who is it?"

"Just come down and see for yourself and hurry up because if my mom catches us we're in big trouble. Go ahead just take him around back and talk to him, my mom is on her way home, though."

I ask, "Edgar what's wrong with you coming over here, you're embarrassing me! Maria is very strict about boys being around Liz and her house only because she knows how you boys are and she ain't having it. Wow! You making it look like I asked you to come over here! Don't be doing that!" "I'm sorry, I just wanted to talk to you." "What's up, what do you want to talk about that it couldn't wait until we saw one another at the park later on?"

"Well, I guess I couldn't wait for your response to what I'm about to ask you."

"And what's that?"

"Do you want to go to the movies this weekend?"

She laughs… "Oh that's sweet, you walked your Puerto Rican butt all the way over here to ask me if I wanted to go to the movies on the weekend? Do you realize today is Saturday? What day are you talking about?" He laughs and says, "Come on I gotta go!"

"What is it?" He grabs and kisses me, only this time I wasn't so reluctant in pulling away. I was definitely digging him. When we stopped and looked at each other, it was weird because I had never kissed a boy like that before. For months we were friends and now our friendship grew into something much different, something I never felt before. I was so nervous after that long kiss all I could say was "I gotta go!" and I ran off.

As we began to walk around the corner, "Yo, Edgar make this your last time embarrassing me." Edgar says, "Okay I won't what?"

"You heard me!"

"Okay, okay I'll see you later at the park!" Edgar and I always seem to get along, especially if it was something that we enjoyed doing on the weekends like going to basketball games, skating or just chilling' out with all our friends at the park.

The weekends that I didn't go skating, I went to Virginia with my mother to see her in-laws. I happened to meet some of Ben's cousins, Sarah, who is my sister's age and Niecy who was about my age. Niecy had a twin brother named Mark.

All my friends made Skateway our get-away spot for the weekend. Everybody and their mama was out. This place was jammed packed every weekend; couples, single skaters and even the smaller kids hanging out with their parents. It was jumping! The exciting times were the all-night skating parties. Who am I fooling? It was the boys. When they all got together they had a lot of fun. It was something different than just being in school all week, hearing the bells ringing every period and passing everyone in the halls. In passing, I saw a lot of people I knew.

"Hey girl, what's going on"

"What's up?"

"I gotta get to class, we'll holla later."

We all skated so much that Saturday, we all still had blisters on our feet feeling like they were on fire by the time Monday rolled around. It was like torturing ourselves for a great cause. We loved it! I always wanted to learn how to speed skate. It was always exciting watching the speed skaters skate backward because they were always doing some kind of trick. About eight of them performed wild routines and all stepping in the same direction to Michael Jackson's "Pretty Young Thang". Their performance was siccccc!

They called for couples and couples only. My friends go, "Yo, look who it is? It's Robert from Governor." I say, "Whaaaat!"

"Right! You have a serious crush, don't you?" All the girls follow his every move. I always wanted to tell them, girls, "Backup he's here to see me," but I stood back and played him cool. Whenever they announce couples all the girls would flock to him. Of course, he already knew what I wanted when I finally got up the nerve to ask Robert to skate couples with me. I'm ecstatic that he even said yes. Robert has always been a respectful dude. All the skaters joined us in the middle of the rink!

We danced the night away. The skates came off and we did the damn thing. Okay! We had a blast! Skating was all we loved to do besides working up a grub and bum-rushing the snack bar. The night was slowly coming to an end; we all said our goodbyes while some grabbed an ice-c's for the bus ride home.

Next weekend my mom threw a huge fourteenth birthday house party for me. Everybody was there it was so crowded, we had a blast, plenty of food and drinks to go around. I loved Tweety bird so that's the theme my mother went with. The disco lights and the music was booming, Salt and Peppa, Run-DMC and Rakim blasting. "It's been a long time, I shouldn't have left you." Some of my friends wanted to battle in a dance contest; the girls battled, but the guys battled even harder. They were hyped when Michael Jackson came on. Na, Na, Na, - Na, Na, Na - Na! Say pretty young thing repeat after me! Yeah, there were some lames too, who just stood there holding up the wall.

Teresa called for everyone to gather in the dining room, it was time to cut the cake. The cake was cut and handed out. Someone had a brilliant idea. Terry was plotting and called my name and before I knew it, when she turned around Teresa got me good; she smeared cake all over my face and they caught it all on camera! Great Memories Hunnie!

What a complete mess? I tried laughing it off although it was too funny because I never saw it coming. Wow, what a surprise! Quickly I ran upstairs to change. Edgar thought he was slick. He invited himself upstairs and before we knew it, Teresa was up there in no time. No sooner than Teresa realized he had disappeared from the crowd she was on him like a hawk; she knew he went looking for something and she knew exactly what it was. Before he knew it, Teresa was standing in the doorway. "Umm, excuse me, Edgar, what the hell do you think you're doing up here? You must be looking for the bathroom or something? It's that way" and she pointed him out of my room."

Edgar says, "No, I don't need to use the bathroom!" Then my mother said, "Then it looks like you need to be taking your ass back downstairs with everybody else. We're all here for a party" Teresa already knew that we were kissing by this point. Teresa made sure that she embarrassed me too. She said to me, "You know better than to have him up here in your room! Show off if you want to, I will embarrass you in front of all your friends!"

"Mom I didn't tell him to come up here."

"Did you try to stop him, no thank you? No, you didn't!"

"Mom, what's that supposed to mean?"

"I know you better act like you know!" I mumble under my breath. "Whatever!"

When we finally decided to engage ourselves unknowingly, we cheated ourselves of our own future. Edgar had been going through some changes and after about the third year of our friendship/relationship, he changed altogether and things became rocky. Once I found out that he had been experiencing marijuana and cocaine, I was through with him. By this time, he had changed for the worse.

The summer was flying by and we were all returning back to school, which seemed all too soon. This year, I knew I wanted a change and began thinking about my career and interests. So, I decided to take advantage of the technical school at Vo-tech. I attended Reading High during the morning and caught the bus to the vocational school for the remainder of the day.

The first day I arrive, I run into dude. "Hello, Scooty!"

"Damn, Edgar I'm pregnant." Of course, he was in denial. Edgar says, "We're too young to even picture ourselves as parents. Are you sure? Scooty did you take a pregnancy test yet? What did your mom say?"

"Damn, Edgar slow down! To answer your question, yes I did take one and it came out positive and no, I didn't tell my mother yet, I'm scared! Let's talk after school." All I could think about was how irresponsible I was along with him at such an early age. Shoulda, coulda, and woulda, what a stupid way to think now, huh?

Planned Parenthood and contraceptives go together so what was I thinking? The crazy part is when I took the pregnancy test over the weekend, it read positive. Instantly, I said what am I going to do? My entire life lays directly in front of me, no father to run to; how dare I tell my grandfather. I was ashamed that I had embarrassed my family for getting pregnant outside of marriage.

"God, what am I going to do? Hell, I mean I love my unborn child, but am I going to let it hold me back from my future. No!" Of course, at seventeen I knew that I had no business having a child, but I stood tall and persevered.

After school, Edgar and I got together and briefly talked. I became upset. "Edgar, what were we thinking? You know what?" She hesitates and shakes her head, "Forget it!" What? I tried to avoid looking at him. I knew I had two options, either I was going to keep the baby or end the pregnancy. My mind began to race. The question came up... "How am I going to attend school and graduate with a baby?" Realizing at that moment the serious consequences that I had begun to face, I also began to question myself. I refused to fail. I didn't care what it would take! Thinking about my own childhood and where I come from, did I want the same lifestyle for this baby? Listen, pregnancy didn't start with me and that's what I had to realize.

Later that night, I repeatedly told my mother that I needed to tell her something. Putting it off until my paper read, La Shana Spann has been to our women's center today, her pregnancy test results are positive. Teresa, who is extremely loud yelled at the top of her lungs, "Scooty, come here right now!" This was the first time that I had ever heard my mother call my name the way she did that day.

Teresa reminisced on her past when she became pregnant for the first time and dropped out of school. I became frustrated, thinking about one of the biggest mistakes I had ever made, but kept my cool. When I finally came downstairs, we sat and talked for a while. In the softest voice, she says, "Scooty, baby you have your whole life ahead of you, it's important that you finish school. I want you to ask yourself, what do you wanna to do about having this baby?" "Mom, I'm determined to finish high school. I wanna go to Temple University majoring in photography, film or journalism, but now I see that I have to settle for R.A.C.C." The moment came when Teresa asked her again, "Scooty do you want to keep this baby?" Scooty hesitated, the question plays over and over in her head. Scooty says, "How could I live with myself if I aborted my child. What kind of future will I have if I have this unborn child that's now growing inside me?"

A few minutes passed and s-l-o-w-l-y she responds to her mother. "Yes, mom I want to keep my baby, really feeling as though I may have answered too soon. Deep down inside I didn't quite understand what I was up against. I was scared because I knew I wasn't ready to become a mother at such a young age. Think about it, what intellectual mother would allow her child's future to be on hold because she chooses to have a baby so young? See, Teresa's thoughts were that Heidi and Scooty were supposed to follow in her footsteps. Not!

I thought about it long and hard and decided to love my family from a distance. Who wouldn't want out and away from all the constant drama? What Teresa should have done was take her butt down to Planned Parenthood much early on so I could have made better choices in planning out a future for myself. Again, leaving the decision up to me was the last thing Teresa should have done. Teresa's hurt and a lot of things resurfaced. Teresa abruptly says, "You're not having this baby, you're getting an abortion!" After all that, I decided to keep the baby, but still wanting to fulfill my dreams of going to college.

Let's put it this way, giving up was just not one of my options because I became pregnant at a very early age. No matter how hard the road may have seemed, I wasn't going to use this as an excuse to give up on my goals, as I always dreamed of being on top. I had a desire to major in textile and clothing. It has always been a passion of mine. I'd say, "I love clothes so I figured why not try something new?" Since her throwback days, she has also had a strong passion for photography and writing too.

Sally was a friend of mine for about three years. She practically knew all my personal business about me and Edgar. She had been hearing the rumor all day. You know that saying, be careful of what you tell your friends about the dude your dating? Yeah, oh girl wanted him bad. Women will be women, but there are lines that certain people just shouldn't cross if you can understand.

Hey, it's life and I got over it real fast.

One evening after school, Sally felt the need to call just to inform me about her new deadbeat fling of a boyfriend. "Scooty I just wanted to let you know that Edgar asked me to be his girl. "Oh yeah, well good luck, you won a pot of coal! By the way, Edgar's a real mess, that's if you don't mind being with a junkie because he's hooked. Sally, you know what, all he can really do for me right now is just take care of his responsibility!" The baby is crying in the background. "You know what he and I share? A son, who needs my attention right now, I have to go!"

Day in and day out me and Sally rode the van together to school, so I continued to communicate with her because I refused to let Edgar even think that he was somebody, for real! At the same time, I realized we both were young women with kids, trying to keep our focus on school, putting our differences aside. As time progressed, in her words, Sally said that she got to know Edgar a little too well.

Surprisingly, Edgar would stop by, maybe twice a week to visit his son or simply to just drop off a check. Put it this way, childbirth is absolutely something serious for one to deal with. The chain of emotions that you go through, from the excruciating labor pains to the actual delivery is something that is truly miraculous. When it's all over, it's a relief of tears and precious moments to remember. Being in labor for 16.5 hours is truly not the norm.

On April 21, 1990, I gave birth to a baby boy weighing in at 7lbs. 4oz and 20 inches long named Myles. I truly believed that I conquered fear by experiencing childbirth. I refused to let it get the best of me. I was always determined to graduate with my high school class of 1992.

It's graduation day and Teresa approaches me with a dozen roses. Wait that's not it, she then blindfolds me and guides me outside and says, "La Shana, now you can take off your blindfold!" I was astounded with tears rolling down my face. I embrace my mother tightly with a grin on my face, filled with joy upon her graduation present. "Mom, you got me a car! Awe and it has a big red bow on it too. Thank you mom, thank you so much!"

"You deserve it, baby, you worked really hard for it and with a baby by your side too, you did it!"

Overall, Teresa was filled with joy while witnessing her youngest daughter graduating from high school. Later that night, Denise and I threw a graduation party in the yard where everybody came through, plenty of food and drinks to go around. God knows that was a beautiful day. All I could say was "Thank You, Jesus. You Blessed us to make it!"

For a brief second, I reminisced on how grateful I was for her grandparents providing an opportunity for stability for my mother on the avenue. The quote, "God, grant me the serenity to accept the things I cannot change, the courage to change the things I can and the wisdom to know the difference" will forever stand.

Time passed and Sally and Edgar dated off and on. Come to find out, Edgar had another girl name Mari pregnant too. Sally became engaged to Edgar and eventually got pregnant four years later, having a baby girl named Sky, but they never married.

Lucia was Myles grandmother. She was a loving, humble person with a beautiful spirit who loved to share her wisdom with her grandkids, she loved them so much. It wasn't until 2002 when Lucia's health began to deteriorate. It was December of 2004. I continuously dreamt of Lucia as I slept. Once she traveled back to Reading, I decided to go and visit her. "Myles we're going to see your grandmom today." Myles became excited.

While searching for Lucia's residence the kids stayed in the car keeping warm. The weather was bad as usual, it was snowing. Mountain weather never seems to change. I knocked on the door at the old house, which leads us to her new residence. Some kid walks by as I began asking around for her and her son. "Yeah I know him, come talk to my mother." I became anxious. The kid introduced us to his mother and once I received the disturbing news of Lucia's death tears began to roll down my face. Wow, I just couldn't believe after all this time, what I had been really experiencing. Lucia had been sending me a message all along.

Every now and then I would take Myles to visit his great-grandmom and she would be so happy to see him. Only this time when we stopped by, she was in a wheelchair. She broke her leg, but it never seemed to slow her down. She got around well and was very generous. She would cook her famous dishes for us, chicken, Spanish rice and beans with fried bananas and a salad on the side. As I heard many times, a Spanish dish isn't complete unless you have a salad on the side. It puts a special touch on the meal, as we all sat at the table eating; she entertained them with some of her beautiful artwork.

Detri, my cousin, would come by to pick me up for school

because I was seven months pregnant. He was so much like his father, my favorite Uncle Eugene, very protective. "You shouldn't be taking Barta to school, I'm going to pick you up in the mornings for school."

"It's not that serious, I can walk to the bus stop, plus its good exercise for me and the baby."

"Yeah, I hear you!"

"I'll be by in the morning by 7:30."

One morning when Detri picked me up he mentioned about his father, Uncle Eugene was in the hospital. Not thinking that it could have been anything else different than his usual. In and out of the hospital as Eugene and Teresa shared the genetic trait of sickle cell disease. I assured him that Uncle Eugene would be okay. His red and white blood cells were attacking one another. Uncle Eugene just needed to be hooked up to an I.V. for a while, assuring him that everything would turn out fine. Briefly, we spoke on how close Teresa and her brother Eugene were and how they would share pain pills, trying to help ease one another's excruciating pain.

By the time lunch rolled around Detri had just left the office receiving a call from his mother, his father wasn't doing too well. "Scooty, I'm heading towards the hospital right after school to see what's going on with my dad."

"Detri, is he okay?" Sadly, he says, "I don't know!"

"Well, wait for me I'll ride over to the hospital with you!"

When we finally arrived at the hospital, the family immediately began to pour in asking questions. "What room is Eugene Wilson in?"

"He's in intensive care."

"What happened, who's his doctor?" Teresa says, "Damn it somebody answer me!"

While the family is consoling one another the doctor walks over.

"Hello, my name is Dr. Drego, we're running some tests and now we're waiting for them to come back so we can determine Eugene's diagnosis." An hour later tests come back. The doctor heads towards the family and informs them of Eugene's diagnosis. "He's not doing well. The test came back with the result that antifreeze was found in his system. "What?"

"Eugene's organs are shutting down and right now we have him on a breathing machine. More tests are being done as we speak!" The doctor pauses, "It doesn't look good. We're giving Eugene a few hours to live, so I want you all to prepare yourselves for the worst, at any time."

Instantly, Teresa falls down to the floor banging her fists, screaming at the top of her lungs. "Nooo, why, why Eugene!" I'm distraught too and grab my belly as it tightens, tears began rolling down my face. "Noo, Uncle Eugene, don't go!" Devastated, the family crashes.

Time passes into the evening; Uncle Eugene is getting worse. The family couldn't fathom the thought of losing him; so, we began taking turns visiting his room to say our goodbyes. When it was time for me to go in, I felt an instant coldness. Slowly I approached the side of his bed I saw the whites of his eyes rolling back into his head and his stomach blown up as though he may have been eight months pregnant. I scream out, "Nooo, Uncle Eugene don't leave me. My heavenly father, please let him live! Don't take him away from us…PLEASE!" I become upset and felt the baby tightening up more and more. My pain turned into loud screams. "Oh God help us…please, please help us!"

A nurse rushes in asking for someone to take me out of the room. I didn't need any stress because it could send me into early labor. Just as soon as I left his room I demanded to return, only this time sitting next to his feet rubbing his legs, asking him to hold on. His parents stood beside his bedside holding onto his hands. "Eugene, if you can hear us squeeze my hand." Eugene slightly squeezed, as a tear rolled down the side of his cheek. Mom-Mom says, "Eugene, hold on baby!" His father cries out, "Son I love you hold on!"

Me and Uncle Eugene shared a special bond and many great moments together. Eugene always gave me a reason to smile as he took Junior's place. Uncle Eugene was the comedian in the family. This was a man who gave from his heart in everything he did. Uncle Eugene always knew how to put a smile on everyone's face. He enjoyed bringing the family together. He was a tractor-trailer driver who traveled from state to state. He was the nickname Giver and named me Scoot-Noot, whatever that meant. Uncle Eugene was vibrant and always the life of the party.

Many times, when the family would come together at his parent's home, Uncle Eugene would set up the movie projector. They all sat around reminiscing on old times; those were the good ol' days. Uncle Eugene and his wife, Aunt Darla used to hold New Years Eve parties at their home with food for days to come. They would leave all the kids at the house and they would go out on the town for the night. During my early pregnancy, Uncle Eugene always found himself rubbing her belly. He would say, "Come here girl, let me rub that watermelon."

As the doctors warned the family, Uncle Eugene's death is slowly approaching, the life support machine flatlines and God calls Uncle Eugene home. We family members become very emotional as we receive the bad news. Many start crying and screaming while others pass out. The little kids were crying because they witnessed their parents crying. It was very loud in the hospital room, as the entire family released their sadness and sorrow. Nurses rushed in! Some of the family members were asked to return to the waiting area. All you heard were people screaming, "Why, Why Eugene!" The room became very uncontrollable while friends of the family began removing kids trying to settle things down in the hospital room. Uncle Eugene we love you…R.I.P

The Wilsin family planned two funeral services for Uncle Eugene one to be held in Reading, PA the other in South Carolina. By having two services in both locations, it gave family members the opportunity to have closure and deal with the loss of their beloved son, Uncle, and cousin "Eugene Wilsin." Once Uncle Eugene died the immediate family began changing for the worse. Certain ones began feuding with others, making it rough for everyone else. It has been 22 years since Uncle Eugene has passed, and his spirit lives on in all of us. Since that day, I have been searching for what it is that would bring me true happiness and peace. I discovered happiness in my soul through faith.

I rarely ever agreed to go along with my sister. Let alone going anywhere on a daily basis. We already lived in a deadbeat town as it was. There was hardly ever anything fun to do. We really never enjoyed ourselves unless a few of us girls got together to hang out in Philly. "Heeey girl, let's get together tonight!" "Who's this?" "Shameerah, oh you don't know who I am now? What are you two doing tonight?" "Not much, same o, same o!" Let's ride down to Philly tonight and check out Transit and Palmers!" "Who's all going?" "Denise and myself. I think Cheryl's going." "Hell yeah, what time we leaving?" "Be ready by 9:00! We'll call you when we're on our way up there, later!" "Aiight later!"

We damn near hung out to early the next morning. They found themselves tired and hungry, grabbing a bite to eat while discussing who was going to drive back. When it came to finding a designated driver, those silly ass girls always managed to pick me. I dreaded the drive back just as much as they did, but I did it anyway. I surprised them too! No sooner than we hit the highway, they realized that choosing her to drive was the wrong choice. "Damn, Scooty put the windows up, it's cold!" "Oh, ya'll don't think I get tired, huh!" "Yeah, just put the window up! Stop playing, come on the windows!"

When Sundays rolled around, we seemed all too well to come and go so quickly and Monday's were here before you could blink your eyes. It wasn't easy trying to stay focused on school work and taking care of my son. Every time I turned around, I was getting a call in one of my classes as my son Myles was prone to accidents while in day care. When the weekends came, we always looked forward to something fun to do. It's sad, but the only two choices for us during the summer months were either to attend the Puerto Rican carnival or the city carnival that travels from town to town. Wow, and it always seemed at any given moment a fight would break out.

There was one particular evening when Heidi invited me to go along to a New Year's Eve party that one of her old high school buddy's was throwing. I only wished that I would have stayed home that one particular night. When they arrived at Isriel's house, I met some more of her sister's old high school friends. As the night went on, we all socialized ate and drank. There was some guy there who happened to be very intoxicated. He was persistent in making himself known all night, truly becoming a pain in the butt to everybody. After a while he became annoying and Heidi and I were ready to head home asking Isriel for a ride. Well, this guy who was so intoxicated and happened to be a friend to Isriel's named Donald (Don). Of course, he asks Isriel to ride along too.

Right away, we think, damn! This guy is getting on our nerves; we couldn't wait to get out of the car. The entire ride back to the house, he repeatedly asked me, "What's your name? Do you know some girl name Jala?" I ask him, "Why do you keep asking me that?" I look at him then look away, and say, "We'll get out here, we'll walk the rest of the way," just so Donald wouldn't know where we resided. "Thank you!"

At that time, it had never dawned on us that it was Denise's friend, Jala, who lived right around the corner from them. Prior to all of this, Donald had asked me for my phone number. I refused but never expected my sister to give the digits anyway. It wasn't until the next day when I came in from school, my mother left a message. "Donald called for you." I say, "I know that Heidi didn't give him our number!" A few days passed, Donald calls again. "Scooty, I know I was drunk." She cuts across him why are you calling me anyway? "You got on everybody's nerves all night constantly asking the same questions."

And... Hell, he had to know from the door. "Look, dude, ain't nobody looking for no relationships around here, it really doesn't matter, okay! I don't mean to be rude, but I really have to go!"

About a week later, he calls again. The phone just rings as she checks the caller I.D. You know them days when you just don't feel like being bothered. Plus, things were beginning to get crazy with Myles' dad; acting stupid about his son. The next time Edgar came by we had a serious talk. "You need to be more supportive of your son. You know he didn't get here by himself." I know, I'll drop something off by Friday!"

"Yeah, okay!"

Meanwhile, Myles is growing like a weed, teething and bouncing in his bouncer and already trying to take steps at 10 months old. Every evening I prepared my son and nephew for the next day. As they said in daycare, you're a great mother and auntie through all the feedings, sterilizing bottles, cleaning diaper bags daily, packing extra clothing and preparing plenty of bottles. Never once did she complain, as she made sure everything was done for the kids daily.

Lord only knows just how much schoolwork she had to keep focused on, in order to keep up and graduate.

Donald was persistent in pursuing me. He called, again and again, that very next evening. "Scooty I been calling you for a few days, can I stop by to see you?"

"Excuse me, no I don't think so! My time is very dear to my family, plus I have some other things I have going on right now. Why do you keep calling anyway?"

One afternoon, while I was in town running errands, Donald happens to ride by noticing me coming out of the pharmacy. I heard someone calling my name and turn around to see who it was. Of course, it was Donald. Dude came off too strong, she wasn't even interested.

"Scooty how are you doing?"

"I'm good just out picking up some things for my family."

"So, what are you doing this evening?"

"Look, I don't have time okay!"

"I just wanna get to know you, we can take things slow!" Knowing that I wasn't being serious, I just told him that I would think about it so I could leave. Why did I do that?

The next day he called again. "Scooty do you have any time today for me to stop by and see you? No, I'm busy all day! Why are you so stuck on yourself and so damn determined?" He laughs... "Sweetie, I'm not. That's just me."

"Listen, I have to go, Don!" Hours later there was a knock on the door. "Uhh, Don you have a lot of nerve just showing up and knocking on my door unannounced. How did you even know where I lived anyway? Are you stalking me?"

"No, I just stopped by to see how you were doing!" I frown. "I'm doing good and yourself!" He must have thought that he was going to be invited in, so we stood there at the door for a few minutes.

"Look, I'm really busy, time is of the essence, you know!"

"You're always busy; what do you have to do?"

"I have a seven-month-old son and two nephews that I help my mother take care of."

"Oh, you do, you have big responsibilities!"

"Yes, I do!"

Teresa offered to watch Heidi's kids. This offer was to give Heidi an opportunity to attend Randy Rick Cosmetology School, allowing her to better help her family and plan for a better future. Problems began when Heidi decided not to call or come home directly after school. Coincidently, the day I stayed home from school due to my son being sick and having a doctor's appointment, Heidi decided to run around after school with some girlfriends.

The day finally came when I had to approach her about her ghetto ways of life. Hell, it was obvious that she didn't care what anybody else had going on. As a result of her not coming home on time, it made my son miss his doctor's appointment! Bottom line is that Heidi is selfish and ungrateful at times; she would rather be stubborn instead of appreciating a good thing. Well, I waited and waited for hours. By this time, I was furious, no sooner than she walked in the door, I let her have it. "Excuse me, but where have you been? Myles had an appointment he missed today and all because you want to be inconsiderate to others. In no remorseful way, she says all nonchalant, "Oh, did he?"

"Heidi, you must really think that you have a built-in nanny. Well, I'm here to let you know that you don't!" She says, with an attitude, "No, I had to finish something up at school then I just rode with Shanel to get some supplies."

"Heidi, you could have called one of us and said something. I could have probably called the doctor and got a later time for today, but you don't care about nothing else, but yourself that's so obvious!

You know what you are so damn pitiful!" Heidi says, "Whatever!"

Already upset. I jump up walking towards her, "What you mean whatever? These are your damn kids so start taking care of them and stop leaving us to do your job as a mother!" Teresa steps in loud, "Alright, ya'll! Heidi, you get out of school at 4:00 o' clock, keep thinking that you can keep walking up in here anytime you want. You have a responsibility here. I don't watch these kids for you to be running the streets after you get out of school. Stop taking me for granted! Heidi, Myles had an appointment today and you messed that up. This is going to stop today I mean it, I'm sick of you acting like you don't give a care in the world about what's going on here!"

I was fed up by this point. Certain things were getting too redundant so I had to get to the point. Heidi has yet to show us any appreciation for helping her. For some odd reason, she acts as if she's owed something here. The fact of the matter is, I love my sister and hope and pray that one day soon, she will learn to become a responsible mother because this is hurting her family. As a result of her irresponsible ways, her son Levi at age five began living with his dad. Her other children Toi at the time was four and Shan two months old were growing up without their mother really being present in their life. Heidi refused to change.

Teresa says, "Heidi you fail to recognize, Scooty has been helping me with your kids and this is how you pay her back!" With an attitude, she says, "I'm sorry!"

"Yeah, I bet you are!" Her family supports her in the choice she made in going back to school to receive her cosmetology license, but I should have nipped her selfish attitude in the butt much early on. Teresa and I couldn't blame anyone but her as we practically let her get away with it. How crazy it looks that Heidi controlled us with her own kids. With my big heart and my sister's horrible ways, I was always left feeling that I had to step up for my family. My family means so much to me. My conscience wouldn't sit still if I didn't do what was necessary for the children, they didn't ask to be here.

The bottom line, the generation curse that Teresa had placed upon herself was now passed down to me and my sister. The chaos in my life never seemed to dissipate or ever slow down. The phone rings. "Scooty, how are you doing, I wanted to stop by and see you." "Well, at the moment I'm not feeling like any company, I don't even know you like that! Plus, I had a long day today with tests and the kids." Donald didn't seem to get that she simply wasn't interested as he persisted on and on calling anyway.

In the meantime, words must have gotten back to his girlfriend. After I walk in from school, about an hour later the phone rings. "Hello, is Scooty there?" "This is she. Who's calling?"

"Jala, I want to know what you and Donald are supposed to be doing." She goes on and on about him being her man. You know the girlfriend syndrome whenever she thinks another woman is involved. Straight drama… I say, "I should have seen it coming." Jala continues to say, "We just came back from shopping in King of Prussia." I was like, "chick, I don't care because I don't want him, how about you're both bugging me now …Helloooooo! Listen, sweetie, he and I hardly even know one another and furthermore, why don't you just tell him to stop calling my house because he doesn't seem to get the picture after only telling him about five times. Look, I didn't give him the number when he asked for it!"

Jala wanted her man and wanted me to know just that! She got mad and hung up. This time I waited for him to call just so I could blast him. Phone rings, I looked at the caller I.D "Hello! Scooty," he says in a nice way. "You sure have a funny way of showing respect and integrity in your relationships." Of course, he plays stupid.

"What are you talking about?"

"Don, you played yourself! You really wanted to see that bad just how far your ego could take you by trying to cause a problem between the two of us. You have a serious problem within yourself, just get over it!"

"What are you talking about?"

"You know what, you're a damn mess!"

I knew then he thought he was it. Not! Now, I'm pissed. It wasn't because of his girl calling; she was only doing what most women would do, minus her lack of class and all. But, it was her intuition warning her from the very beginning; from the first time they met, I avoided him, he was a drunk. I go on to say, I'm not a rude sistah by no means, but when it comes to some grown ass man-child who's in college, who I don't know like that, has the audacity to bring drama to my front door, all I can say is, "Oh hell no and keep it moving!"

Time was flying, and Myles was getting bigger as each day passed, it wasn't too much longer when he began walking as they informed me of the good news one day as I picked him up from daycare. I was extremely excited! Myles had been taking some steps and falling down, but now he was finally walking. I was a very proud mom. I run in the house and put all my things down and call my mom from the kitchen. "Mom, look Myles is walking, he takes a few steps towards the couch and he falls down. I pick him up and he takes a few more steps, falls again. I pick him up! Yayyy my baby boy is walking!" I kiss him and couldn't stop smiling.

More excitement unfolded months later. It's Myles's first B-day party. A few friends, family and their very active children come by to spend Myles's birthday with him. The kids had fun as they played themselves out. Bozo the clown showed up and some of the kids were scared, so they played some games too. Denise's daughter, Ava, and Myles are five days apart in age and were close growing up.

At one point, I began wondering which way my life was headed by residing in a small rural and racist town called Reading, PA.

Realizing then the longer I stayed the more uncomfortable I would become. It was simple to see as African-Americans, they have allowed our school systems to conquer and endure a righteous indignation way of living. There's absolutely no way of covering up great leaders, nah! As African Americans we have many great leaders such as Dr. Martin Luther King Jr., Mrs. Coretta Scott King, Rosa Parks, Harriet Tubman and the list goes on and on. Black people are from Africa; but if you think about it, some of us refuse to embrace our culture and that's what Reading is truly missing, an African American culture.

In the city of Reading, the people there who are black say they're black. But where does the African-American culture really stand? The question being asked today is how much do people really want to know about their culture by educating themselves in order to pass it on to the next generation? I can remember while growing up there was no one in my household teaching me anything about my culture and I now wonder why?

When the time finally came I taught myself about black history and I'm still striving today, I refuse to not know what's most important. It truly wasn't until I visited Philadelphia and Harlem, New York as a kid when I recognized something different with her people, she couldn't put her finger on it, but she did know that education and intelligence can get you far in life. She often wondered what rights do they really have living there in Reading? As they say we all been hoodwinked and bamboozled by our city and school system. The school system didn't make it a high priority educating the children about the importance of all the Afro–American great leaders. It was these great leaders who have paved the way for us today and I'm so grateful!

What about the next generation? Oh, or don't they even count? What a crazy way to think. Right or wrong, I just got to a point when I felt that I needed to change things for the next generation by educating my children, nieces, and nephews. It was just a ridiculous way of living, seriously. As weird as this may sound for a long time, I felt like I had been in total darkness. It's like being in a cave, stashed away somewhere, for years. Finally, I surfaced and the light began to shine. What's in our Lord and Savior is in me and that's exactly what I've been witnessing.

My grandparents had many achievements, which were far less than the accomplishments that they could have had. Not once did they complain about raising Heidi and me. It was very unfortunate that Tot was forced to quit school while only in the third grade, but he did as many grandfathers did back then. He stated that his father said, "You must help the family. It's about survival!" He never turned back to see another day of school. Sadly, enough Tot became illiterate but always knew how to count that money. He believed in another cause for his family. This belief may have caused him to treat the family as a colt.

Tot developed a certain mindset, ways as result of not having a great education. He only had certain beliefs, which also had my grandmother thinking on a whole different perspective, one-way syndrome. It was very unfortunate that he didn't have an open mind. My grandmother refused to settle for less, paving the way for herself and her family. With determination, for many years, she became a licensed practical nurse. Gradually, she looked for another job paying a higher salary.

Mom-Mom was blessed to get into AT&T. She retired from AT&T after thirty years of working second shift. This was before the plant closed because there were some who weren't so lucky, as they were forced to resign with a package.

Tot also received a letter for hire from Carpenter Technology for swing shifts; overtime was all he knew. His family hardly ever saw him from day to day. The summers were really hot, and he stood diligently in what felt like 110-degree rooms to get the job completed. He was a real man and he did what he had to do for his family.

He always wanted more than he ever had. To him, it was like he had a million dollars; simply because living in the south was much different than what we may think. Why, because we didn't have to endure the harsh struggles of racism and hard labor of being outside in the blazing heat and sun that beats you down which so many others had to bear.

I remember, many times sitting and talking to my grandfather about his past life in South Carolina, Tot would say, "We would have to go deep into the woods and gather up some coon's just so the family could eat dinner and we would get hungry while out there hunting for dinner!" So, for all the days that I missed Tot not being home with them, God had another plan. I was the chosen one to have to experience all this but look at the outcome now. God doesn't bring any of us this far to leave us and there is no turning back now.

Time passed, Valentine's Day is the next day, so Donald wanted to know if I would accept an invitation by riding to Kayztown University with him as there was some kind of event going on. The phone rings. "Scooty, I want you to ride with me to Kayztown." "I can't just up and go with you, I have a responsibility and plus I hardly even know you." Refusing for the second time he stops by again, unexpectedly. When she answered the door, his manipulating way showed up; he handed her a little brown bear with a balloon attached to it saying, "Happy Valentine's Day."

"Awe how cute! Now you're bribing me, huh!" He thought he was slick, trying to work his way in the front door. "Nah, it's not gonna happen, wait right here" and I push the front door closed." Now, as I look back, he just wanted to see how weak I was by letting him in.

Donald was persistent and I was very naïve.

I figured since it was later in the evening and my son and nephews were already asleep for the night; why not invite him in for a few minutes. We sat and talked for a few minutes before there was an abrupt knock on the door, it was Jala, his girlfriend. "Hello!" "Can you tell Donald to come to the door?"

"Your girlfriend is at the door!"

"Don, what are you doing here?" It's already 9 pm and she was loud standing in front of the house. He tried to calm her down by moving her from in front of the house. She refused. Out of nowhere, she takes off her belt and literally, begins beating him. They're both screaming and yelling. Next thing you know her mother's walking down the steps. "What the hell is going on out here?" Jala's mother turns the corner trying to get her to leave; she refuses. It was so obvious that she was hurt; she refused to leave until he did. All hell broke loose when I heard her 7-foot 350-pound grandfather out in front of the house.

All I could think about was all damn, they done woke up the damn neighborhood now. In his deep voice, while towering over them as he spoke, "What's going on here? Don, you need to take this mess to your parent's house and get from around here with all that noise. Where do you think you're at making all this damn noise out here and for what?" Her grandfather was serious, he let them both have it. "Who do you think you are coming around here with this bullshit and involving my granddaughter? Take that shit somewhere else!" Donald had a stupid look on his face; he was speechless. Jala refused to leave until she witnessed Don pulling off. Don had nothing to say. He got into his car and drove off.

Can you believe this man-child had the audacity to pick up the phone and call me the next day? Was this a test? Not looking at the caller I.D. "Hello! I'm sorry Scooty, I didn't mean for all that to happen last night!"

"Excuse me you don't have anything else to say to me after all that drama." He called himself apologizing like she was supposed to say, "Come over so we can talk or something."

"Listen, I ain't looking for anything, I just ask that you do me a favor and lose my number." And she hung up.

It was all a game and his plan had crashed. Now, I guess this is where I'm supposed to let you know, somehow or another I started caring for this character and why I was asking for trouble and all his drama lifestyle. Instead, I should have been praying for God to give me common sense. Lol.

Well, the next day, Jala started her drama by calling the house then hanging up and now I found myself in the middle of some bullshit. Being young and naïve wasn't even an excuse anymore, misguided and stupid is what I called it. Well, as we all live and learn from our mistakes, it was simple, she was hard headed and didn't want to listen. Hey, it just goes to show you that anytime we go against God's word, look what happens. Karma is truly something else when it comes back around. I hate to say it, but I even began to start liking him too and we began to see more and more of one another.

Now, go ahead and say it, how dumb could I be! A month later, he invited me to go to Kayztown University, but this time they were having a step show. Guess what? Step shows are my weakness, so I went along this time, I couldn't refuse.

By this time, a year had passed and my family was off and moving again. Only now it was for the last time as my grandparents purchased a home for their daughter Teresa. "God bless her grandparents for all that they've done for her!" I was now wrapping up my 11th year of high school and was overly excited about becoming a senior. Denise and I were always trying to find something fun to do with the kids. Anything else besides settling in the house day in and day out just doing the same ol' Reading thing, which gets boring very fast.

Back then Reading lacked parents who cared to have unity and integrity. Standing strong for their children is what they should want to do. This leaves a higher percentage of kids straying away and not having the confidence in knowing who they could be today. I know because I lived through it, sadly not finding out until much later in life.

I mean, the parks are cool, but the arts have so much more to offer to kids, which Reading lacks in that area too. Hell, traveling was the only way I could maintain my sanity. I was a young mother who was very responsible, striving for independence while living at home. Now, if I could do it all again, she would have chosen her degree first in directing a film and of course get married and have children much later in life, "Instead of letting the stroke, keep her broke!" I knew for sure, a broke ass man-child would have never been a choice. Again, you live and learn!

Don's friendship began to develop which headed into a much different direction. Time had gone by so fast that I didn't even realize I had let him get so close, so soon. I admit one thing, though, I was looking for security, but instead I received the worst treatment any woman should ever have to experience.

The phone rings. "Hello Scooty, how's your day going?"

"Not too good!"

"I wanted to see you."

"No, because I have some studying to do for a test tomorrow!"
"Okay then, good luck with your test tomorrow!"

"Thanks!" I was only a week and a half away from my final exams. I knew that I had to stay focused, but every time I turned around someone was gossiping about what Don was doing out in the streets. The town isn't but so big and we all know how that goes. Everybody's in everybody else's business.

My associates were really my critics, I knew what was up. Who did they really think they were fooling? Thank God, one day I finally woke up after hitting my head too many times with this guy. Hell, there's no better way of putting this, Don is someone who has this big ego who obviously thinks he can treat women any way he wants to. Does anyone else know someone like this? Huh, his friends know him best.

What time is best then right now to leave town; my girls and I go and hang out in Philly for the night and damn near the morning too. Damn, the brotha's staking us out like we were fresh meat in a market. Although, it felt good to know that we were away from Reading and breathing air from a major city now.

Edgar Still's Day was special to some such as myself. Drill teams came from all over to participate in the competition against the best. They had traveled from cities to states. Yes, we were one of the best teams called The Playgirls.

The day of the parade, three mascots including myself kicked the doors down. First place is all we knew and worked real hard in earning it too. Ya'll remember just how sharp we were, right! The Playgirls practiced like no others around, literally felt like boot camp. The Playgirls were confident in our performances and knew just that. Anytime today when I hear a drill team, it takes me right back to those moments when we brought our 1st place trophy back home. We were very proud! Today is the parade, I can hear the judge on the microphone. "Everybody step back! The Reading Playgirls are coming through!"

As the years grew, the next generation was ready; my daughter and nieces became a big part of the drill team and now they love it too. For sons, they would play sports, which taught them to believe in themselves. It groomed them to be strong young black men with optimism, drive, determination and to have big dreams to one day become someone great. There is one true statement that I believe in so much, which is "Her crown has been paid for and now all she has to do is bend down pick it up and place it on her head," as Oprah once quoted.

Is it a natural thing for a male to introduce boys to sports, especially if they're around him on a daily basis. Someone answer this please, as Don didn't think so. As of matter of fact, Don played sports damn near every weekend for years, not once did he ask Myles to play catch. You would think if you're dating the mother then you would take more initiative in preparing the kid to learn what he should know. As Myles grew old enough to play sports, I had the pleasure of introducing him to football and the Blacktop Basketball Team. Remember, I didn't have any brothers growing up.

My uncle Mark took up boxing and wrestling. He always fought in the streets. I attended a few of his tournaments, which was another experience that kind of taught me a little about sports.

Do not change yourselves to be like the people of this world, but be changed within by new ways of thinking. Then you will be able to decide what God wants for you; you will know what is good and pleasing to him and what is perfect.

Romans 12:2

CHAPTER 8

We All Had One

S omeone thought we could have at least showed a little integrity, but when the truth is revealed, it turns out to be a deceitful person who pretended to be someone else. Take Barry Bonds, tall dark and as they say handsome, one of the best baseball home run hitters of our time. One who broke our beloved baseball hero Hank Aaron's baseball record of 755 home runs. Who would have ever thought that steroids would be needed as a crutch to do so?

Well, that's just where I come in, as I was a crutch for guys who appeared to look like they needed help in being a man. These dudes turned out to be tall, dark and stupid. They had to manipulate me to get my punany and used me like a crutch getting it if you know what I mean. Take for instance this guy name Edgar, of Latin descent. By the way, he was tall, dark and handsome created like those characters in those old 1940's movies. Edgar and I met in seventh grade, knowing one another for several months we began dating, and a friendship developed. We often went to the movies, hanging out with friends at the park. Skating is what we loved most. There were times when we were curious about being affectionate. After a year or so later, we did the damn thing.

It was the new year of '88. My cousin Misha and a few of my associates went to the projects to see our boyfriends. We all were having so much fun that we pulled an all-nighter. Lucia, Edgar's mother, proposed an invitation for all of us to stay over for the night. We stayed up all night playing dominoes, telling stories, laughing, and just having a good time. The whole time I already knew that I had messed up, my stomach began to do something new, the hell with the butterflies, I was worried about what would happen to my butt once I got home. None of us asked for permission from our parents to stay out.

Pulling my keys out and hesitant about turning the knob when walking into the house, instantly I felt the steam coming down the steps. "Scooty where the hell was you all night?" I was so scared the truth rolled right off my tongue. I stayed out all night like a woman, how could I lie? My mom tore my ass up. "I'm going to make sure you think about it next time," as she grabbed the belt. "There won't be a next time." Believe it or not, I walked around with a long welt on my leg for about a month.

A year later, I met a kid named Mac of Caribbean descent. Mac and I became close friends. Mac thought he was one of those sexy guys, only one problem he had no clue how to work that sexiness into a business aspect. It's all about them Benjamin's brotha! The funny thing is a man can be sexy, but if he has no money, sexy doesn't get him too far. Ladies we all know one of these, don't we? I really don't know what we called ourselves doing at the time because it wasn't a relationship it was more of a friendship than anything else. Although, we really cared for one another as good friends do.

We would take trips to Queens, N.Y. to visit our families. When my mother moved to Virginia, back in 1998, I would come into town and Mac would swing by showing us a nice time, sweet guy. Early on, I met another kid named Derick of African-American descent, a comedian, always had us laughing. Derick was like a brother to me also, we took the bus to school every day, walked the halls and even ate lunch together. By the time prom rolled around who else better to ask than my God sent brother Derick. We had a great time on the dance floor. After we graduated Derick moved away.

Now I have told you my history with Donald. I have recognized that God is my heavenly father and Jesus is my Lord and savior as every day I praise them. There are two things that I had to recognize, time heals old wounds and God loves me. How could I have let someone like Donald get so near who wasn't of God!

One day I struck up a brief conversation. Donald, why don't you go to church with us one Sunday?"

"No, because I'd feel like a hypocrite."

"Why?" No response. In no time, he had proved himself of what kind of person he could become. As a young woman, I realized that I wanted better than Donald. He was a man who claims to come from a great family but never goes out of his way to show compassion or empathy. Simply, it's not like him to act this way.

On the other hand, I was young and naïve and have always felt that I had a beautiful spirit inside and out. Once he took me for granted, it changed who I was inside. Of course, meeting him rubbed me the wrong way and that's a rap. When a man is involved with a woman, his integrity enables him to shower her with love, support and protect her in many ways. Every woman deserves to be treated like a queen. Anyone agree?

When you think of a man and how he respects you, you never think that he would ever be so blatant to flaunt another chick in your face. Right! Well, Donald invited me to a basketball game one weekend, as he happened to be home from college. Little did I know there was a surprise waiting for me. He showed his butt the entire time up until the game was over. As he walked off to his car, I continued to walk on. Oh, let's not stop there! Pulling up on the side of me, he offered me a ride or was he just trying to get rid of me? I had to climb into the back seat because he had company. He states, "it's just a friend", as we road in total silence the entire ride to the crib. He drops me off at my front door.

Hell, I wasn't mad at the fact that he was cheating again, just really fed up by this point because he's been showing his true colors since we met. It was how he continuously thought he could switch the light on and off. It was the level of respect that he neglected. As I think about it his deceitfulness was a clear example of how he lacked a sense of class. Do you want to know why I say this? Dude pulls up in front of the house, I get out. How dumb is this? I'm standing there in the middle of the street expecting for him to look back, which he never did. For the umpteenth time, where was my head?

For twelve miserable years, I have been antagonized and not to say again prejudged. Guess what, though? It's cool because he helped me get my big break on stupidity. Dude's pattern never seems to slow up. Now it's a white girl! (lmao!)

She was white, but let her tell it she was trapped in an African-American's body. How hilarious is that where you claim you don't know your culture and you been white your whole life. How stupid could I be? Now I'm crazy, I had to find a way out for myself.

Later that night, I scooped up a friend who rode along with me. Lo and behold, I was right. This nasty chick had her trashy ass out there at his job, doing who knows and what? Nothing surprised me anymore. Let's just make a long story short. All hell broke loose and I was ordered to pay her restitution. I was just playing myself by being stupid or thinking that I was in love. Damn! When we finally arrived at city hall, dude instantly became her witness. Ain't that a bitch! Tell me, what true brotha' calls himself a black man and turns his back on a sistah like that, all behind a broke piece of ass? Do I need to go any further? You can see where his head was? After all that, he still came knocking at my door and ringing my phone. "No! You can't stay here with me."

"No! You can't lay here with me, be on your way." Bottom line is that he couldn't help himself; portraying me to be the crazy one here.

Enough was enough. It was time for me to do some soul searching of myself in getting ahead. I got the final message. "Leave well enough alone." No sooner than I told myself, I was done. My name was slandered with many rumors. First, they said, my mother wasn't shit, my grandparents were broke because they were still living on the same block after retiring and I was supposed to be this hoe. Well, guess what? Your dead wrong! So much I learned through this entire time of my life. When you are in the midst of a storm, hold your head up high. People who have morals don't stray and dudes who don't have any Integrity will disrespect women each time they can. We as women must demand the RESPECT that we so well deserve, wash our hands of the relationship and just walk away, PERIOD!

One night, a friend and I were out for the night and Donald shows up out of nowhere, offering me a ride to my car. Hell! Can you believe this by now? As he gave the ride, my foot kicked a wallet of someone he had just dropped off. I knew then that I was done. I've been through hell and back. I'm stronger than I ever thought I could be, thanks, Donald!

Realizing that I could never stop working on myself as a person; God expects the best in me. It is God who drives my spirit. As I see, my lessons in life have been taught as God definitely, makes a way. Today is a new day and Jesus is the answer. So, guess what people?

I'm still standing tall because nothing can hold me back from prospering. It was God who gave me a second chance and I'm so grateful.

When I decided to move away to get a better focus on life, God had more in store for me. Each time I held onto my past, my future was put on hold, slipping right before my very eyes. Hold it! Now writing about it all becomes a therapeutic lesson for me in moving forward with my life.

The question is knowing just how great God is, even when you make the wrong choices in life. God is truly awesome... To all my critics, now since we're all gathered here any questions? You people of no faith, you know exactly who you are. How can I judge you without judging myself first, really? That's just how I felt through the entire second half of my life.

SECOND SHIFT

Father's do not make your children angry, but raise them with the training and teaching of the Lord.

Ephesians 6:4

CHAPTER 9

The Drama Unfolds

Sssss! Only be afraid of the living snakes, they can bite you when you least expect them too. Now I was the idiot, Donald decides to stop by his parents on our way back from King of Prussia. "Mom, this is Scooty." The look this woman had on her face gave me the impression that something was terribly wrong and not with me. I mean I shortly experienced this after knowing her. Where he often wondered why I refused to visit their home.

Something was definitely wrong! Man, I was twenty-two years old and hated the person I was. The word pregnant never came to mind especially since I already knew that I was one child knee deep and a careless father of one. It was what I said that I would never ever do again, like a dumb ass I got knocked up again. I was angry of making the same mistake twice and no college degree. I actually promised myself and it was the worst thing I could have ever done. I made the decision to get an abortion.

I scheduled for an appointment, a friend even supported me by coming along., Abstinence is no nonsense. Children aren't cheap and they can be very costly. What do they say, practice what you preach? Well, on June 17, 1994, I gave birth to a nine-and-a-half-pound big baby girl. She was beautiful and huge like her dad. Everyone was happy except me, I mean I was happy to see my daughter; I just didn't realize what I was getting myself into by having this bundle of joy. Why?

A week after my six weeks check-up my gynecologist calls me with some disturbing news. Can anyone guess? Yes, I had an STD and guess who gave it to me? Hell yeah, I was pissed at myself. Refraining myself, yeah right! It's not like I didn't know he had his nasty ass out there like that again. I was stupid, but he has no respect for himself. Praise God, Zoë was protected. Did it ever cross his mind that he could have given me herpes or even worse, AIDS instead of chlamydia? Attempting to wake him surprisingly, one day we drove to Planned Parenthood. "Why did you come here? So, we can get an AIDS test done and for you to educate yourself." I couldn't thank God enough. After confronting him, he denied it for a day and it's sad because Don tried so hard to convince me, that I gave it to him. Really!

The hard part is that he's a mess and he knows it. See, God says to forgive them father, for what they may not know. There comes a time in our lives when we meet people who refuse to change, and that means to run for your life.

His mother asks, "When are you two going to get married?" I already knew that I was young and naïve, but I didn't need anyone dictating my life in buying a home or let alone marriage. From that day I knew that I deserved much more. Whatever it was, it was. I'm twenty-two with an open mind. Now I want to venture out with an apartment preparing for the new birth of my child, moving into the suburbs. What was I thinking? Through the five years of living on my own, I continued to be the sucker.

Don manipulated me. No excuses! I wasn't focused! Whenever I said no, he took advantage of me. Excuses, excuses! Honestly, there were many times that I called myself being strong, avoiding his calls. He would even persuade me that he would change. Here he had been working on buying a house with his parent's help. Out of nowhere, he says, "I want to become a family." Where did this come from? "Scooty, I'm serious." Months later he asked me to go along while he signed papers. We talked and I decided to give the rental office a thirty-day notice putting my things into storage.

A month before moving in Donald decides to show his natural black ass, he tried to manipulate me out of $4,000. When I refused, he denied us a place to live; his daughter, his flesh, and blood. "Didn't you just get some money?"

"Yeah!"

"Well, I need at least $4,000."

"For what?"

"A down payment on the house." It wasn't the principle of the money, it was the integrity that he was totally lacking and it was disgusting to me.

I immediately backed up asking myself, "Why did I take my family through all this mess?" We were content in our own place with less drama. Don can only control those who are weak. Here I found myself starting over and having to cover my butt for the sake of my children. He moved in and we moved on. Actually, it was one of the best things that could have ever happened for the kids and me. We had no other alternative moves besides moving back in with family. For a long time, I felt like I failed my family and myself. Due to their waiting list, the choice of even moving back to the townhouses was not an option anymore and all this for what?

Ladies, never make decisions during an emotional state of mind because you will regret it. I know I regretted it like hell. The neighborhood was beautiful for raising kids. Don's sister eventually moved in across the street from me. I could always talk to her about how comical her mother would be. How long does it take for one to learn? Years later, Donald was married and still, he decided to show disrespect to his new wife and family.

Asking myself, was he ever really taught how to treat a woman? Only he can answer that. It was Don who also decided to play mind games with two women and why? It was very obvious that he wanted his cake and eat it too. It's the day before his wedding day. Of course, he's at it again and it really surprised me. He had the audacity to ride past my mother's house checking on my whereabouts. He parks and rings the bell for however long, I don't know. Finally, I decided to walk to the front of the house looking out of the window. I noticed Donald's truck across the street so I decided to ignore the bell. Plus, I had a few friends visiting from out of town.

Marc says that he heard something downstairs in the kitchen. "Shhh, be quiet and listen." So, I got up and slowly went down the back stairway and surprisingly enough, Don was standing in the kitchen looking startled that he was caught. First of all, his t-shirt he was wearing had dirt across the front of it, something felt strange right then and the expression he had on his face was a dead giveaway. "Donald, how did you get in the house?" I looked and noticed the kitchen screen was up. "What do you think you're doing climbing through the kitchen window?" He looked me dead in my face and lies again changing the conversation, refusing to answer me.

"Scooty, why didn't you answer the front door?" He heard my friends talking upstairs aiming for the steps, as I stopped him, "You know what? You're supposed to be getting married tomorrow and here you are worrying about who's in my house. It's really none of your business. You just committed a crime in my mother's house I should call the police for you breaking and entering. You gotta go!"

He refused not until he knew who was upstairs in the den.

Meanwhile, Marc walked towards the steps as Don reaches the top of the staircase. Walking towards Don, "What's up Don?" Don insisted on arguing. I step in, "Look, Donald, you have to get out my house."

"Why?" Finally, he decides to leave, walking out the back door. But then stops.

"Scooty, can I talk to you?"

"About?"

Right away, I knew something was wrong because he was acting strangely. "Wait a minute," excusing myself from my friends. When I opened the screen door to go outside, I couldn't believe how nervous he was acting. He was actually shaking while talking to me with tears in his eyes. He says, "I knew you were home, I was curious as to why you didn't open the door for me. I drove around back and came through the yard. Scooty how could you even have Marc and his friends in the house, I still love you!" He goes on to say, "I really needed to talk to you because I'm not sure if this is what I really want to do tomorrow."

"Donald if you didn't want to marry her, then you should have told your mother no when she asked you to get married. Don, it's one thing that you must realize sooner or later, you'll have to make your own decisions one day without your mother demanding you twenty-four seven. Damn!"

Don gave me a look as if to say you're right! "You know what Donald I love you too, but only as a friend now." Surprised he was.

"Why don't you love me anymore?"

"You must first learn what it is to respect a woman before entering into any relationship, I gotta go."

"Look, as long as you're happy, then I'm happy for you. Good luck! Scooty, before you go can I have one last kiss?"

"No, that's not necessary." He turns and walks away.

As time progressed, Don refused to stop calling me even after I asked him to stop. One evening unexpectedly, he decides to drop by my grandparent's house. "What are you doing here?"

"Scooty I still love you!" I looked at him with such shame, here he's a newlywed only two months into the marriage and now he's complaining to me about mistakes he's made. By this time, I was fed up. "Look, why are you telling me all this?" I walked out the front door to leave. Can you believe this dude followed me to my car, pulling on the door to get in so he could talk to me about his marriage? This was a weird moment as we sat there talking for a few minutes, up until I pulled off heading in the direction of his house.

"Scooty I'm stressed!"

"Why are you putting yourself through drama and stress, all this just to satisfy your mother?"

"Ain't no way in hell you're crazy! I just don't know what to do?" Call me crazy, call me what you want, but he left me no damn choice. "Scooty where are you going?"

"Your house!"

"What?"

"Scooty pull into Wal-Mart please."

"No, I didn't come this far to pull into a Wal-Mart until you get yourself together. You got yourself into this mess and now you need to clear it up."

"Don, your wife deserves to know how you really feel and since you can't be man enough to tell her, then I will." When I finally pulled into the driveway; he was a nervous wreck asking questions. We walked in and I approached the top of the stairs as she breastfed their newborn child.

"Kerry, Don needs to talk to you downstairs."

"What's going on?"

"Your husband just tracked me down to complain about your marriage."

"What, Don why did you go looking for Scooty anyway?" Now he's speechless. Funny how tables turn, now it was our turn to antagonize him. After a while Don finally surfaced. "I didn't mean any of this, but I still love Scooty." Oh, and she was hurt. "Don, you didn't have to have me move from New York to figure out that you still love Scooty; you know what Don, all you had to do was tell me no about the marriage."

"Kerry to be perfectly honest with you, it was all his mother's doing just like she tried to do me the same way." Kerry was devastated, "Don, I can't believe you did all this because of your mother. Don is this why you decided to start sleeping on the couch?" Before I left, I said. "Listen, I'm sure you two have a lot to discuss," as I walked out of the door Don follows me again.

"What's up Don?"

"I need to get my truck!" Still nervous, "Scooty you know I couldn't stay there with her." Out of nowhere, Don says, "Scooty thank you!"

"For what?"

"You just relieved me from all my stress." He was actually being honest I could see the relief on his face.

You wouldn't believe it, but all hell broke loose. You might as well say Action News was involved because, by the time Kerry called her mother-in-law, she then called everyone in the phone book by the end of the night. Let's just say, Reading now had something new to talk about. Hell! Now Kerry was a part of all the family drama. I was done with all of it. What the hell do you even call that, some kind of plague or something? Someone else I know calls it a cult.

What I found out and learned, which took me a while to realize is we as African-American people, who live in Reading refuse to stand up for our own culture. Why because we already know the truth especially when it comes to how the Caucasians think as biased as they do when it comes to our culture. Not once did they ever allow for any African-Americans to run for mayor and it's so sad.

Think about it, living in a small town like Reading only makes us feel like we're being treated unjustified because we can never be heard. Did you ever have a black mayor run for council or even think about doing it in the town you live in? Am I right? There's nothing like stepping out on faith and discovering who you really are without that small mentality around you. Sooner or later there comes a point in your life when pessimistic ways don't faze you not one bit. Eventually, reality comes to the surface and I grow up through all the madness in my life, now realizing that life is about making others happy and living out one's dreams to the fullest. I've grown and only God can judge me. God has delivered me in more ways than one, so I say this as nonchalantly as I can, "Whatever it was it was. Lord, free me of myself, so I can please you.

Now that you are obedient children of God do not live as you did in the past. You did not understand, so you did the evil things you wanted, but be holy in all you do, just as God, the one who called you, is holy.

Peter 1:14-15

CHAPTER 10

Patience

Did you ever experience a time when you felt like you were all alone due to certain things that maybe you had to experience? You know that feeling where you just can't seem to shake it off because you felt like no one really cared. It feels as if you don't have a true bond with yourself, or even knowing who you are as a person. My mind seemed poisoned for so many years often telling myself to shake it off and to be strong and faithful.

One day I realized very abruptly what I was faced with day in and day out. Unfortunately, the realization was that I met someone who I may have thought was special, turned out not to be so special. You think they care but they really don't. When you find out that you opened yourself up to a can of worms, the trust gets broken and a whole mess of things begins to happen. Yes, when we meet a guy do we really think about who he really is or just how he looks? Hmmmm! Is he all cracked up to be who he says he is? Good question right? Do we as women, really understand what it is to be a real woman? Maybe! Since birth, we were all taught to trust one another right? So why does Mr. Right turn out to be Mr. Wrong?

After one relationship fails, we've become vulnerable to whatever. After some time, we then start to put our defenses up. Damn! What ever happened to the trust? What happens psychologically? Why do men cheat, lie and screw us over, in turn making us out to be this crazy woman only because we ended up meeting him? It was he who tore me down and it was he who made me come out of my bag, but with no hesitation I allowed it to happen. Real recognizes what's real...lol

They know exactly who they are. If I didn't know then, I definitely know now that trust is supposed to be one of the main components in a relationship. Nine times out of ten, the woman gives the relationship her all, and all she gets in return is taken advantage of again and again. Say that I'm wrong! So, what do we do? We ask questions of his friends, find out who he really is, before getting serious. Why? Because some men will try to hook, line and sink you, no sooner than they see you coming, it's all game. You have some older men that prey on the younger woman to get a closer look at their credit score. They then use you up and ditch you just as fast as they met you. Apparently, that's all they seem to know; which is enough to make some of us very aware of our surroundings.

When a man lies, cheats and basically steals your joy, he expects for you to stick around for his repeated brutal mind games. Once again, he who preys on the weak will have his day. Smile, better days are coming. I say, we as young women needs to recognize who we are and our surroundings and capture the moments of true happiness. No woman is put here on Earth to be taken advantage of by no means. Strong women stand up! After we done all we can we just stand!

We all had one dude who may have thought he was the shit, turned out he was a piece of shit. No disrespect, recognize it when you see it and call it what it is. They say it's the women who make these men go into their next state of mind. Nah! I don't even want to believe that for one second. As they say, there are trashy women and there are classy women, which one are you? Are you a woman who constantly has an attitude? How much time alone does it take for serenity to embrace you? Think about it, could it possibly be something going on inside of you which makes you react this way of course, after meeting him. Right!

After all, is said and done and the relationship is over, your spirit has turned for the worse. He tested you just to see how far you'll really go. Men, who are egotistical, tend to be more of the controlling ones. I only know from experience, but also know that there are good Godly men out here too. As women and men, we must recognize sooner or later, that what we may think is right, sometimes isn't. We all must recognize sooner or later, what we may think is right, and sometimes isn't.

Sometimes life may not be all cracked up to be what someone else life may be and we may not meet people of great character and they may take advantage of you. Get out fast! If you haven't received a second chance, then that simply means you truly haven't sought God enough for God to recognize who you are. I mean you must love God more than you love yourself and even them chaps that you gave birth and tend to every day.

Ask yourself, "Who do I think I am to put anything else before God? Second chances bring success, so get on board. We often think well, it's never too late. Let me say this, I witnessed a miracle from God, me. Once I learned to trust God and his work, he made all things possible for you and me. Believe me, God's works are truly amazing! Now I know happiness is important, so I will never allow myself to settle for far less than what I'm worth. When you allow yourself to invest in a friendship with God, you have invested in a forever friendship. I live to say this, again and again, just continue to have faith, put God first and he will handle the rest.

We all are gathered here, to know our differences in life to think about where we're going. Reality begins to sink in, only to make us understand that God is real and an on-time God! What are you happy for today? Your dreams, how far do they extend? Mine are vast and immense to dream bigger than I ever thought before.

And after you suffer for a short time, God who gives all grace, will make everything right. He will make you strong and support you and keep you from falling. He called you to share in his glory in Christ, a glory that will continue forever

1 Peter 5:1

CHAPTER 11
Babies

Babies are a true blessing from God. If it weren't for the Lord, think about it, where would you be today? Now, think back when you were a baby; can you remember? From the door, you know it takes a strong woman to give birth to a bundle of joy. It's not any way easy and please don't let anyone fool you in telling you differently. It's unfortunate that some women aren't blessed to carry babies due to complications. How important is a child to you when you don't have any? A question I ask myself.

How could a mother of two neglect her daughters at such a young age and feel at ease with herself? The children are distraught; chewed up and spit out. What could possibly keep our mother away from us; I mean what was so important out there? How does a grandmother become so comfortable in shifting her very own grandchildren around in between families? Will the family ever be normal? Huh! Will there always be problems, drama and much more? Well, this is just what my family went through very dysfunctional, sound familiar.

In these days and times, no child in America asks to be born into this world of neglect, although it happens and why? There is a generational curse going on, not only that, when does it stop? You go to baby showers or even help put one or two together. Children come through you, but not from you. Parents create a bond with those children for the remainder of their lives.

A majority of teenagers out here today are having babies too early. What they fail to realize is that having a baby isn't an oops kind of situation, it's a lifetime commitment. Ladies, it's very important that you have full control of your dreams and your destiny. There are so many positive things you can do for yourself in and after school, so don't become a part of this epidemic. Listen, babies are being born into poverty every day sometimes they're even deprived of their parents love.

So, I'm advising you to stay in school and live out your dream first. When the time does come for you to meet someone get to know your mate first before you ever think about getting serious and losing focus on what's truly important for you. Taking off your clothes and laying down for him is just not it! This is a very SERIOUS situation where we are today as young women; again, fulfill your dreams and aspirations. When you wake up in the morning and you look in that mirror, ask yourself where am I going today? Where does my future lay? What am I going to work hard on in trying to fulfill my goals to become one day? Where do I see myself in seven years from now? As I always share with Myles and Zoe love others, help many, live your dreams and have lots of fun in life in creating many memorable moments, but always make wise decisions in what you do on a day to day basis.

Oh, and how can I forget a must share! Whenever that day comes, always remember to do yourself a favor in making sure that your mate is not a momma's boy, still living under her roof as a grown man with no job only because she wants to control his every move with her credit cards. I cannot stress this enough. Make sure he comes from a great family of respect, morals. Bottom line be sure he has some damn sense, so he won't ever try and take advantage by living off of you. As Spike Lee says, "Do the Right Thing!"

Remember we all were babies once, I'm very strong willed and most times underestimated. I just want to say that I was a lonely child once who made it out by the faith of God; that's what enables me to be as strong as I am today. A true factor, wisdom is good for the soul and a wonderful thing to know. I was ecstatic by the time I finished high school, although I never quite felt prolific enough. My problem was that I was naive and sometimes weak which lead me to focus on the wrong things in life.

Eventually, Don witnesses that I had no strong male role models in my life. I mean I did, but I didn't because they never stood up for me and he preyed on just that fact. Now I realize much later just how focused I should have been towards my career and not that so-called man-child that I, unfortunately, ended up meeting and sharing a child with today. As I look at my young adults now, I ask myself, how could I allow for someone of such character to disrupt my life in steering me off the right path? Damn! What the heck was I thinking?

As I see now, God wants me to aim high for myself. Unfortunately, getting pregnant with my son at 16 years old was something that I simply had to accept. I could have chosen something different for myself, I know. So, I believed and became motivated because anything is possible.

Late that evening, I began to have excruciating pains. I was already five days overdue and had a doctor's appointment that afternoon where my doctor stripped my membrane to get things rolling. Early that morning I was admitted to St. Joseph's Hospital where I was in labor for 16.5 hours. What a hell of an experience it is to give birth to a newborn baby. I mean it was rough, I went from yelling at my mom; to being very irritable with his dad, up until reality set in realizing this innocent child didn't arrive here alone.

Due to our newborn's arrival, he and I had already split up and just like that, he went his way and I became the responsible one. I was a young woman, yet strong enough to get through the struggles of life. I said to myself, "Regardless of what Edgar's decisions were, we managed because I was determined to finish high school." I always knew that I was a responsible caring and loving person from a young age. Due to my sister Heidi having her first child, I was forced to step in and help take care of my nephew Levi, while I was only in the eighth grade.

Myles went from taking his first photos in the hospital to going home to his brand-new family. A typical mother, I just couldn't stop staring at his little precious face. Myles enjoyed warm baths, warm milk bottles, bright colors and off to sleep he went, the story of a newborn. No sooner than he began to eat cereal he got thicker than solid food, he was off and crawling getting into everything, time was moving all so fast.

Every morning Myles and I prepared our day by getting picked up by the teen parenting van to go to school. Myles was blessed that he could even join the other children on a daily basis in the high school daycare, while I continued to focus on my diploma for us. Every day before lunch and study hall we would go to the daycare to put our kids down for a nap, where Myles slept on his knees with his butt in the air, which was so very cute.

Today is Myles first birthday party. I will never forget all the precious moments with him as a kid. The terrible two tantrums were truly an experience too. Woo Hoo!

The day he became potty trained, my baby hated to have to sit on that potty chair just before his naps. Tears would roll down his little face, and then sometimes he would even drift off while sitting there.

When Myles reached his first-year time began to move faster. Carnivals, B-day parties and skating he absolutely enjoyed.

We all had a time in our lives where we can relate to making wrong decisions, whether it was yesterday or today. Now, ask yourself the question early on are you ready to take on a responsibility in raising a child as a teenager? You should think about it long and hard. Make sure you keep in mind just how far you're trying to aim in your life and know that you deserve so much more for your future because education is the key.

Listen, having babies before your far more than ready is so hard, it completely shortens your learning path and having the knowledge for that child. It stomps growth for you both mother and father as teenagers. You don't have a clue what you're getting yourself into at such a young age. Think about it! Today you have adults that refuse to have babies until they complete their education and have met certain milestones in their lives, their dreams come first. There are finer things in life you could be doing. The bottom line is that you have your whole life ahead of you so aim as high as you can because the sky is the limit. I cannot say it enough!

Feeling lost and despaired I was tempted to try certain things that I maybe shouldn't have, like sex. Look where it got me... young, dumb and pregnant at 16! So, I say this, ladies really think about what you're doing with your life before you put yourself in the wrong path as teenagers. Sex is not that serious, it's when you make irresponsible decisions that can land you in a more detrimental situation, where you don't have to be if you just say no. "I'm not ready yet."

We as beautiful young women should want to wait so we can give something special to that child and your future husband. It's called marriage, where you love someone deeply and plan on spending the rest of your life with him or her. I'll tell you when young women take it amongst themselves thinking they're grown and growing up too fast only leads them into places where we will later analyze and look back and say, I shoulda, coulda and woulda wish I did this differently. I promise you that's the truth! So please enjoy your youth while you can, it's worth every minute of it. There's really no need in rushing to say that you're his baby mama, it sounds crazy, doesn't it? You're the one who has to live with this. Sistah, you're so better than that!" It's simple, just let him know that he doesn't qualify.

Listen, when a child is born, he or she deserves the best of both parents. Nine times out of ten, if you decide to have a child while you're young, it will only be you who will be short-changed out of life, believe me, I can relate. One thing my grandmother always told me since I was young, "Treat other's the way you would like to be treated and take care of your responsibilities." All children are a gift from God.

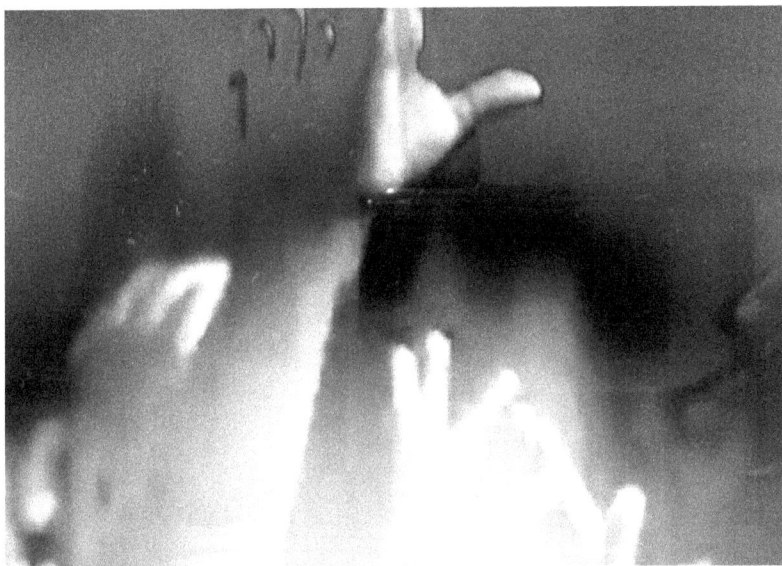

I am the Lord, the God of every person on the earth. Nothing is impossible for me.

Jerimiah 32:27

CHAPTER 12

Mom Mom

There's A Big 'O World Out There!

After all those lonely days and nights of sitting up through the night wondering if our mother was ever going to return, I repeatedly asked, "Where is she?" They didn't know and that's all I ever heard. Until one evening my grandmother, who has always inspired and encouraged me to pray, reminded me that everything was going to be okay in time. Mattie called me into her bedroom where she enjoyed relaxing and watching her favorite black and white movies.

"Scooty, come here." As I approached the doorway she says, "Sit down baby so we can talk." She held my hand, "What's wrong? I noticed that something was bothering you over the past few days."

"Mom Mom, could you ever imagine being a kid, worrying day in and day out about your mommy and trying very hard to keep your grades up in school the best way you know how? Well, I am that worried kid."

"Listen, baby, there will be a lot of things in life that may not go the way you want them to, but that doesn't mean that you have to give up, you must keep your faith in God and He will see you through! If Tot and I can make it through poverty without an education and have made it thus far then you know you too can get through these tough times because your strong-willed God loves you, baby!"

"Okay, I will!"

"Let's not forget, we had to help support our families too. I can make it, we're going to make it mom-mom!"

"I still want to know something, what did Heidi and I do that made my mommy leave us? I mean my mom chose to be somewhat absent from our childhood. She thought it was acceptable to have left us with you and the gentle giant."

As I look back, there were a lot of mishaps that I had to really overcome. I had faith in God that he would have our backs and provide us with his guidance and strength to make it out of all the turmoil. I am very grateful today.

"Mom Mom, I want to thank you for all you've done for us. Smile, God is watching over you for taking on the responsibility in raising us. When I think about why God is watching over us, it's because of your daughter (Teresa) that you and CW raised us, she decided to walk off many days thinking that she didn't owe you all any explanation. I often wondered how you two really felt having to raise my sister and me." She stopped me right there. "This was the only way to keep you and Heidi together. We were not going to let you two go into any foster care system or have you two going from one place to the next, no not none of mines!"

I hugged her and began to cry, thanking her for the support that they gave us all these years. It was so painful at that very moment. As always she prayed for us. As we got older, the reality of life set in and my perspective was much different. It was so sad because the life that we were forced to live before our grandparents got full custody of us, began to discourage me in so many ways. Our self-esteem, respect, levels of trust and love were unfairly torn apart. I managed to hold on to my faith and my strength, which seemed to be all I had left to hold onto.

Heidi always managed to show me that her being promiscuous

was her way of not dealing with any of the pain that we both shared. Without the love of our mother and fathers, Heidi and I shared rough times together. At that time, I felt as though I was smart enough to say no whenever a boy asked me if I wanted to join him in sex. As time went on, I later found out that I ended up being a part of that generational curse too. As I am constantly reminded of those times, I try to understand that we could have possibly had better opportunities in life, if our mother had an educated background and if she would have been there for us by sharing her love in building a strong foundation by providing a home with stability much earlier on.

After all these years, I now realize that she couldn't provide all of that for us because she obviously didn't have a great education growing up with her parents, she rebelled. Teresa gave us what she could in providing for us the best she could in surviving. When I think about it, I don't think she really knew anything about being a mother, she was too young to truly understand it. Especially, when you're out there having children so very early in age and depending only on yourself to make ends meet. I recall the times when Heidi and I had to get split up and go into different homes. We really fought deep down inside knowing, in keeping the faith in God, we would one day reunite with our mom.

One day we would have what you call a normal life. We always knew that we wanted the finer things in life, but we shortchanged ourselves by settling for a lesser quality of life in staying in Reading. We didn't venture out into the world like we should have to experience something new for ourselves. I can only speak for myself; although I was always independent in wanting to work and live on my own. An unfortunate and unforeseen circumstance arose in my life, Don. I allowed him to manipulate me in moving out of the townhouse my kids and I had for eight years.

This was a major setback as a result of Don's selfish ways that forced me to move back in with my grandparents. Now that years have passed, I realized that if Junior were a major role model in my life as my father, maybe I would have never been taken for granted. Junior should have laid down the stipulations in my life from the beginning.

Caring is all I could do for my grandparents, choosing to stay close by, whether I was in the suburbs or living in the city. It was always about making sure they had what was needed. Now that they have gotten much older and really needing all of us around to give them moral support, I now feel a sense of guilt by not physically being there.

I have prayed about it time and time again. Realizing that I did all I could do when I was there. As I think about it, I have my own life to live and business to tend to. So, I knew then I had to move on if I wanted to make them very proud of my accomplishments. After all these years, it has honestly taken me 29 years to learn that there is a big o' world out there waiting for me. So, I had to gather all my things together and see for myself. I'm so grateful for the time that has passed; it has allowed my soul to surrender from all the hurt and turmoil that I've been dealing with for many, many years. I just thank God each and everyday day for giving me a second chance in making things much better in my life. No matter where I am, I find myself crying at times only because I'm happy and praising God for all his grace and mercy in all he's done for me. Now, I'm actually living each day as though it's my last and never taking life for granted anymore.

These nine years of being away from my grandparents have been a beautiful learning experience for me. Actually, living in a different state doesn't stop the way I feel inside for those who really cared for me. I reminisce on those precious moments growing up with my grandmother. She has shown me that her inner beauty is what shines. I have often tried to show the inner beauty within myself. However, the hurt and pain are what always seems to shine through. At the end of the day, I know that there is a beautiful person that stands before me. Although, I've been judged over and over by the standards of how my mother lived her life. Why? I guess I'll never know.

After walking in these shoes for so long, I say judge me not because it's been a long road. I may have been forced to live under these circumstances as a child, but I'm all grown up now and I know the difference. I'm not perfect and I don't pretend to be, but there are certain things that I often ask myself, have I ever done anything wrong that I'm not fond of? Yes, I have. Everyone on this earth has done something, but they may refuse to admit it. As each day passes, I am grateful and blessed to be here. I have been enlightened which has humbled my spirit. I have come to grips in knowing that my life must go on and I must stop blaming myself for the mistakes that my parents created for me while growing up. When there's a will, there's a way.

Those who go to God most high for safety will be protected by the almighty. I will say to the Lord, "you are my place of safety and protection you are my God and I trust you".

Psalm 91:1-2

CHAPTER 13

Strength

There comes a time in your life when you must call on the higher power to give you guidance and strength through all things that we may come face to face with each day. I'm aware of how far I've come even through all my trials and tribulations. The higher power has a better plan for me only this time around and it's called a second chance. Who would have ever thought, by me craving and going for a slice of pizza crazy things would instantly develop?

It's so crazy! I'm eight months' pregnant and craving a slice of pizza; my sister rides along only because she wants a beer. As we are sitting at a red light across the street from Maria's, the pizza shop. The light changes, but we never make it inside. We notice a white Audi going through the light so, right away Heidi and I looked at each other knowing what we noticed was our mother's car, only this time it wasn't our mother who was driving or presently in the car. It really looked like it could have been a white girl from a distance. With no hesitation, we followed the car up until her husband Benny decided to park. Exiting the car these two-people entered an apartment building, as they say, "Crack is Wack!"

I couldn't recognize her and unfortunately, we were determined to find out who she was. Attempting to open the door to the apartment building it was locked. Heidi began knocking on the neighbors' window who lived downstairs. We were in now and asking the neighbor questions. "Yo who lives upstairs? "Some crack head named Ali. "Are you talking about that nasty chic Ali?" "Yeah, you know her. Ali who?"

The neighbor was even nice enough to open up Ali's door too, so we were really in now. The only problem was that I was wearing some flats that were loud and each step I took on the hardwood floors were undeniably noticed. Plus, I was carrying a ten-pound baby. Heidi went ahead and once she reached the top of the steps she began to listen to their conversation. Once I had finally reached the top I could also hear two people talking, which really sounded like they were trying to whisper now since they heard us standing in the hallway.

"Ben, what are you doing here and who is the crack head?" He ignored me. "Come out of her apartment because I saw both of you when you got out the car and walked in." I began knocking on the walls. I can actually hear them inside walking around as for a minute it was nothing but total silence. Heidi quickly ran downstairs because we heard a door open we weren't sure if Ben was trying to get out by the fire escape. Minutes later after I finally got downstairs, Ben came walking down the street trying to play it off as if someone had just dropped him off and he was walking to get the car. As I walked up on him, he looked like he was already high.

"You are caught in your own act and I'm telling my mom." Heidi started questioning Ben, "Why were you in a crack head's apartment, if you weren't trying to get high and what are you doing here anyway?" As usual, he made up some lie and really expected for us to believe him. Heidi and I just walked away from him and walked back to the car. We waited until he pulled off following him back to the house. As he got out the car and walked across the street I asked him, "What were you doing with her?"

No sooner than I got in the house I called my mom and gave her the 411. Once I told her, she wanted to speak to Ben and the next thing I knew, she was walking in the front door from work. She was hot as fish grease. I don't know what went on in that bedroom that night, but I do know that Teresa wasn't playing with him or that nasty crack head he was spending his time with.

Teresa personally drove to her apartment, but the crack head refused to come outside to even talk. The next few days Teresa found out what job she was working at. Can you believe that this crack head had the audacity to phone the house trying to apologize by calling Teresa by her married name? Teresa said, "Bitch, you wasn't thinking about calling me anything when you was trying to sleep with my husband" and she hung up the phone.

Teresa wanted revenge and she went after it by finding out where her job was and got her fired from the first, second and now the third job which was a bank. One morning Teresa walked into the bank pretending that she wanted to open a bank account. She sat down waiting for someone to assist her, as the lady approached her, my mother announces as loudly as she could, "I would like to open an account here at your branch, but you have someone here that's working under the influence of crack cocaine" and then she pointed to the teller, Ali. Soon after Teresa shared some more information about Ali with the lady from the bank.

It was now days before Teresa was going into the hospital to repair a herniated disc and to have spinal fusion surgery. As Teresa prepared herself for surgery her husband was very persistent in keeping the drama going in their marriage by him hanging out all night with his so-called friends. It started way back when I was in the seventh grade. He would bring one of his friends over and they would go into the back room to get high. How much weed does one smoke until they realize they need a different high such as crack cocaine?

Teresa's surgery took approximately two and a half hours and everything went well according to the doctor's words. She stayed in the hospital for a week for observation. My grandparents, Heidi and I were there every day making sure she was comfortable and anything else that she needed. By this time, Teresa hadn't received any antibiotics from her doctor so she requested some, which he deliberately refused. The entire time Teresa was in the hospital, she became stressed and irritable. Literally, she cried out worrying about her husband's whereabouts, more than thinking of herself in getting better so she could go home.

The week that Teresa was in the hospital for her surgery, if Ben came up to see his wife it was maybe once. He kept doing his disappearing act. This is what repeatedly upset her. Instantly, I became pissed off. You would have at least thought if he wasn't going to show up then he would have called to see how she was doing. Hell, it was very obvious that he had no respect for his wife or what she was even going through. All the while we were trying to keep her positive, so she could get well enough to come home. However, she only continued in worrying about him. The morning came for her to be discharged and I went up to the hospital, I don't know how Ben got word that she was even coming home, but he decided to be there too; although nothing seemed to change with him.

One morning as he lay there asleep on the couch, the smell of alcohol reeked lingering in the air through the house. No shave, dude just looked worn out from getting high constantly and out running the streets. The situation got even worse. Ben began stealing from his own family, literally wiping out his wife's account. I mean their mortgage payment and bills were literally in arrears and all behind his weakness.

As it turned out the doctor was right about her having possible complications after her surgery. Teresa began to get depressed and we began to wonder why. Dr. Sharmaei prescribed her Paxil and not an antibiotic first. Teresa briefly explained anytime that she took these particular pills, she didn't like the way they made her feel. She would cry for hours at a time. We even cried together on many nights. It felt so uncomfortable to see my mother go through all this tremendous pain, mentally and physically, but it was when she mentioned to me, "when I fall asleep I wish not to wake again to this agonizing pain", right then is what drew the line for me. The Paxil had to go and something had to be done.

You would think that Dr. Sharmaei would have shown some compassion for his patient in prescribing her an antibiotic, instead of Paxil, so she wouldn't catch any infections. Now I'm questioning what the hell is he doing as a doctor. Who the hell goes into the hospital for a major surgery and comes home without a prescription for an antibiotic? This simply bothered me!

Since the first day she came home, I was up with her through the nights, changing her dressings, listening to her cry, watching her be depressed day in and day out. These were some of the toughest times my mother had to endure. I, of course, had to stay strong for her. The first time I changed my mother's dressing, I was amazed at what I saw; a seven to eight-inch incision that was being held together by surgical staples. Everything seemed fine the day she came home. I often wondered what went wrong?

My mother briefly mentioned that she wanted to stop taking the Paxil cold turkey, so it could exit her system. The more I changed her dressing, the more her incision became soiled within minutes. It wasn't until that next evening her stomach began to reek, the smell was so bad it smelled as if she was decaying from the inside side out. "Oh, my goodness mom the smell of your incision is so bad." Instantly she began crying as I dropped down to my knees and started praying. "My heavenly Father touch my mother, heal her body and please restore her strength and give her divine health Lord in Jesus name I pray, amen."

I wasn't a nurse just yet, but I knew something was definitely wrong, repeatedly I tried to get my mother to go back to the hospital, but she refused again and again. No sooner than the doorbell began to ring she became embarrassed due to the foul smell of her wound. She calls out, "Scooty!"

"Yes!"

"Spray some air freshener downstairs."

"Okay!"

My mother knew something was also wrong. So, I called my grandfather and he demanded that she go back to the hospital, but she still refused. I refused to stop until she gave in. I called my girlfriend Aisha, who is an LPN who rushed over right after work. The doorbell rings "Hey girl...hmmm what's that smell?" As we were walking upstairs she asks, "Is that her stomach smelling like that?" After taking a look at her incision, she says, "Mom Dukes your stomach is infected" as I continued to quickly give her the run down about her doctor and the medication. Aisha became upset dialing the emergency room. "Emergency...This is Aisha I'm an LPN, I have an emergency."

"Yes, I have a 46-year-old woman here, who's had stomach surgery three days ago who has been sent home with no antibiotics and now her stomach incision is severely infected."

My mom begins crying out, "I don't want to go back to the hospital for them to have to cut on me again."

"Mom you have to go back, they have to scrape you or you could die from this infection, it's that bad." My mother was emotionally distraught but insisted on not going to the hospital. Prior to calling her doctor's office for the earliest appointment that next morning, I had been up all night trying to console her. Here comes Ben walking in as we were walking out the door, so now he goes along for the appointment to see the doctor that performed the surgery.

Dr. Sharmaei why didn't you prescribe my mother an antibiotic after her surgery?" I asked. His response, "She didn't need one." He rudely cut across me. "Teresa, I need for you to lay down on the table so I can look you over, instantly he begins to cut the staples from her stomach while my mother lays there moaning. Then he begins cutting out the damaged underlying tissue from her stomach. I had to look away in disbelief at what I was seeing.

After the doctor performed the procedure he ended up leaving her stomach open, eventually packing her stomach with gauze covering it up with a bandage. Now her incision had to heal inside out, instead of the staples being attached and closed up. Finally, Dr. Sharmaei prescribed her an antibiotic by the time we left. Surely, I informed him of a malpractice suit due to his poor decision by not prescribing her an antibiotic after surgery.

No sooner than we were done there, I had my mother back home in the bed so she could rest. Surprisingly, Ben finally decided to come around by getting her prescriptions filled. There I was lying next to my mother, praying. Fighting back my own tears while holding onto her as she cried, rocking her to sleep.

Early that next morning her hospital bed arrived at the house. As fast as I could, I got her set up in the den so she could rest even better. "Mom, I prepared dinner, are you ready to eat?"

"Yeah baby, I could eat a little something." An hour later Aisha came by to check on her too. Everything seemed to be going well at this point. The following week she had a follow-up appointment, the healing process was going just fine and she began to gain her strength back each day.

In the meantime, Heidi and Sher, my mother's longtime friend, sat with her while I went out for a few hours with my girlfriend Sandy. We were out shopping for her boyfriend's son Jon. Just as we parked and got out of the car, we decided to order some Spanish food from the restaurant across the street from my house. As we walked in, we noticed Luzette sitting by the door eating as she gritted on Sandy. She stood up.

"What the hell you doing with my son, where's Che?" Knowing me, being short tempered, I stepped in because Sandy had mad respect looking out for her man's son. "Yo, you need to chill out with all that Yahdy, Yahdy and be grateful that someone else is even caring for your son, while his dad's out there hustling. Sandy just bought a bag full of clothes for your son and you have the nerve to be buggin' out right now! What the hell is wrong with you?" Luzette says, "Whatever, just give me my son!"

Luzette started back with all the nonsense and Lord knows I didn't want any problems with this girl and before you knew it, I snapped and banged her right up against her head with the mask that I had just brought. Yeah, I probably was wrong as I look back at the situation now. But it was the three of them who thought because they were from the Bronx, we were supposed to be intimidated or something of that nature, huh not me!

Prior to this Luzette and Sandy were already having beef. The baby mama drama was truly deep. All I ever knew was that this girl was from the Bronx along with her and her coke addicted sister and aunt all trying to make it known when walking through the streets.

They hung out on the avenue where I lived, they all hustled, so their kids could eat. I mean every day these girls walked the streets as if they took over the block. It was obvious that Luzette had beef with Sandy for a minute now.

Luzette suddenly turns from fighting me and she swings on Sandy. Sandy swung back only, this time, Sandy had a toy truck in her hand hitting ol' girl upside the head too. Che's dad comes from behind the counter, "Stop fighting inside the store" as he grabs Sandy, Luzette left the store. As she rode off, she began yelling out the window, "I'll be back!"

We blew it off, ordered our food and walked across the street to the house. About a half an hour later, Sandy and I were sitting on the porch and the next thing we knew we were on a movie set because there were about six girls who came walking across the parking lot with baseball bats talking about, "You wanna jump Luzette!" As they stood in the middle of the street, waiting for someone to make a move, I stood up from the steps as Sandy sat there on the porch. Within minutes there were people coming from every direction. I can't lie Sandy was shook and my heart was damn near in my throat, but we refused to walk away from them. Luzette's sister Dana walked up on the neighbor's porch standing directly next to me, trying her best to intimidate me, but I blew her off. She kept insisting for us to walk down off the steps.

I told them, "What did ya'll come here to do, then do it? Dana told Sandy to come down off the porch. I told her, "If you want her then come up here!" This short dike looking woman who happened to be their aunt always felt the need in making someone fear her, so she leaped up onto the porch so fast climbing over the banister. Sandy jumped up and stepped back. She forcefully took Sandy's $200.00 leather pea coat right off her back. Well, it was on from there, we all started banging it out.

The plot was that they all wanted Sandy so bad they jumped her in the middle of the street as they held her head down everybody began kicking her from every direction. Huh, not one person used their bats. Here I found myself fighting Lissa, one of the girls that came along with them. I backed myself up against my railing so I could see where everybody was standing. We began tussling back and forth over the bat.

By this time, I don't know what my mother was hearing from the second floor, but you would think after all that she's been through in the past weeks with her surgery she wouldn't be able to make it. Somehow she made it downstairs, when she came to the front door she witnessed at least twenty-something people standing outside her house. When she opened the door, she scared Lissa and I grabbed the bat from her. As I began to walk into the street to help Sandy, my mom came down off the porch grabbing the back of my shirt forcing me to get into the house.

Now, I found myself being worried about my mom being safe out there in the middle of all this. Walking her back inside the house, I turned to go back outside, she locked the screen door yelling, "What the hell is going on?" No sooner than she locked the door Lissa ran up onto the porch forcing a screwdriver through the screen door trying to get at me. My mom screams, "I called the police and they're on their way."

Dana's brother pulled out a gun and shot up in the air, "The cops are coming clear it out!" They all scattered like rats before Luzette ran off she kicked Sandy in her face, it was so loud I thought she broke something. I opened the door and ran into the street. Sandy headed for the bathroom, her jaw was swollen, but she was fine. After all that we looked at each other and started laughing. "That was crazy they thought we were going to run from them."

Teresa is pissed. "What the hell is going on with you two? Ya'll need to get your acts together because them damn streets ain't no joke!" "Mom you only know half of what's going on." I didn't say any more about it; Sandy just looked at her. Now, every day before I left home my mom would tell me to be careful out there. "Yeah okay, mom!"

One afternoon my mom and I were out riding and when we stopped at a light, I thought that I had noticed the girl Lissa who had approached my front door with a screwdriver. I said "Yo." When she looked over I noticed that it was her. No, I'm no tough guy but I told her, "Remember my face because you will see my face again!" Deep down inside, I really had no beef with this girl; I just knew I had to be prepared whenever I saw her again.

Days later, word had gotten back to me that Lissa didn't want any problems, so everything was squashed. A month or so has passed and my mother's health was getting back to normal, by the Grace of God. Out of nowhere, she mentions that she would be moving to Virginia. "Yeah right mom, I won't believe you until I see you packing up the U-Haul on the sidewalk."

"Alright! Scooty, listen I want you to keep the house while I'm gone."

"Okay, but tell me, mom, what is Heidi's plans? Is she still going to be staying here, if she is then she will contribute to the bills, food, and her kids." Teresa talks to Heidi and she agrees to contribute to the house.

Well, as it looks, it didn't take Heidi long to break that agreement. The bottom line is that I did what was expected of me and I continued to be humble towards my sister. In return, I got walked on several times, but it was okay because I tried my best to get past the negative things that I had to go through with her and her bad habits. I fought very hard in doing all this alone; the kids became my main focus. I knew if I didn't stand up and do my part as an aunt in providing a roof over their heads and food in their mouths then my nieces and nephews would have ended up in a place where my grandparents refused to see my sister and me; in the system. So, I dug down deep, going to work every night pulling off third shift in order to take care of us.

There was an associate who lived three houses down from us and one day she stopped by the house while the kids and I were taking groceries in. "Scooty, I just wanted to let you know what's going on with your sister, while you're at work. Heidi is hustling from the back of the house and there are always people in and out your back door, you know these so-called drug dealers from around the way. Did you know that Heidi's getting high?"

I responded in a way of being surprised because she never appeared to me like she was losing weight or anything, but then again anything was possible when it came to my sister. She was always liable in doing a lot of things that no longer surprised me anymore. I saw her every day, I guess that may have been the reason to why I didn't take any notice. Oh, and it gets even deeper than all that!

Can you believe Heidi so boldly stole my identity right from under my nose? Originally I had a credit card in my name. Whenever Heidi decided she took it upon herself in making her way into my bedroom and into my purse. She then went online and requested for an additional card in my name. She ran that card up to $1,600 as I later found out.

Instantly, I dealt with the hassle from the credit card companies in clearing my name up. I also inquired about identity theft. It took a while, but it all was eventually cleared up. Heidi practically knew my schedule from working third shift and how tired I would be when I came in. I'd get the kids off to school, shower and lay down for about six hours every morning. Bottom line, she became absolutely ridiculous on how she preyed on her next scams. Imagine yourself just being dead tired early morning from working third shift and finally being able to climb into bed and instantly drift off into a deep sleep. The devil is always at work and determined to disrupt something.

There's a knock on my bedroom door and they knock again. I ask, "Who is it?"

"It's Heidi."

"What's up?"

"I need for you to do me a favor." I unlock the door as if I'm a prisoner in my own home. "What's up?" She says, "Can you write me a check for $600.00 in exchange for the cash I have right here?"

"For what?" She says, "I need to pay something."

Right away a red flag goes up thinking about it for a brief second. Was she being honest or just being slick again?

Heidi had obviously thought this out, she knew that I would be half asleep and that's when she would make her move. At that moment, I figured if she had already given me the cash, then how could there be any problems later. Hmmm… later on, when I got up for the day, I thought about the situation again; hoping that the situation would work itself just fine. Until later that afternoon when there was a knock at the front door only this time when I answered the door it was a man wearing a baseball cap that read Fulp Car Rental, asking for La Shana Spann. I replied that I was La Shana.

"Hi, did you rent a 2001 Nissan, Altima from Fulp Car Rental."

"Huh? No! I own a 1994 Nissan Altima" while pointing it out

to him across the street. He briefly explained, "There was a 2001 Nissan Altima rented out in your name. That car has been out for two months now without a payment being made in the amount of $600.00." All I could say to myself was o' no she didn't! He continues to say, "If the rental car isn't back into the office or if a payment isn't made today by 3:00 o'clock then we're going to turn this matter over to the Reading police and further actions would be taken." Smoke was coming out of my ears by this time.

Wait a minute maybe I need to fill you in on something that came across to me this morning with my sister then I ran it all down to him. "I will definitely look into what's been going on sir and I will get back with you. Do you have a card?" Now I'm heated! I mean, I knew there was going to be hell the minute she walked through that door!

Approximately an hour or so later, here comes Heidi all nonchalant the minute I heard the door shut, I met her at the top of the steps, "Heidi is there anything that you need to fill me in on about that rental?" Heidi looks me dead in my face and says, "No what are you talking about!" I'm past furious, sound the alarm!

"Oh, now you want to play dumb to what I'm asking you right now, so you'd rather look me in my face and lie instead of telling me the truth?" I became so disgusted just from having to clear up my credit upon her destroying my character. Lord knows I tried so hard to stay calm, even after I gave her a chance, to be honest with me. She still wanted to play stupid. Honestly, I don't know what came over me, but all I knew was that I had hauled off and slapped her so hard her face turned red. She grabbed her face walking back to her room, "I'm calling the cops!" I told her "Go ahead and call them because you're the one who did me wrong!" I walked back to my bedroom and sat there waiting.

About twenty minutes later there was a knock on my door.

"Who is it?"

"It's the police, Ms. Spann!" I opened the door.

"Do you want to explain to me what's going on, your sister says that you hit her?"

"Yes, but let's start from the very beginning," as I explained everything. He listened, and this is why you are here right now. "Okay, I see, Heidi didn't say all that had happened."

"I guess she didn't because she's the one who is guilty here, not me. I want to press charges on her for stealing my identity."

He asks for my name and jots down a few things. As I walk him to the door, I could hear her bedroom door open and she goes into the bathroom.

As I head back to my bedroom, I explained myself, "Heidi, I'm so tired of you trying to destroy me, I have been nothing but good to you and all I get is your ass to kiss. All these months you and mommy have taken my kindness for weakness and I'm sick of it! Oh, and not to mention that you keep leaving your two kids here for me to raise while you wonder off without a care in the world and of course, you refuse to help pay any bills around here!"

Ughhhh. I felt like I asked myself the question damn near every day. I loved my sister too much to want to kick her out. No sooner than I got in my room I cried like a baby, I knew deep down inside I was doing the best for our family, it's what a mother and auntie supposed to do. Why didn't Heidi care enough to be here as a family? I often wondered and wept because it wasn't easy or fair to me.

Here my sister and I have been struggling with our very own insecurities for many years and now I address her in saying this, "Heidi all that we've been through has been a trudge, but we can't blame no one now for own decisions in life, all we can do is try our hardest in making the best out of life. Be strong and that maybe even easier for me to say. Heidi, God put us here for a purpose, being prepared to be challenged and fail, but we can never give up. I love you!"

Schuylkill Avenue was the block where we resided at one time. Once the drug dealers began hanging out there, it became a dangerous territory. After Ted was shot and killed on the block, I was determined to move my family into the suburbs. Only living there for about seven months when Myles and Zoë met two young Caucasian girls who happened to live in the same building. One morning while walking to school, Myles and the older girl Erica got into an argument and she called him a ni****. I was appalled that a child of her age would even go this route, right away I thought, "What kind of parents does she have?"

The minute that I asked the kids to follow me downstairs my blood began to boil. I knocked on the door, no one answered. Later that evening while we were out, upon returning home the neighbors were getting in at the same time. I approached the mother by letting her know what was going on. She claimed that she was unaware, and then I approached Erica asking if she could explain what happened. While they were walking home from school, she gave us a different story of course, although she did admit to calling Myles a ni****.

There was something inside of me that was fired up, but I held my composure. Then I asked Erica, "Do you even know what the word ni**** means as you directed it to Myles?" Ericka had this weird look on her face not knowing what to say, so her stepfather (the bully) told her "you don't have to answer that."

"Erica, I have a strong need to let you all know something knowledgeable, Myles is an African-American kid, not a ni****. A ni**** is someone who is inferior and ignorant; you're the one young lady who doesn't know what the word ni**** means, Myles knows and understands who's being mean to him when they call him a bad name. When you use the word ni**** it doesn't feel nice. So, Erica, if I were you I would focus more on learning what certain words mean before you try using them. Ericka, I think that you owe Myles an apology." Her stepfather wasn't too happy about Ericka apologizing, but she did anyway because she knew she was wrong. As I witnessed from that moment, the stepfather was the main problem in this whole situation.

Myles and Zoë came home from school about a week later. "Mom, David tried to hit us with his car."

"What?" You know one of those moments, when you really want to hurt something for real with no hesitations, this time, around. All I can say is you don't know how hard it took for me not to go knocking on David's door with my bat. I prayed and prayed for God to forgive me because I wanted to do some damage to this guy and I didn't care what happened at that moment. I was just praying to keep my cool. As my mother would say, "You can mess with me all day, but don't mess with my kids."

Since that day, it's been like hell for me because now I had a bitter taste in my mouth every time I saw them coming. I tried, again and again, to overcome what we had been experiencing. It gets worse, my kids and I were standing in the hallway checking on our mailbox and the neighbors came in. Some words were exchanged with Ericka's mom and myself, I guess about two hours later someone was banging on my door and my first reaction was to grab my bat not knowing who was at the door. I looked out my peephole to see who it was. When I opened the door, it was David from downstairs screaming at the top of his lungs. Now there was David disrespecting me in front of my children. What was I to do?

He says, "What did you say to my wife?"

"What?" I just banged on him by closing the door in his face and eventually he walked away. Oh, you know I was hot as fish grease, banging on my door disturbing our peace. Think back, remember that time when that certain person pissed you off and all you could do was refrain yourself because you knew just how crazy the situation could get. Well, this was one of those moments.

Right away I began praying because I knew that I couldn't take things into my own hands, although I wanted to so badly. The rental office became aware of everything. I even called the police and made a report over the phone. Coincidently, the police were aware of who David was because he had just had an accident and his information was still on the computer. The police officer confirmed that he would try and get things straightened out.

I was so upset explaining what had happened to Don thinking that he would care enough to go downstairs to address it. He refused for weeks until I finally told him to be a man and at least step up for his daughter, then finally he went down. When I complained to the office about the occupants they gave me a choice of moving into another building not too far. I refused. Instead, I put IN my two months' notice to vacate the premises. Briefly, the decision I had made crossed my mind. Where would it lead us in the end?

The next two months came and I was packing up to move again only this time in with Tim. By this time, Kerry had already moved in. They married and divorced in a matter of six months. She found herself moving back to New York. Now here I come with my crazy behind believing all his lies. All the I love yous, and we can make it all work this time, all the bull because that's exactly what it was all day. I was the sucker. Little did I know he only wanted us to move in just so I could help him pay his bills now since Kerry was gone. He pressured me into taking him off of child support because we were now living together. Kerry and I both put him on child support actually paying us both $248.00 bi-weekly. He had a mortgage payment of $971.00 and every month and he was struggling to make it.

"Where's mommy and daddy now?" When we moved in, the first day the kids missed school due to paperwork being transferred from the other schools. Don's personal life was never his own, there was never a day that his mom wasn't in and out of it. When it came time for him to fess up in telling her the truth about when we were moving in, he refused. The day after we moved in we had visitor's come by unannounced. I heard the screen door open, then I heard a key enter the door and next thing I knew, it was his parents walking in. We were shocked as we sat there, finishing up our breakfast, while Don was at work.

We greeted them with a hello, they responded as if they were shocked and displeased to see us sitting in their son's house. I guess his mother, couldn't resist showing her disrespect as usual in front of my kids, as they came in and out. When Don got off work I explained to him that his parents had been by. He seemed a little shaken up, "What did they say?" They came by the house again only this time when they entered, she approached Don by actually removing her keys off of her ring in front of us with no class, of course, she states, "I will not be needing these anymore!" Don was speechless. She turns and walks into the kitchen gathering the rest of her things that she had given to Kerry and then exited.

November is when we moved in and no later than three weeks Don stepped right into his mother's footsteps in showing his disrespect too. As the old saying goes the apple doesn't fall far from the tree, huh?

Kerry lived in New York, but she would actually come to Reading every two weeks for a week and stay at his parent's house, which they all thought was cool. Don would come home from work, shower and off to his mom's he went, making sure that his daughter was his last priority as he never offered to take her along. I was upset at myself because I had allowed myself to continue to go along with all the chaos, instead of avoiding it all together. It was very unhealthy for me and my children and the cycle had to change and fast. So, I began praying to God to get me out of this rut that I had put us in, but God never said how it would all end.

Get this, I was arrested on account of Don telling my son to call the police because I actually let this amateur get the best of me. I not only pulled a knife, I completely snapped. I chased him down, as he ran off. Kerry practically went through the same thing with him; only she chose to cut the seats of his truck and dumping his clothes into the pool. I chose to take it a step further. After all the lying and cheating and continuous disrespect he had done and thinking it was okay to play with my emotions, I had to show him that I refused to tolerate it any longer. Kerry and I were the fools for love. LOL

The games never seemed to let up. As Don says, he was going to New York to see his son and he asked to take Zoë along to see her half-brother. Wow, how true was this? Don tried so hard in convincing me that Kerry had a boyfriend. I find out later that it was all lies because he and Kerry were still having an affair as Zoë witnessed them kissing. I felt like kicking my own ass for moving in with this lying, cheating, son of a gun and boy the way he did us was so ridiculous. Hey, what can you possibly expect from a man-child who simply refuses to be a grown man, a momma's boy that is?

While I was on the phone with my mother, an officer arrived and called me downstairs. "La Shana, I need to talk to you." Hell, I had to surrender to the officer wearing a white t-shirt and my leopard slippers. The officer questioned me, "La Shana you're now under arrest" and my rights were read to me. We arrived at the Ex Police Station. The officer fingerprinted me and then sat me in this nasty ass holding cell that had feces all over the walls. I was a bit chilly while nodding off and on.

After about four hours they finally decided to transport me into Reading to see the judge. Well, the day of court Don and his dad showed up. Don's mommy told him not to press charges because she didn't want Zoë's mother to go to jail.... Really! Finally, I was fed up with all his family bullshit, so again, I questioned his integrity and all the continuous disrespect from his family. It was enough to send us packing and out the door, hoping to never see his face again. But as they view it, Zoë is supposed to be satisfied just living under her dad's roof as if she doesn't have a mother. Yeah okay!

Here, I found myself moving out of Don's and back in with my grandparents, starting all over again. I was angry, but I still had a lot to be thankful for as we had some place to live and blessed to still have my job. I changed to day shift, as my grandparents needed my help. This allowed me to be closer to them, so it all worked out in the end.

Meanwhile, my grandmother and I go get her prescription from Rite Aid where I happen to bump into this broad Ali who had an affair with Ben, my mom's husband. Long story short, words were exchanged and now I was arguing and fighting with her too. I was arrested again and jailed due to giving that officer a false name. My grandfather thought one-way. He never wanted to understand that I needed support from them, even after my mother moved to a new state.

When I wanted to step out on faith and believe in my future my grandfather told me to get a job. He refused to believe in the company that my partner and I had established, "Scootymack Inc since 2004." Many have turned their backs on me, but please know that God is great and God will always do great things for me, I have faith. Pessimistic ways get you absolutely nowhere. In the words of the late great Lou Rawls and the NAACP, a mind is a terrible thing to waste. We all have family members who we look to for support, but whenever you need to lean on them, they seem to fall short on giving you the support that you so desperately need. Instead of lending support, they talk about you behind your back, which is absolutely absurd and truly embarrassing.

Let's face it, I am a part of a very dysfunctional family and there's no other way to say it. Family, when you read this book, it is my hope that you will finally begin to analyze your inner self and try to change for the better. Every day, I realize something new about myself. Being a good person inside and out wasn't good enough for the people I was around. We all go through certain things in life, but I just felt like I was on my last straw. There comes a time when you get tired of certain people taking your kindness for weakness. I decided to go after a real change for my family. As I hand everything over to God, I began to witness constant changes in my life.

Prior to this, my new business partner walks down to the corner store as I was sitting in the house talking to my grandparents. Don happens to call asking if he could come by to pick up the kids for a few hours. Don pulls up and beeps, the kids embrace me with hugs and kisses and they leave out the door. I walked back into the kitchen to grab a drink. As I'm walking back towards the front door, Don's standing outside of his truck doubled parked in the middle of the street while the kids were waiting on him. When I opened the door wondering what was wrong, he walks towards me stating, "I see your new boyfriend's in town."

"What? Don, why are you making my life your business, it's not of your concern? You came to pick up the kids so let's leave it at that. As a matter of fact, aren't you supposed to be happily remarried, so why are you still here?" He refuses to leave trying his best to cause a problem. "Don, you know what, you really need to grow up and move on with your life!" Suddenly he has the audacity to ask me while tearing up, "Scooty, why are you doing this to me?" Turning away, I walk down the street towards the store. Don got mad and drove off.

He returns twenty minutes later and parks in the middle of the street again with two of his friends just sitting in his truck like he was looking for a problem. My friend and I happen to be walking back up the street. Don proceeded to get out of his truck, approaching my friend by introducing himself. I guess he was trying to be smart and arrogant. Don proceeded on with his nonsense until we walked away. I hated to see my kids witnessing Don acting the way that he was. But I left saying, "Kids have fun okay, I love you, call me later!"

My friend would ask, "What's wrong with that fool ass Donald? Why is he acting like he don't have no damn sense? "He's buggin' because my life has moved and he simply can't." A few months later, Jane has Thanksgiving dinner at her fiancé's house and who shows up, but Don, uninvited. The whole twelve years that I have known him, he has never come to any of our family holiday dinners, but this one time, he made it his business because my friend was visiting for the holidays.

As I tried to make a move with my family, critics began popping up, like crazy. Jane, Misha, and especially Don were all determined to make my life a living hell. Jane and Misha are my biggest critics. The last time I checked, they were supposed to be family and how convenient. They constantly betrayed me by feeding Don all lies. They had the audacity to tell him that I stole a credit card from my grandparents, I committed fraud and now I'm supposed to be running from the law. This is the kicker, after reading the court papers I was like damn! Really!!!

I didn't even know half of this that was supposed to be going on. I may have been through many things in my lifetime, but I would have never expected for these two to be as cold as they were to me. My family critics have too much time on their hands if all they do is discuss me. I mean for real though' this is truly craziness. They think they're always right even when they lie. Listen there is so much more positive energy that could have been created then to be so damn negative about false accusations. When you focus less on your life, you absolutely get nowhere with achieving your goals.

Since the day I left Reading, I have moved on to bigger and better things. I'm traveling many places and meeting wonderful people. Scootymack, Inc. is growing each and every day. Honestly, I'm very happy about the success of our company, as no one back in Reading believed that it would ever come to fruition. It has been eight years since the first day that Sccotymack, Inc. was created and we're going strong by the grace of God!

I had a long talk with Tot and he knew that I had wanted to vacate Reading long ago. He agreed that we, meaning my kids and me, deserved a new start in a new state. My grandparents gave us a monetary gift as a token of their love in supporting our move to Atlanta. This gift was to help us find a home.

Now, back in February of 2003 when I began to make the move to Atlanta, Myles, Zoë and I were so excited about looking for a new home in a new state. We looked at maybe six to seven houses before finally deciding on which one we would enjoy living in. The realtor ran my credit and a $2,700 deficit was listed under my name. I was in total shock, "Are you sure, I didn't apply for anything to be on my credit. Wait a minute we have to try and figure out what's going on here?" I actually asked her to run my credit again to be certain. I explained everything that I knew especially about when my sister stole my identity.

The realtor was really nice in working with me on this unfortunate situation and extended me some more time in getting this matter resolved. Well, come to find out it wasn't my sister; it was Donald Jack who was causing all the chaos for my family in moving forward with our lives. When I called to ask him about it, he denied it, again and again. While I was on the phone he asked me if I was moving. I denied it, as I never owed him any explanation to where or what I was doing in my life. After all, he has left me with no other alternative moves, besides being this way. He threatens me by saying, "I want to know if this is when I should draw up the custody paper's to stop you from moving." I hung up. Every day I would ask him "When are you going to fax over all the information that the company requested to clear my name of this $2,700 deficit?" He would repeatedly lie to me as if he had already sent it off. The bottom line is that he still wanted his cake and eat it too, but I was so done with him and all his family drama.

I discussed this situation with my friend. The next day I called again, this time demanding an answer about the deficit. He again denies for the second time. It wasn't until the fourth time when I asked that he finally admitted to it. "Okay, Don why did you lie? You know what? That doesn't even matter, why don't you just get on the phone and call whomever you need to speak with and get my name cleared from this deficit?" He deliberately decided to take another month and a half to clear everything up.

Remember now, this process all started early February of 2003. It wasn't until late April 22, 2003, when he finally decided to fax over the documents that the bank of HSBC had requested and I still have all the documents with his name on them to prove it. They simply requested for him to fax over a written statement saying that he would take full responsibility for the $2,700 deficit that he put on La Shana Spann's credit card. They also wanted a copy of his social security card and his driver's license.

Well, unfortunately by the time he decided to fax over all the information to the bank, the extended time that was given to me by the realtor has passed for clearing this matter up and my $500 deposit that was put down on the house was now lost and I couldn't get it back. I truly believe this was all done because of the hatred that he had for me in wanting to see us move on and be happy starting a new life somewhere else. Prior to this, I told him I didn't want to have anything else to do with him. I truly think this is what triggered him in trying to get back at me. Last time I checked, it was my so-called family who said that I was supposed to have been this fraudulent individual. Huh, now look who it really is? "Anything that hides in the dark will always surface" as my mother always shared with us.

Wow, once again Don degraded himself in signing my kids' names without their consent for some BMG CD's. Seriously, it looks like he's been the one robbing me and the kids of our identity. Damn! When I approached him, he denied it trying to change the subject, of course. I really don't think Don understands how serious identity theft is. So, now I wasn't gonna be so calm just because he wanted me too, not this time around. I don't ever wish this on anyone.

Atlanta is the Black Mecca, a great city that can afford my family many great opportunities for growth. I love the fact that Atlanta is a progressive metropolitan city where many people of all cultures can benefit. The city of Atlanta is definitely a better city for my family to prosper in, anything is better than where we come from. It makes one keenly aware of all the possibilities life has to offer compared to Reading which has little to no progression and no real opportunities for development. We deserve to have so much more as a family, than just a small town filled with chaos and drama. Living and raising my kids in Reading was never the lifestyle I dreamed about for my family, it's about growth in many ways. You would think the critics of this small town would understand this mindset, but they chose to be used by the devil again and again.

Tot wasn't just my grandfather he was someone special sent from God, as we were really close. After a while, I truly felt that Tot became envious of my relationship with my partner and what we were trying to build together for Scootymack Inc. The truth is Tot only thought one way when it came to finances.

In Shillington, we checked into a hotel and stayed there for one month paying $69.00 a day. It really got crazy because none of the places we considered living in were sufficient enough, but God made a way for us, which we are very grateful for.

One day when I called to check on my grandparents, they shocked me with some disturbing news of my mother being in the hospital due to her sickle cell. It was only a few days later she had gotten worse. Her lungs collapsed, her kidneys were failing and the most devastating situation had happened when she slipped into a coma and died. The room became chaotic in a matter of seconds. The nurses and doctors rushed in. Minutes, that seemed like hours had passed, and my mother was revived. Thank God!

Once again, my grandparents found themselves worried about their baby girl's life because they have been down this road before. It was then they began heading towards 95 south to be by her side. Meanwhile, I was mentally devastated, very emotional and literally collapsing from everything that I was forced to deal with. Still, I couldn't understand how Don could be so cruel in having so much hatred in his heart for me. When my mother was on her deathbed, he and his family refused to show any compassion in what I was faced with, but it was God who gave me the strength to get through such a difficult time. God carried me through it all.

Every day I called to see what was going on with mother's progress. No changes yet, the entire time I just held onto my faith and prayed for her to get better. My phone rang and the call was coming from the hospital. Instantly I became numb, I didn't know what to expect as I picked up the phone. It's my sister, "Scooty, mom came out of her coma, she's much better!"

Finally, I arrived at the hospital; I walked into the I.C.U and saw my mother lying there. I felt helpless as tears rolled down my face like the mighty streams of justice. Here my mother was lying in front of me suffering from a horrible illness and all the tremendous pain and there wasn't anything that I could do for her, I was so hurt.

No one ever thinks that the day will ever come when you have to witness your mother fighting for her life. I mean the notion of even thinking that my mother could have died, while I was away from her, made me feel sick. I didn't think that fighting for custody of my daughter and moving away from selfish people would be downright depressing. I sat there trying to focus on why the devil was after me? I looked at my mom and picked up her right hand, "Mom, you know that I love you very much. You also know that I've wanted to leave Reading for a long time now. So, when I go back home, I'm coming back here to live, so I can be closer to you!"

My mother responds, "Okay" as the tears ran down her face. The minister from her church walks in and begins praying for her. We all begin to feel the spirit of God's presence in the room. She begins worshipping him through all her sickness, "Hallelujah, thank you, Jesus, oh thank you, Jesus, you saved me!" There was not a dry eye in the room. We stayed for hours. God knows it felt good rejoicing with my mother again. I was stressed but relieved that she was alive and going to be well again. I just needed to try and focus on something else for a while, so I could clear my head of other things I was now faced with. What else could go wrong?

There were nurses in and out of her room monitoring her for what seemed like every two minutes. Once we walked over to the nurse's station to get her progress, the nurse informed us of her intake of meals and how they really needed to increase. "We'll try and get her to eat something." When I tried at lunch we coached her on until she ate at least 75% of the meal. Teresa knew that she needed the energy so she could be herself again. We lifted her spirits and she was smiling for a while before we left the hospital. The nurses were surprised at how she progressed as fast as she did.

As we left the hospital we went to take care of business on a property we were interested in purchasing. Approximately, one week from today my mother was blessed to walk away from another hospital stay due to her sickle cell illness. Once again, I praise God for allowing her to be here another day with us. This has been her third scare with death. She had a brush with death once when she gave birth to my sister as her sickle cell took over. The following month my mother was back in the hospital again. Only this time she collapsed from her sugar level being too low as she found out that she was diabetic. She would constantly say that she never wanted to claim it, although she stayed for a few days and back home she went. There were times when she had to battle her sickle cell and neuropathy and other times when she would battle with trying to keep her sugar level regulated, but overall she's still blessed to be here with us. Thank You, God! Thank You, God! Thank You, God!

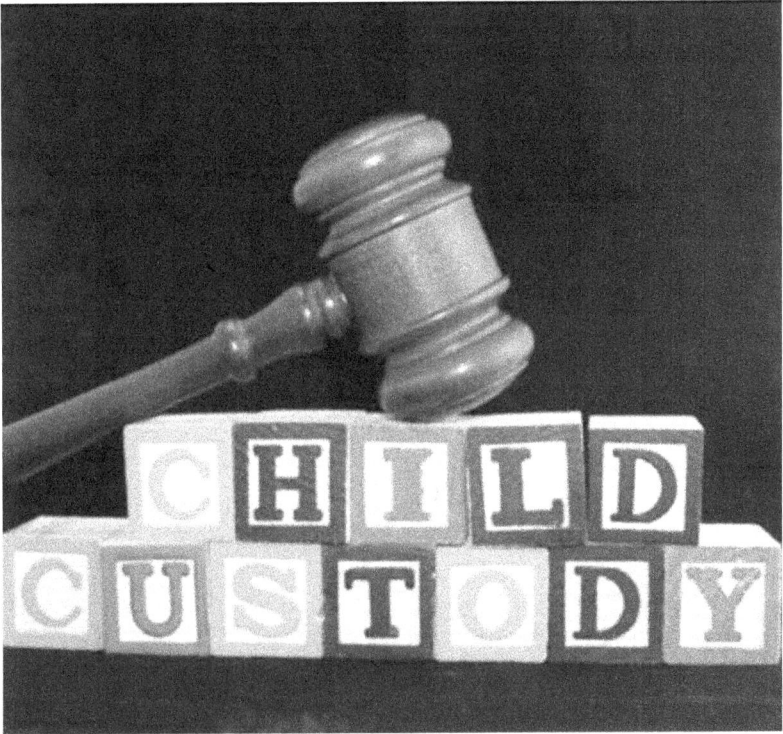

Don't let your hearts be troubled. Trust in God, and trust also in me.

John 14:1

CHAPTER 14
Custody

Just when I thought that I had an opportunity to purchase a home in Atlanta, I was forced to return to Reading. I had to endure a twelve-hour drive for a custody hearing that I was unaware of. I get a phone call from my son Myles. "Mom you have a court hearing you have to attend tomorrow. Don wants sole custody of Zoë!"

"What?" Immediately I knew that I needed a lawyer. Once I finally arrived in the courtroom there sat Don and his lawyer waiting for the preliminary hearing to begin. A preliminary hearing was held to determine what accusations were brought against me and why it was so relevant for him to have sole custody?

Days later I received a letter from Don's lawyer stating that he wanted sole custody of our daughter Zoë, due to me allegedly neglecting my kids and doing some harsh things to my grandparents. The letter listed multiple reasons including the stolen credit card accusation. Can you believe that? However, his lawyer still chose to push it in that direction. It's simple, he and his lawyer were trying to build a case against me, and so they did whatever it took to do so. As time went on, I had to deal with my name being slandered in so many ways it all was intolerable. It didn't surprise me anymore because I already knew what kind of people I had been dealing with for years, not excluding any other critic who wanted to be nosey and butt in.

What was surprising to me was how these people could sit and make up false accusations about me just to make them look good. Here the problem was extending from my so-called family; Jane who was supposed to be an aunt and her two daughters became haters too. They didn't like the fact that I chose to take the chance of doing something absolutely remarkable for myself and my children; like building a business from the ground up with an angel sent from God. While they sit being pessimistic thinking of ways to try and destroy me, we're busy creating ideas for Scootymack Inc. since 2004. Need I go any further and tell of all the drama?

In the meantime, my grandparents were in need of some support from the family. Frequently, I would go by to check on them as my mother would too when she was in town. I would travel back and forth to Reading to support my grandparents in any way I could. There are other family members that could involve themselves, but they chose otherwise. Let's just say, adults are supposed to understand what their parents are going through as they grow older and everyone should want to help out. Right! But they don't and if they do, it's only if someone complains. Then there's bickering back and forth between siblings, it's so crazy. A family of dysfunctional people is all it really is and it's so sad that they choose to be this way.

My mother is another one at times who thought differently of me because I chose to move on with my life, aiming higher towards my dreams. At the time I saw no one in the family having a dream to even call their own. They had no planning of their future. This lack of esteem within the family was enough to make you mad because you had to grow up around these people. Man, what a mind trip. Again, you try and find a way out and that's just what I did. Now they want to continue to pull me back. It's unfair that the kids are raised to think as past generations do unless their parents teach them to think outside of the box by growing and working towards their future goals.

My mother had become envious at times because I was never around whenever she came in town to visit. The way she acted was ridiculous! The fact of the matter is I have always been there for the ones who needed me. Now, where is she when I need her? Right now, I'm after something in my life that is bigger than I ever thought. For the ones who refuse to see or think the worst, shame on you. I think it's funny if you really want to know. People find enjoyment in kicking someone down instead of supporting and believing in that person who has aspirations. No one can accept the change in me and what I'm after for my children's future. As they say when someone says, "You've Changed" it simply means you've stopped living your life their way. Hey, they enjoy knocking me down instead of praising what's being accomplished by the grace of God. Just know, no one can keep a great woman down, believe that!

It's mighty strange the entire time I was going through the custody hearing, I never heard a word from my mom and I wondered why. Until one day, someone pointed out to me, that maybe I had been around a sickness of people for so long that I couldn't even recognize it.

There are certain things you must understand about my mom. Teresa can be loving, caring and smiling one minute, and then turn around and become this vile person. Teresa can push me aside, but I still find some way in my heart to love her through all the madness. I mean, I have to she's my mother and because God lives in me.

Jane is the oldest daughter definitely set in her ways. There's something evil in her too and I mean deep down inside. If all she could ever do after all these years is help contribute in taking care of her mother. Really!

A month into the case I received a form in the mail from my lawyer. The letter requested information on if and when I decided to leave the state with my daughter. This letter came at a bad time, as I was upset with no help in assisting my grandparents, and having to attend major meetings in Philadelphia. Again, it's the critics who don't seem to understand. If it weren't for my kids and I being there for my grandparents, they would have been helpless. Instead of pointing the finger, my kids became a big part of helping out their great grandparents who were very grateful.

So, for the rumors that were put out there about my grandparents being elderly and being taken advantage of is a false accusation and plainly put, "You're a liar!" This is odd to me because my grandparents never felt this way, not once. So, this means at least to me, that critics will lie and basically do whatever they feel is necessary to have someone believe in what they're saying is really worth hearing. NOT! Again, critics don't get far in life, trust me only because they're so busy worrying about everyone else's business. They continue to stand up for the same old garbage and that's just what it is.

Once there was a time when I would do absolutely anything for my family. Until the day when I witnessed them saying f*** you. Why? When I look back, it truly felt as if I had been raised in a cult that refused to let me grow in so many ways. How fair is that to my children or myself? I simply don't need it. Since then I've learned to love from a distance.

About six months into the case, the judge orders both of us to see a psychologist to help determine our case. Neither one of us set up an appointment early on to see the psychologist that was mandated in court for us. Finally, I called for an appointment to be seen and coincidentally the day of my appointment, there was a snowstorm.

"Stay home the emergency broadcast warned!"

As time progressed, Reading was like a damn soap opera, a complete mess. Instead of the people being honest, which obviously was too hard for them to do, they became dramatic. Don fed on this drama his lawyer turned out… Huh! Let me even stoop that low. The slandering of my name was continuous, "Scooty's a crack head and her friend is a drug dealer and that's how they bought their car." It's hilarious as to how wrong people can be. The people I'm speaking about know exactly who they are. Give me a break! Man, the first day I met Don's family, I immediately felt a draft of cold air and it was all during the summer! Instead of his mother raising her son to have integrity and respect in life and for women, she taught him to be judgmental and disrespectful. This was evident that I was being prejudged, it was a mess from the beginning.

It's April of 2004, having to attend another meeting in Philadelphia. I had my neighbor watch the kids at my grandparents until I got back three hours later. Jane showed up at the house while my grandparents were out of town, which she barely ever attempts to do. One day out of the year she pretends to make herself useful by cleaning out the kitchen cabinets. Anyway, one thing led to another and I commented; "Now you want to make yourself useful!" She says, "Who are you talking to?" How dare any of her nieces or nephews talk to her with such authority? Oh, now she's this pit bull in the family. I've always given everyone respect. While looking away from her talking to the kids, we walk outside onto the porch as I talked to the neighbor. I left to go handle my business. So, the evil spirit surfaced, and all hell broke loose.

Jane orders Myles and Zoë to find some place to go as she was leaving. She informs them that she was going to be locking up the house and putting on the alarm. Myles and Zoë sat there on the porch playing their games. Now you tell me, what aunt takes it upon herself to even think that she's right by trying to kick her niece and nephew off the porch. Jane simply couldn't help herself, revenge I guess. Of course, this all happens while I'm not present. By the way, Jane happens to be my son's Godmother, but this was her way of showing her love to him and his sister.

As I see it, Jane who informed Zoë to call Ursula, who is now involved and the drama continues. Ursula sends for Zoë for the night, it happens that Myles goes and stays at a friend's house for the evening and of course, not informing the neighbor. When I returned from Philly and my kids were nowhere to be found my intuition told me that something was not right. Instead of Jane doing what a real aunt would normally do, she chose to cause major problems within the family. This family has been going through crazy situations for a long time, I'm surprised that I'm still sane, seriously!

Right before I left the neighbor, a few houses away, the kids were fine sitting on the porch playing their games. In between all the chaos that happened, our meeting today for Scootymack Inc. went really well and things are moving right along. "Hey girl, how are the kids doing?" Drai panics. "What, the kids were still at your grandma's a few minutes ago. I just saw them sitting there, I only ran into the house to check the food and to put the clothes into the dryer, seriously?"

"Well, no one is there right now, the house is pitch black. Listen, I think I have a strong feeling as to what happened to the kids since they aren't here with you. Girl, listen, it's not your fault, I just have some very ignorant and hateful people in my family and they just can't manage to help themselves."

"Huh, don't we all!" She goes on to say, "Everything just happened so fast! Let me go, so I can see what's going on, I'll call you!"

"Make sure you call me as soon as you hear something!"

"I will!"

If anyone truly knows me, they know how I am when it comes to my kids and they know how much my family means to me. It wasn't until early the next morning when I finally heard from my son as he gave me the run down. "Mom, Zoë's at Don's mom's house, Phil picked her up last night."

"For what?" The phone rings, Ursula answers. "Hello, may I speak to Zoë?" She took it upon herself to question me, "What happened yesterday with the kids?"

"Excuse me, last time I checked I didn't have to answer to you. By the way, I'm on my way to pick up my daughter." The doorbell rings. Zoë answers the door and exits while Ursula looks on.

A few days later, we rented a U-Haul and began separating clothes and packing our things. But here's the kicker, prior to what had already happened, Zoë had no clue of the outcome of the phone call with Ursula regarding the Walkman that was left at her home. As we were sitting there I noticed Don's parents slowly approaching the front door. As I walked over to the door she handed over Zoë's things, looking into the living room. She asked, "Are you moving?"

For that moment, I paused because I wanted to deny her knowing the truth. Then I figured, why should I have to lie to her or anyone else about anything I choose to do with my family? By this time, I was frustrated and upset; fed up with her and all the vexed years that she caused me while being with her deceitful ass son. God lives in me, so I did what I knew was right. I reached out and hugged her goodbye.

"Yes, I am moving because my mother isn't doing too well. She's in the hospital and needs me by her side right now." Not once did she nor he have any remorse to what any of us was going through with the hurtful news of my dear mother. No sooner than she pulled off, she called Don trying to put a stop on our move to Virginia on the count of the custody case. The phone rang and rang and rang. It was this day that I refused to allow anyone to steal my joy anymore! Early the next morning about 4:00 am we were all packed and ready to pull out heading towards a new start; at least that's what we thought.

My mother takes a turn for the worse, now she's in a coma state and her organs were shutting down before we knew it she died. My mother has always been a fighter. A fighter in the streets, in her relationships and now she's having to fight on her deathbed. Where did I stand, by the grace of God looking on wondering? This time in my life was like hell. I was suffering beyond extreme deterioration as my flesh and soul were completely drained. I became mentally and emotionally stressed and hurt. As they say, God takes you through things for a reason.

Now, I find myself writing about those times as it's been a way to release all the emotions of anger and frustration all these years. I have been antagonized so much by listening to all the false accusations said about me and my kids and it was necessary to find an outlet that would help heal me spiritually and mentally. It was God who brought me to this realization and humbled my spirit. It's very deep when I think about it. I found myself feeling all alone knowing that my mother was suffering from an annoying sickness and having to fight to keep my nine-year-old daughter because of what certain people thought and said about me.

Honestly, all I could do was pray for them again and again. A tough ride, but my faith lead me through it! The fight wasn't easy although I tried my best to stay focused by standing strong with the support I did have. It's now day five and Easter vacation is now over.

The kids were now missing school due to my mother's ailments in the state of Virginia. Unconsciously, I began thinking that the move to Virginia hurt us more than it helped us. That's another crazy situation as I think back to the many days when Teresa and I had been apart for weeks and sometimes even months. Who would ever think as loving and caring as I am to my mother and others that they would try and hurt me as they once did? A day later, I got the call from my lawyer.

"La Shana did you move?"

"Yes, I did."

"La Shana you never filled out the forms to leave the state so you will have to return to Reading sooner than you think." Can you imagine as a mother having to go through such an experience? I then also had to go through a process of getting permission from a judge in order to take my child anywhere out of state, I bared down sixteen and a half hours of labor to have a child and now someone else is telling me what I can and cannot do with my child. I mean I raised this child for eight and half years bending over backward and forward for her to have a stable life. Man, anger ran through my veins like a rod of lightning that makes a very loud BOOM! Really, for this man-child and his family to have iniquitous treatment shown to me since the third day I met him is very wrong on so many levels. I could have screamed so loud in that courtroom just to inform the judge how much foul play I was up against from the very beginning. Literally, it was like being in pure hell for twelve long horrible years.

"La Shana, the judge has filed contempt against you for leaving the state without permission, you must have your daughter back in Pennsylvania by tomorrow or a warrant will be issued for your arrest."

"What, you mean I have to drop my daughter off to this?"
Goodness, can you believe that all of this extends from the day I
chose not to give Don's mother the 411 on my life which was the day
I picked Zoë up from her house?

Don demanded to know my whereabouts too and it didn't
take a genius to figure out who lead him in doing this. It was his
benevolent mother who pushed him to go after custody of his
daughter just to get back at me. I was pissed off because of the fact
that they together were trying to control my every move just because
we shared a child together. "Yeah okay, I get that!" But their actions
will never stop my determination of getting out of Reading, and I
will continue to do whatever it takes in doing so and I did just that!

My partner and I stayed on our grind just to make it out of there.
As you see, Reading has nothing to offer besides the drama. You
stay there long enough and you find yourself sitting in the damn
courtroom for something ridiculous. We needed a drastic change
and we were headed towards something great. As they say, I changed
for the worse, but we simply decided to step out on faith. What's so
wrong with that? Again, it's my faith that leads me, not the gossip.
As we step away from those who relish in the small mind mentality,
suddenly I see a change in me as I began to grow more and more. A
job is all they say I should have, but I believe in my God who says
that I should have much more.

The shame in all this is my children had to go through chaos and
being around people who called themselves Godly human beings
but were really evil people in disguise. Having to accept all Don's
bull made us miserable and unhappy for years. No sooner than I
began to move on with my life and family, searching for peace and
serenity, sure enough, the devil shows up at my front door to destroy.
Don says he can raise Zoë much better than I can. They claim that

it's a better life. Yeah okay! While he was fighting for sole custody of our daughter, he was off living in New York with Kerry, while Zoë was living with his parents, but that's supposed to be okay according to what they say.

It's so weird to me how critics supposedly say I'm this unfit mother, but anyone who truly knows me as being much different. Hmmm.... It was I who provided for my daughter for eight and a half years and it wasn't until I repeatedly asked Don to provide for his daughter, Yesss I had to ask him, he refused until he received them papers from child support. Then he cried about that. It was his mother who gave him this and that instead of making him become a real man in getting a job. By the grace of God, Don couldn't see anything else but mommy before he ever thought about moving anywhere on his own.

Hey, as usual, it's all talk. You see it never seems to really amount up to anything. Besides them now pressing me for cash, Zoë living there with them something is bound to happen, I can just taste it and it has again and again. The slandering of my name never stops and the unclassy behavior on their behalf is sad because Zoë has picked up some of it now! Later Don begins to lack one on one time with his daughter, Zoë's hurt and complains to me. I mean really! Come on, how much more incompetent do they want to look? What father fights to take his daughter away from her mother, which is totally wrong from the gate? Turns around then leaves her with his parents just because he can't accept the truth that the relationship is over? Hello, just how far does a mommy's boy get without mommy's GPS (global positional system)?

A real man gains wisdom and searches for change, not concentrating on how to manipulate two women to stay underneath him to use and abuse! Don then disrespects his daughter's mother some more to the point of making himself look good. You and your family should be ashamed of yourselves, as you have made it all too personal to truly love and nurture Zoë. I truly feel sorry for my baby. An innocent child should never have to grow up this way. Tell me this isn't unfair.

Mannnn…every time I turned around there was someone intentionally trying to make my life a living hell. Why? Scootymack Inc. was being built which no one wanted to believe in and that's okay because as they say, critics will always show up when they refuse to see greatness. As a mother, every child deserves to have a great start in life and that's all I wanted for my family. I was determined for my kids to have just that by making a move to Atlanta. Now, if I was such a bad mother, don't you think her dad and his family would have tried to get sole custody of Zoë much earlier, as a newborn, instead of waiting until she's eight and a half years old? Idiots give it a break! God doesn't like ugly!

Don was so determined in trying to show off his manipulative ways, he began to lose focus himself. Bad karma follows…the bank foreclosed on his property and that means placing him back home with his mommy and daddy. Sometimes things aren't always what they seem to be. Huh! By this time, we have attended maybe five court hearings and I had no one from my family supporting me. Not one time! All I had was God, my lawyer, my business partner and myself.

Don's in New York living with his now remarried wife. What was so odd about this was that I couldn't leave the state and my grandparents would watch my children from time to time. Don, however, could make moves to New York and leave Zoë behind with his parents for at least ten months. This is someone who wanted sole custody of his daughter, not time away from her.

There were two hearings that I attended while Don was off in New York refusing to show up or even giving a courtesy call to the judge. But somehow or another his persuasive a** lawyer shows up and the courts show us just how biased they could be in letting them get away with it not once, but twice. After that second hearing, Don had the audacity to call me.

"Scooty I didn't know anything about the hearings." Abruptly I responded, "What are you calling me for, you need to be calling your lawyer?" What the hell was he thinking? When it really came down to it, my lawyer asked the judge to throw the case out since Don refused to show up for the second time now and stay in touch with the courts. The judge refused to do it due to his lawyer addressing the bench, "Your honor, I know the family well and I will be getting in contact with someone a.s.a.p." So, the judge allowed for a continuation of the hearing.

Soon after that day, unexpectedly I received word from my legal firm that my lawyer was maneuvering and leaving my case. This happened so suddenly and now I find myself left unrepresented just before the final hearing. Can you believe this? What luck? The most important time of my life is being put to the test to see if I could come up with more money. Being in an extreme situation in a town like Reading where the deck is already stacked against minorities, meaning black folks, was absolutely unbearable. Since the sixties, Reading is known for having a different political and unethical viewpoint within the justice system. The stories I would hear are how Reading's politics resembled more of the Deep South than I ever knew.

The $4,000 that was needed for a new lawyer would be impossible to raise in such a short time. I had to find a new legal team and quick, but where would I go? As I searched for my new legal team I needed to keep in mind a contingent method of payment, which I could afford, only time was running out. The more I struggled to try to come up with a plan the more it seemed impossible to bear.

I tried to get a few lawyers out of Philadelphia, where I was told that maybe I could make a deal with a firm, but they refused to take my case. As one of the lawyers mentioned, "I'm being straight forward with you, when I say this. I really don't think you'll have a chance in Reading at all. The court system is just too biased towards African Americans. Right now, I think your only bet would be to seek new counsel in Reading." He went on to say, "Did you know back in 1968 they were lynching black people in Pennsylvania?"

"What, are you serious?"

"Yes, I'm serious and I'm advising you to read up on it."

"Oh, and I will!"

Here the courts had ordered both of us to pay $700 apiece to see a psychologist. My back was against the wall so I couldn't set up another appointment. For a brief second, I figured it probably would be counted against me, where was my family when I needed them most? Can you imagine that?

It's February 8, 2005, the big day was finally here, my stomach felt weak, but I was told to keep my head up whenever I'm going through a storm by any means necessary. Alone and devastated as I stood there, strong even when my knees wanted to buckle, I called on God. The clock was ticking away; I was late on one of the most important days of my life. Yet, still trying to find a lawyer up until the last minute. Everyone turns and looks into my direction once I entered the courtroom. Heading towards my seat in front of the judge, the psychologist was already sitting on the stand making me out to be the bad one here because I wrote the truth down on paper and never paid her a dime.

Prior to her being at the final hearing she sent both parties packets to be completely filled out and sent back to her office by a certain time. I answered the questions as honestly as I could, but as she says, I affirmatively said things of Mr. Blooper that weren't proven. Well, I can't really fault anyone else but myself for not showing up, so she could witness just what the raw truth was as it was on paper. Don's family was there for his support, again where was mine? I was so determined trying not to make myself look any worse than I already did. I tried very hard to refrain myself at the time when I knew that lies were being tossed around about me. I had no choice but to sit there and take it all in like a real woman would have done in my same situation.

George, my new attorney, called Don to the stand to be sworn in. George started questioning him in the angle prepared. "Donald I want to go back on that day when your daughter Zoë was at your sister's house in Virginia and she slept overnight."

"La Shana left Zoë at my sister's house for three days." I sat there looking him straight on as he knew that he was not only lying under oath but before the judge too. Hell, his family already knew how much of a liar he was. I cringed, this mother flower! There was nothing that I could do, I instantly became annoyed.

The truth of the matter is Zoë called me the evening she arrived at her cousin's in Richmond. We spoke briefly and she asked me if I could stay the weekend. The next afternoon she called asking if she could stay for another two days. I didn't mind because I knew she hardly got to spend any time with them during the school year. So, I was really being humble to the situation, but of course, when I said yes, they plotted and used it against me. Cool, now who looks incompetent? God is great! Now to set the record straight, I never stole my grandparent's credit card. I never wrote bad checks and I'm definitely not running from the law because of it.

In closure, to all that Don and his lawyer tried to pin against me as being this unfit mother, none of these accusations were ever brought up in court for the judge to hear. It was only written on paper to get the case started. Strange huh?

Instead of Don finally trying to show some integrity to the courts, he chose to take another route. This dishonest man-child resurfaced again for the umpteenth time and his family was very much aware, as this was nothing new to them. Honestly, it was he who set himself up to look like a liar over and over again. Anyone who truly knows Don knows exactly what I'm saying, Kerry, I know you know. Point blank, Don has lied so much in the past, where should I start? He tried to get a job working as a police officer and lied on his application saying that he never stole a thing as a child. He was never hired. Kerry has even informed me in the past of him swearing on his own daughter just to prove something to her that he and I both know is the truth, but he chose to lie once again. Oh, and this one just takes the cake, back when his parents asked him when my children and I were moving into his house, he even denied his parents of the truth. Now come on!

After Kerry moved out, he desperately came running because those bills started kicking him, asking me to move in. To all who attended the final hearing, you really expected to believe what this man-child was saying was true. You suckers! The apple doesn't fall far from the tree that's very obvious as you see. These gossiping ass people never knew my partner's occupation, so they took it amongst themselves to make up lies.

Instead of Ursula and dude showing some kind of class by personally asking him times we arrived in front of their front door to pick up my daughter, they chose to call him a drug dealer. Yeah okay! What normal person wouldn't just ask, if they really wanted to know the truth, instead of being phony in saying hello when they saw him? Gosh when does it stop, even after the relationship is over with their son, they insist on continuing the drama, but what really took the cake was when they tried to convince Zoe to be negative by having her believe that being there with them was supposed to be better for her. Give me a freakin break! Where did the word manners ever come up in this family? It's so obvious that it never ran through the gene at all. Didn't I say, the apple doesn't fall from the tree?

Why? These people chose this lifestyle, I just happen to be the unfortunate one to have to meet them. Oh, and let's not stop there! The worse thing they could have ever said about me, "Scooty's is on crack" and you know that even sounds crazy. I notice when I came back to visit, I honestly had people looking me up and down or even asking questions about a rumor that Don and his parents made up. Certain ones would run with the rumors, instead of trying to get ahead. People get a life because I'm living mine. All I have to say about that is seek God, I'm sure if you do, you will get much further in life, I promise you that. God is the only one who can judge me, as he knows me inside and out. You're only guessing that you know me and that's the truth.

The day had finally come when I not only had to deal with the thought of taking my baby girl back to Reading. I had to take her and drop her off in the hands of his mother, someone who has been manipulative, deceitful, outlandish, repulsive and extremely infuriating to me. As I approached the house and knocked on the door she answers, addressing me in a way I least expected.

One particular time that I forgave, but I will never forget; which was the evening we dropped Zoë off from spending a lovely weekend together, of course. We rang the doorbell, Ursula answers. I must have asked her for the umpteenth time, "Hello, did you ever get a chance to make Zoë a key so she doesn't have to stand outside in the cold waiting for someone to finally answer the door." She refused to answer. I kissed Zoë "I love you, baby, keep your head up because God will handle all things in his timing, say your prayers."

It wasn't until Zoë stepped into the kitchen where Ursula decided to become vindictive by abruptly shoving Zoë further away from the door and shutting the door in my face walking away turning off the lights. I had so many feelings of resentment. Ursula is someone who has such a horrible demeanor, someone who has gone out of her way to show her granddaughter that evil vibe that exists in her by trying to turn Zoë against her own mother. As I said before God is great, God will make a way for us; no matter how hard they try to rip us apart, I have faith!

God knows I forgave, but I will never forget the miffed look my baby girl had on her face because she was confused and hurt at the same damn time. Oh, and it's best that Zoë lives with them, I don't think so. I just stood there, not surprised, but furious. As I walked back to the car, tears rolled down my face, something inside of me didn't feel right. Now my daughter was being mistreated and being put in the middle of this vindictive, phony ass grandmother's lifestyle in which she acted as if she was in control now and that's all I've ever witnessed from her since the day we met. I prayed on it and eventually I became pacified, saying to myself that God was in control of this whole situation. As we drove away I became numb. The entire ride home I thought of how sorry I was for Zoë and Myles to have to go through any of this from the beginning to the end.

Only God can humble me! Yes, of course, Zoë was upset about

Ursula's unpleasant behavior. Ursula and I have exchanged words on different occasions and the conversations really upset Zoë. Ursula had the audacity to tell me, "You have your daughter brainwashed" and I told her that your son would never be a real man because of her and I hung up.

By this time the case had gotten to a point that Don and his lawyer wanted to put Zoë on the stand to testify against me. All I could think about was why should a nine-year-old child have to be put on the stand to be torn apart between two parents that she loves dearly just to get closure in a custody case. Well, it's just this simple; it wasn't going to happen to Zoë not if I had anything to do with it. It wouldn't be fair to her and I knew it, but they only thought of themselves, again not putting Zoë first, not once. I really thought this case was supposed to be about the best interest of Zoë, but that's not what was going on here.

Now the time has come for the closing of the hearing, as we stepped forward towards the judge. His lawyer had already drawn up a legal document that both parties would compromise in sharing partial custody of their daughter Zoë Blonc. She will reside with her father Donald Blooper during the school year and La Shana Spann will pick Zoë up for Spring Break, Summers, holidays, weekends and whenever La Shana's in town. Donald Blooper and La Shana Spann will meet half way to exchange the picking up and dropping off of Zoë.

Well, this document was Don's idea of how he wanted things to happen because he thought he was in charge now. Remember he is his mother's child and they love to be in control. I informed him that I would travel back and forth to pick up and drop off Zoë, which he agreed too. Once I finally walked out of that courtroom and we slowly walked toward the elevators, his family passed my partner and I to stop and talk. Ursula stops and reaches out to rub my shoulder saying, "Scooty everything is going to be okay."

God had already told me, but it was Ursula's demeanor that really had me twisted. They all stepped onto the elevator and we caught the next one down. I walked out of the courthouse dialing my mother's number to inform her about the case that she cared so selfishly about. My intuition was already telling me that there would be a problem where Zoë resided. It would be on my family's behalf that I wouldn't get a fair case, due to the custody of Zoë and sure enough it unfolded right before her pretty little eyes.

Trying to hold back the tears, as I explained on the phone, my voice became weak and I began to experience a crying spell. "Mom, why weren't you there for me? Zoë's with her dad now and something tells me that they will start acting unfair sooner or later? Why, what's going on?" Full of rage I just hung up. All my life I had to fight, but it's that one time that I felt vulnerable it was my family that had let me down. It was his family who wanted to war instead of thinking more civil. If you were paying attention then you know where it all comes from.

God is my witness since the first day. I have been nothing but a respectful person to everyone until they stepped over the line. As rumor has it, my family was never strong enough financially to move from the hood. Yes, of course, I was tremendously hurt behind the fact that Zoë was not only back in Reading, but also now the devil is at work and he uses them as an impostor to show up again and again, against me. Reading is one place I've been trying to escape for many, many years. I felt trapped!.

My family has tried so hard to move forward to another state just so we could be happy together and grow, but again you have vindictive evil spirited people who love to cause conflict. Listen here is closure to all this garbage, a man who says that he can raise his daughter much better than I can don't go running to domestic relations, he just handles his business as a real man would. I didn't know talking trash about your daughter's mother to all your friends would be of your choice to make you look good. Then again you can't help yourself, as you have to vent, instead of just manning up to your responsibility! That's all he's ever been about was that damn tick for tack trivial stuff. Just like that my crossroads changed like a bird in flight.

As Don says, "Scooty, look at your life and look at mine."

What was so great about his life when he was living with someone else's mother? Why I was living in Virginia, working on providing a home for our daughter, Zoë, and her brother Myles, where Zoë had her own room. But back at his parents' house in Pennsylvania, she had to share a small room with someone else.

Dude absolutely loves revenge. Now the fight comes. Really and how stupid does this sound? The freaking audacity of this man-child to even think about taking me to court even after I raised our daughter while he chose to run around doing whatever. He then finally decides to settle down because a sistah refused to settle with such a character, so he decided to challenge me. See tick for tack! That's his game.

Ladies, never let a man take something from you that you bear of your flesh behind a judgment call. It was unjust and plain scandalous of him. If you really want to know the truth, here he laid my ass in a bed at an age where I should have been preparing for college and my future. Instead, I give a life to a man that turned out to be a true idiot and what did I get? You got it, as behind door number three we won partial custody to our daughter. Not only did I get the third prize, I got no respect for bringing a bundle of joy into this world from any of his family.

As my days grew longer, my strength in God grew stronger. You see Don didn't want Zoë to leave the state because that meant her growth would increase. He would rather stunt her growth in minimizing it for living on a hill and calling it a life of where Zoë grew up. Come to find out Don never really wanted the responsibility of raising Zoë and neither does his wife. She states, "I wish Zoë could go and live with her mother." Hmmm... but what happen to that day in court when you stood beside your man trying to take Zoë from me? Strange how things change in a matter of time, huh! Zoë, as any child, deserves to grow up in the strength of a healthy environment. Not a bunch of drama and chaos.

Last time I checked I thought this entire situation was supposed to be about the betterment of Zoë. Bottom line, these folks have lied to themselves because they pretended to act out on something that was never taken seriously on their behalf. Pure selfishness, again Karma is something else.

As I mentioned earlier, God has blessed us with a company called Scootymack Inc. and calls for me to travel quite often. Little did I know how all this would take off, it's all God's doing we're just living it out. Again, what no one seems to understand is that God already had this planned out from the beginning and what I understand now is that God will provide for us as long as I continue to put him first in my life. It's amazing how God has lead me to meet my business partner who is quite a unique and Godly man who has a great love for many.

Failure sometimes causes for us to win. At the end of the day, I'm a mother of two beautiful young adults and I pray many nights for a new start. At the age of seven, I remember praying to God for him to bless me to be able to travel one day. As my grandmother always told me, "There's a big ol' world out there." And I wanted to see just that. I held on to my faith and right now is my time because God says so. Every day I fight for my existence in winning and when I invested my time into God, I know that I invested in a forever friendship with him.

THIRD SHIFT

The eyes of the Lord are on the righteous, And His ears are open to their cry. The face of the Lord is against those who do evil, To cut off the remembrance of them from the earth.

Psalm 34:15-16

CHAPTER 15

Whoops

Friends! How many of us have them? Remember that old school Whodini song? Well, that's the way it played over in my head again and again. There are five things I do know. One, if you can have a friend in your life that sticks it out with you through thick and thin, it has to be a miracle. Sometimes you gain some friends and you lose some. Then when you least expect it, you find those that can become backstabbers, "smiling in your face all the time knowing they want to take your place." Well, Niecy Kaves turned out to be that nightmare of a friend.

Niecy and I were like family once upon a time. You know like my mom knew her mom and her mom knew my mom, you know the routine, real close, so close all the way back to the sticks of Goochland, Virginia. Back in the day, I would go to Virginia for the weekend to see my mother. She and I would hook up and go out and get jiggy with it. We would go for drinks and whatever, but the chick was always cool with me and showed much respect. That all changed when I moved to Virginia in 2004. Niecy had taken a bad fall in a supermarket that caused her to sue for damages for breaking and fracturing her jaw. I felt so bad for her because it caused her to have to go through operation after operation and it also made her a different person in so many ways.

The girl I knew and loved had been taking prescription medication for pain, which you know as in the case of Anna Nicole, it can change your personality desperately. When we talked she had always invited me to come down to see Virginia, she even went so far to say she needed help in some of her inspiring enterprises. You see Niecy had come into a settlement for her fall, which entitled her with big sums of money. And everyone knows money can be the root of all evil. Money can also pave the way towards happiness. What I was afraid of most was to see if the money had changed her. Well, just like I thought, she became this money hungry illegitimate slick chick.

Prior to all this early on, I explained to her that I wanted to move from Reading wondering if her offer was still good. "Yes, of course, it would be a pleasure to have you down here. It will be like old times." I was assured that it would be no problem, but she said, "I'm having problems right now with a couple of my tenants, mainly my sister. She hasn't paid me in over a year, she lives rent free!"

I can't imagine why she and her sister would be going through the type of problems that had occurred. I said, "Niecy maybe you guys can work it out, I mean just maybe." She said to me, "No way, I'm sick of her." Shandy has four girls and a job at McDonalds and was in no shape to keep up a mortgage or rent in a run down, need to fix it dump. I said to myself how can you expect something good to come out of something so bad that even a miracle would only be as a bandage to a wound? It had to be more than I could see, but what troubled me so much and got me to thinking, mmmm... would the same dilemma happen to me if I chose to move into one of her properties?

I had faith and put it in God's hands and gave Niecy an opportunity as my landlord, which turned out to be the landlord from hell. She ended up scamming us out of our money that we were paying her for rent over and over. Every dime we paid this fraudulent phony business woman, she used it for her personal use, which meant that she refused to pay her mortgage on the property we were living in for years. Niecy eventually got backed up in her mortgage the first year we were there, turns out she was only seconds away from foreclosure twice since we were living in the property and never, I mean never did she inform us of anything that was going on. Get this, she even had strangers stopping by to check out the property.

The second time around she waited until April of 2006 to sell the property without telling us. During that period a lot had changed between my son and I. Myles was enrolled into Carver Middle School. The school he attended gave him a greater opportunity academically in doing well with guidance towards a strong education. It was all up to him to apply himself in working towards a great future. Myles not only let me down, he let himself down and that's what he will realize later on in life. I gave Myles an opportunity, but Myles refused to take advantage of this great opportunity. Although somehow he passed to the tenth grade, I never once thought at any given time that we would ever have to experience a situation, so hurtful as to what my son developed into.

When he was three years old, you figure all boys want to play with balls, bats, gloves basically toys, but what I found out was that a boy needed his father first and that's his heavenly Father. Can you imagine that? Nine months I carried this kid up and down steps, around corners, in school hallways where I never thought I would be pregnant so young. Eventually, it all became clear to me. A teenage child just seems to think he can do whatever he wants to do and my stubborn handsome son did just that.

He drove me crazy, I didn't know what to do. Especially, when it came to Myles wanting anything he asked for. I didn't understand his generation, his ways or his swagger. I was lost in a world of Hip-Hop, Fifty Cent and every hoochie that you could imagine. I wondered if I had lost my touch, at being the hoochie I thought I was. I mean not a hoochie, but BBW and if you want to know what BBW means it stands for a beautiful black woman. Being a single parent raising a son without the father seems as if I was pushing him out all over again. It's kind of like being pregnant but seeing your child upright and talking.

Myles started to make me understand maybe, just maybe, I did something wrong, then I felt as time went on my son had the same problem as many other African American males and minority young men share. He was scared of growing up. Meanwhile, dealing with a son and a daughter in a siege, I felt the only way that I could deal with this was to put it all in God's hands. Oh, and did I leave out my mother, the take-over artist, who was breaking up a mother and son relationship with such ease and petty thoughts that I could just scream or better yet wrap a hanger around and turn. Feeling guilty in so many ways not having the answers and making a reason for not having the answers is another excuse for leading the blind. It turned out that I had become blind and committed to using something that I never used before. I mean actually have been driven into it by pressure, if you want to know what I'm saying.

Faith carried my son and me, Niecy and Zoë' through troubled waters, so I can say that faith became my best friend because at the end of the day that is all I had left. I walked away from a troubled relationship then, in turn, I was forced into having to compromise the loss of my daughter. You see sometimes terrible things can be looking so vast and unreachable like dealing with some of the news that you may hear every day. It's not whether you can take on a problem, no! It's whether you give faith a chance to be selected as your primary relief through the problems and not choose to surrender to the chaos.

Myles has finally gained some wisdom inside a long lesson taught to him on a daily basis. In this process Niecy, my so-called friend, had lost a prime case in court against us from her behavior and as for me, I have gained a new sense of respect for my problems where I thought once, that I was the blame for so many wrongs, there were other people to point my finger at too. But I didn't blame them, but never the less, as I thought I might have, and most of all I could have if it had not been for faith.

I love the Lord, for he heard my voice; he heard my cry for mercy.
Because he turned his ear to me, I will call on him as long as I live.
Psalm 116:1,2

CHAPTER 16

Club House

Ever since I can remember, my sister Heidi would say, "Well Scooty isn't any better, the only difference is that she made herself useful and she always wanted to stand out." Heidi always insisted on doing things her way, which wasn't always the right things to do. There were days when she would have to watch me and she would, of course, walk off leaving me home alone for hours at a time, but never hungry. Well, I guess I wasn't quite alone. Our neighbors were like family someone was always around. For hours, I sat on the porch waiting for her to come home whenever she finally decided to show up.

"Where were you? You didn't even tell me that you were leaving? Pop-pop called to check in on us and he asked if you were here." Heidi panicked because she knew that he didn't play around when it came to chastising us. I mean whenever he said something, he meant every word of it. Heidi quickly asks, "What did you tell him?"

"You weren't home!" She frowns at me and walks back towards the kitchen to warm up our dinner. "Heidi, you were drinking wasn't you because I can smell it on your breath and your eyes are even red. You're going to get in trouble."

As we sat at the dinner table she says, "Scooty I thought you had my back."

"I do, but I'm not getting in trouble for you!"

For the rest of the evening, she avoided the family as my

grandparents came home because she didn't want to get a beating with his long belt.

In the meantime, our next-door neighbor Carl had a closed-in back porch, so Heidi decided that she wanted to make a girl's clubhouse from his back porch. Carl gave her the okay. He even helped her with some of the necessities she needed from time to time. The weekend came and about five of her grown ass girlfriends showed up for the party. I wanted to attend, so I asked, "Heidi can I come to the party?"

"No, but you could make the snacks and drop them off before 6:00 o'clock." All she wanted to do was use me. Now I was in charge of the snacks and I knew that was my only way in. Of course, I would have to hear Pop-pop complain about the snacks being gone as they just went grocery shopping. "Who done took all them snacks from out of the cabinet, money don't grow on trees around here!"

My cousin Sha who lived across the street from us would supply the Kool-aid flavors and the pitcher. The closer the time came for the party to start, I attempted to ask her again as nice as I could, "Heidi can I please invite one of my friends over for the party?" She said, "No, this is for grown folks!" Walking away disappointed, humbly asking for the second time as she refused again. Hmmm…I had a plan. Heidi was older than me, so I never questioned anything she said. Although, I had a strong feeling she was planning something around me. Her friends were always at the clubhouse hanging out. I hipped myself to certain times when my friends and I could use the club house too.

Carl even had an old beat up car in the back of his house that we use to sit in pretending that we were going somewhere far, far away while lighting books of matches. Yeah, I was one of them kids who was mischievous, but very respectful. The word was out for a few weeks now about Ricky and his crew having a boy's clubhouse around the corner. As I walked passed our bedroom I overheard Heidi on the phone being sneaky, "Yeah girl, Ricky's supposed to be bringing some of his boys. I hope Mitch stops by."

"Who you talkin' 'bout Mitch who wears them serious pinstriped green dress pants, damn near every Friday like it's a Sunday."

"Well, I happen to think he's cute. He has a car."

"Ughh! Whatever!"

Heidi opens the door on her way out of the room, "Damn Scooty, your nosey." Trying to play it off, I quickly run downstairs on my way out the door. While walking through the alleyway I hear music blasting, it was Ricky and them exiting a door into the alleyway. "Hey Scooty with the big booty, where are you going?"

"Excuse me, but that's none of your business!"

"Come here, girl!"

"No" and I ran off. He yelled after me, "That's right girl. Be a good girl so your pop-pop don't tap that ass."

When I arrived at the end of the alleyway, there stood my grandfather talking to a neighbor about Ricky and that loud music they were playing for the past week. Damn, this is the last thing I needed for him to think that I was trying to sneak into Ricky's clubhouse with all those boys inside. He always said, "Them boys are gonna get you in trouble."

"Scooty, where are you coming from? "The house, I'm going to visit one of my friends." He says, "Go back to the house, I'll be around there in a few minutes."

While sitting on the porch I began to wonder where Heidi snuck off to this time. Pop-pop walks up onto the porch, "Scooty did you know anything about Ricky and those boys having a clubhouse around the corner?"

"No!"

"I betcha Heidi knows something about it. Where she got her tail at?" He walks inside the house, takes off his belt and comes back outside. Thinking to myself I know that I didn't do anything, but somebody's about to get their butt whooped. "Pop-pop, why did you take off your belt?" "Our neighbor said he saw some girls going in and out of that clubhouse and I want to know who them girls were?" As I walk back to the front of the house from grabbing a drink, the door opens and Heidi walks in. My grandfather walks towards her with the belt and out of nowhere he started swinging his belt and she kept trying to grab it.

"Where you been, didn't I tell you about walking off and not saying where you're going?" Heidi screams out,

"I was at Tanya's house."

"No, you wasn't!"

"I was at Tanya's."

"Now where do you think you're going now?"

"Tanya's house around the corner!"

"No, you're not!"

"Yeah I know you drinking beer with them boys in that clubhouse, keep taking your rump around to that clubhouse, it's going to get you gals in a lot of trouble you hear me. Don't let me catch you in there, you hear!"

By this time, you could literally smell alcohol coming from Heidi's breath. He wanted to teach her butt a lesson, "Heidi, I'm telling you right now, you better get yourself together before it's too late. You better stay away from that clubhouse too, I won't tell you nothing wrong now!" Heidi was upset but refused to cry in front of him. No sooner than he finished she went straight to our room. Being the loving and caring person that I am, I went upstairs to check on my sister, "Heidi you okay? See I told you!" Heidi says, "Just close the door!"

"Heidi don't be mad at me I didn't say a word, I promise? Why do you keep sneaking off thinking that you're not going to get caught, you're crazy!"

"Just leave and close the door!"

"Huh, don't be mad at me you did it!" I grabbed my radio and head back outside.

At times, I've often heard people say to me you and your sister are like night and day, never quite understanding what they really meant until I got older. Heidi can be stingy at times, more than often. I, on the other hand, likes to share because sharing is caring, it all comes back later on. There were days when our mother would leave us money and Heidi would spend hers the next 30 minutes. Then she would have the audacity to double back asking me for half of mine too. My mother and Heidi have a lot of similarities; I guess that explains why they didn't get along half the time.

Heidi started doing certain things in her life that no parent would ever agree to. One thing leads to another and unfortunately, she's been diagnosed with the bipolar illness, which she says always leads her back down that same road of using drugs. I'm reaching out to my sister today in saying, through all these years, none of these critics out there could ever understand what you and I both been through. Just say to yourself, I will not lose, I will survive and I will persevere. Only God can judge you! One thing I do know Heidi is first you have to try and start by opening up and giving all your problems to God. It's you who will need to want to change for the better.

Reach out and ask God to come into your heart and give you the strength and guidance to get you through day by day. We all have a story that we could share, no one person is perfect! I know this isn't who you really are as I remember when we were young and I would always wake up looking for you because you were my big sister. Remember how much fun we use to have back at the Michigan Fairs. Those were the good times that we spent together with mom. I have to say there's absolutely no other place you can go, God hears you just talk to him. I pray that you can allow yourself to be right in your spirit. Look at it this way, hurdles bring happiness as long as you work at them. You can do it, I believe in you. What God wants for us is to have silver and gold as he will never turn his back on us, because those are the blessings that he's given us. It's your time now to search for the inner you. Love you!

I truly believe that we all have silent powers and it is when we make it known, our brilliance shines. When you've been unhappy with yourself for a long time, you decide on happiness, as it may not be an easy thing to see when you've been sad for so long too. You see God gives us all talents and it's up to us to put them to use. We all have to want it for ourselves and that may be a hard thing to see for some compared to the morals your family instilled in you.

Heidi's first son Levi is now 23 years old and attending St. Joseph's University. He's studying to become a lawyer. I am so proud of my nephew. He has a 4.0 GPA, runs cross-country track and field and is full of life. He also has perfect attendance and has done so since grade school. God has a sense of humor in showing Heidi just how powerful his work is through Levi since she was the one who gave up years ago.

Unfortunately, Toi and Shan's fathers haven't been present in their life since they were born. They both have been living with my mother since they were very young. When Toi turned fourteen, my cousin, Detri decided to lend a hand in trying to help raise him too. Craziness came about eventually moving Toi back in with my mother in Virginia. As a young man, he began to rebel. Since my mother and her family have moved back to Reading Toi began to deplete. Shan and Heidi have seemed to swap the same similarities as her and her mother contained, only this time they get along like sisters. Shan was a cheerleader while living in Virginia, but once she came to Reading it all began to change. Shan began to show a poor demeanor academically.

There were repeated suspensions for fighting, all due to her low self-esteem issues, she also felt neglected by her parents, which is another generation experiencing the same negative truth. As time went on things began to get worse. Shan becomes pregnant at 15. She only needed her father in her life years ago; as you know he's part of the reason too. Due to Heidi going through her battles she ended up leaving her youngest daughter Keish with our grandparents to raise. Mark and his wife Terry raised her for about four years. The great news about all of this is that Keish has been reunited with her father Steve.

Keish travels back to visit her mother, a message to my sister… Heidi perhaps your childhood memories bring you more hurt than inspiration. The voices of your past tend to curse you, belittle you and ignore you. At the time you thought such treatment was typical. Now you see it isn't and now you find yourself trying to explain your past. Do you rise above the past and make a difference or do you remain controlled by the past and make excuses?

Think about this. Spiritual life comes from the spirit! Your parents may have given you genes, but God gives you grace. Your parents may be responsible for your body, but God has taken charge of your soul. You may get your looks from your mother, but you get your eternity from your heavenly Father. God is willing to give you what your family didn't. Sis whether you realize it, you're hurting yourself and other's too, so I ask that you go to God because he is waiting on you. Heidi, I'm saying this from my heart. You need to make the necessary changes in your life today! Do it for yourself and you will see how it will not only affect and change you, but it will affect others as well who are surrounded by you. I'm always here for you and don't you ever forget it.

Even though I walk through the darkest valley, I will fear no evil, for you are with me; your rod and your staff, they comfort me.

Psalm 23:4

CHAPTER 17

Call Me LaShana

Wow! All these years they thought they knew of me, but as I later found out, I was poisoned to show up as someone else. La Shana is who I am like I mentioned before. "Scooty" is just a nickname, it's a name that's been given to me and is now being used for a great purpose. Scootymack, Inc. since 2004! Huh, makes me wonder, was it already planned? Only God knows! As I continue my journey in soul searching, I gracefully find myself taking each day at a time and living life peacefully along the side of God's two beautiful children, Myles and Zoe.

I wouldn't have it any other way. As I reminisce about the times I sat on the porch wondering and looking homely with my two pigtails and 70's outfit. I asked myself was my life going to be only based around a small town like Reading? Naw, it couldn't be! It's all God's timing. Even after all the house searching and coming up empty, I knew then it was time for us to move on, as it seems some couldn't let me go. Hahahaha…. I'm so flattered!

You could never imagine the blissful feeling that came over me while driving down the highway looking over at the kids as they slept halfway through the trip. I prayed thanking God the entire ride to Virginia. With prayer, God understood that I could no longer bear the weight of living there in Reading anymore. I'm a person who absolutely love's to grow with peace and serenity in my life because I (we) deserve it. Rather than being around negativity, I would rather ride around the world and see the glory of God. Let's hope the critics can catch a glimpse of God's grace and seek change for themselves.

In the meantime, I have gratefully traveled many places and even had the opportunity of meeting many celebrities through business affairs. While sitting at Mr. Chow's in New York, the entire New York Knicks basketball team walks in and my partner introduces me to a few players. For a few seconds, I became ecstatic until I pinched myself. Besides, dinner was exquisite. You have to go to Mr. Chows! Have you ever traveled someplace and wished someone you knew were there to witness it all too? Been there done that.

Now, imagine looking out over the Pacific Ocean, seeing mind-blowing views and silhouette mountains. The houses in the mountains are absolutely astonishing. This peaceful time is exactly what I was needing. California has some of the most beautiful people, flowers, and tallest palm trees I have ever seen. Cali just gives me a softer side of life and it's so authentic, it's like a whole new world on the West Coast that I can truly appreciate, really.

Feeling more at home as I always do while being in Cali. And really feeling more at ease with myself should I say. Many times, being stretched beyond measures and challenged often enough, I realize by making my dreams happen is about using fears and frustrations as fuel for transformation. As they say, dreams do come true. As long as you believe and strive for greatness, it will happen, and I do. Well, the truth of the matter is that I'm happy now, smiling and of course living life as I should. God's works are truly amazing!

But whoever looks intently into the perfect law that gives freedom, and continues in it—not forgetting what they have heard, but doing it—they will be blessed in what they do.

James 1:25

CHAPTER 18

My Thoughts

I am on the verge of something new. I can just feel it. I know something special is about to happen. I have spent the last ten years of my life looking back, remembering. Time has passed quickly, and the process has been wonderful. When I was in it, it felt like a painful struggle. When things happen, they are sometimes difficult to understand, especially when there is pain involved but I believe everything happens for a reason, like this great opportunity to write about my story.

For the past nine years since I have been able to make a change focusing only on the good things and appreciating life. I was constantly being reminded of how lucky I am. I hunger for more knowledge, for the opportunity to learn new, different things. I try to push beyond my comfort zones, experiencing all that is new, forever taking the challenge. I hope that this experience serves as an inspiration for each of you to reach for your dreams as I have reached for mine. I don't feel I am very complicated, but I am really happy to have this opportunity to have cleared my soul from all the pain that I have carried for so many years. I see more clearly each day and I want to try and inspire others to make a difference through my example.

Looking back through my life, I see that I am not really angry about anything. There have been many turning points and peak experiences. I have learned a lot about myself, and I know there is much more to come. My personal spirit search has reached new heights. It is my intent to find a way to share this knowledge with my young adults, my family, my friends, my loved ones and with anyone else who cares to use it. Although I'll never be finished looking back, it is with great excitement that I now look to the future. I stand on the threshold, eager for the next step, ready to dive head first into the second half of my life. At this point, I have no real formula, nothing that I can write down and say, "this is what happened and how it happened" or "this is what I did" as I finish this memoir. I know that I will continue to express my thoughts through books, movies, music, all of the above. This is a new beginning for me. All I did was pray and ask God. God say ask and it shall be given. I am looking forward to my future. Although, I miss my uncle, my grandfather and now my mother, very deeply.

One day soon I would love to finally get a chance to know Junior as my father. Most of all, I wish to thank God for everything, especially for the gift of writing. To my readers, this book is my offering. I ask for everyone to continue to pray for my family and me. If and when you arrive at the pearly gates, what would you like for God to say to you? What I came up with is this. He would say to me, "La Shana, my darling you have arrived here in heaven come on in, we welcome you!"

I have been described by my friends as loud, passionate, caring, loving unique and destined for greatness. I am ever changing and on the path of my personal human revolution. Right now, I am learning a lot about my wants, needs, who I really am, my good points and my less desirable characteristics. This is a much-needed time as I transition into another phase of my life, trying to keep my eyes and ears open for the truth, even if it hurts.

"But to you who are listening I say: Love your enemies, do good to those who hate you, bless those who curse you, pray for those who mistreat you.

Luke 6:27,28

CHAPTER 19

Faith

Remember the first time when you began to walk or maybe rode your bike. As long as you believe, you can do anything in life. God is the one who carries you through, not you. We all have our times when we feel certain things appear to be hopeless, and we are in a fight we think we can't possibly win. It's in times like these that we need to remember the battle it, not ours, it's the Lord's. A change is going to come! Just look at Barack Obama. He's our 44th president of the United States of America. Who would ever think that we would see this day? It's a blessing!

There have been times in my life when I felt that I was up against what seemed to be an insurmountable enemy. It's when I realized no matter what I was faced with, God always has a plan. No sooner than I turned my life over to God, a miracle showed up at my front door and I became free of the entire ruckus that had entered my life. Finally, there was a way out!

Sunday mornings when I tuned in to TD Jakes and Jesse Duplantis, they strongly spoke the Lord's words and we listened. Listened so that we could understand what it was that we must know in order to change ourselves by getting closer to God. They strategized their stories in ways that we can so often relate to like trusting God's time. It's a process that takes time and I have discovered that trusting God's timing often means not knowing how or when he is going to do something. I know that God is pleased with me even after my sins and is not surprised as to who I am. As crazy as this may sound I believe that I'm the apple of his eye.

Yes, I've made some fairly wrong choices, I must admit. Since then, opening myself up in so many ways in order to receive God's greatness it is what I was supposed to do. You know, it's every day that I realize what God is doing for me, even on the days that I thought that I couldn't make it. I have come too far to turn back now. Regardless of what I'm faced with today, I know that God still has good thoughts for me.

Remembering, "The accusing voice" would surface and I would beat myself up unknowingly, somehow it took control of me. It was like being inside of prison and never having the right to be free or even having a chance to breathe fresh air.

Now realizing sitting here, looking back. While living in Reading I had an attitude. I mean it truly hindered me and again it beat me up. As long as I was there, it was like a silent voice, the enemy wanted to win, but I conquered over all, the battle came to an end.

I read and thought about it long and hard. If I tried to change my mind, I would be able to change my life. In order for me to have all that God wants me to receive, I work every day to get my mind in agreement with his. So now I ask you: is your mind hindering or helping you? If you feel even the least bit like I felt in my past, being trapped by your very own negative thoughts is unhealthy. I want you to know that the word of God has the power to liberate you once and for all.

As I began to meditate on the principles of God's word, he has shown me many things that changed my thinking and transformed my life. He helped me to understand the importance of the mind and how it effects everything in my life. Since I've turned to God he's shown me the truth by thinking correctly. He also conditions my mind.

Did you know that God also shows us the dangers of having a judgmental, critical, confused, anxious or suspicious mind? Believe it or not, we all can overcome wrong mindsets that can keep us wandering in the wilderness. Think about it! If you think better, you will feel better... You will even look better... Your whole life will be better! Guess what? God will even show us how to find peace and operate in the mind of Christ. I feel good right now, I don't know about you, but I suggest that you get on board because all I want to do is praise Him. All aboard!

CHAPTER 20

Happiness

It is a warm sunny day at Manhattan beach in California. The scenery fabulous. The first time ever catching that glimpse of the Pacific Ocean... The mouth of God. It stretched for a zillion miles. Blue waters glisten while the sunset draws a perfect picture. A perfect picture that changes on a daily basis. Tremendously breathtaking, really. Come see it for yourself! I'm telling you, it's a must.

It's just something about the West Coast and how we are all dedicated to living a faithful healthy, happy, free spirited lifestyle. And having opportunities to live life to the fullest.

Back at the beach, there is always something to do. Whether it's skating or standing with the crowds watching the skateboarders do their stunts, guys playing basketball or chose to ride your bike for miles at a time. Jog, run, swim, walk for miles, watch magic tricks being done, dinner, shopping, even a little fishing on the pier too. Being a part of society just feels so great. People are everywhere just living life.... Cali is green all year round, now that's what I'm talking about.

There's something about a Pisces and nature that just fits so well together. It's sad to know that living on the East Coast for all these years and having to deal with the brutally cold weather and to know that the winter months here on the West Coast are like an autumn fall day. It hardly rains in sunny California. Wow! If you haven't seen it, I would definitely say, it's a must. Wake up people, travel and see the world for yourself. Your minds will open up! LA! LA! Where DREAMS do come true.

Honestly, if we were capable of living on the East Coast in a house on the side of a mountain on stilts, I wonder how many of us would be so daring to jump at the opportunity. Californians literally love nature and fitness. I absolutely love it there…

So, the two weeks we were in Los Angeles something about me began to change. My soul began to speak to me. As weird as this may sound a sense of soul searching had surfaced in my spirit and the harmony in people's spirits spoke to me. There was beautiful energy in the air, I mean everywhere we visited, it's just an amazing feeling and so very real.

The key is exercising, you just feel so much better about yourself when you do. It was so easy to see that, "blight was nowhere in sight" and I was so content as I could be at peace within myself. I had the opportunity to climb the mountains, Amazing! Truly, I can go on and on about L.A. But since the day, I accepted Christ as my Lord and Savior, this is now what I choose to do more in praising him. It's such a beautiful blessing. God has never let me down yet. Since then I know "the secret" and I am happy. For one minute, walk outside and stand there in silence. Look up at the sky and contemplate how amazing life really is. "Thank you, God. I am so happy for the journey that you have me on."

You know what else makes me extremely happy. Hey, just having the dream of a spiritual awakening sweeping the world through the millennium generation. I see the gospel finally being spread to every person in the world, with every nation and groups of disciples with the teachings of Jesus Christ. As I envision this, I see every little girl and boy growing up knowing they are valued, knowing they are made in the image of God, and knowing that they can fulfill all the potential they have within themselves. All of us have talents as I mentioned before, which we were all born with. As in "She Is Gifted Musically," do you think that God has anything to do with that or is He the source of our talents and abilities? Are we the accidental combination of DNA from our parents and other ancestors?

The bible answers this in Psalm 139, where it shows God at work, creating us during the ninth months before our birth. Verse 13 says he knits us in our mother's womb. Our unique fingerprints, voiceprints, retina prints and DNA all bear witness that God was personally involved in our creation. Each of us was handmade by God. Verse 14 says that we are fearfully and wonderfully made. We are all naturally gifted. Think about it!

You were not an accident. It was God's choice for you to be born. Not one of us was a chance collision of a sperm and egg. God purposefully made us. As He was weaving us inside our mothers, the gifts and call of God are irrevocable. They are for life. This doesn't mean that God ignores character to use an unrighteous person with the gifts that He wove into us during the nine months inside our mothers. No! It's not like He withdraws if you turn from Him and break His heart. You can choose to use your gifts for sinful purposes. You know, sins don't eradicate the design, but it mars it. You can use your gifts to become a great artist, a talented performer, a record-breaking athlete or a successful entrepreneur, yet choose to be selfish and corrupt. Or you can choose to seek God's will, recognize your natural gifts, and allow Him to use them in ways that will amaze you.

As you may already know God has called us all from birth. Isaiah was a gifted communicator. Jeremiah was called to be a prophet to the nations. Esther was put into the King of Prussia at a particular time for a special purpose. Paul was called to be an apostle. John the Baptist was called from his mother's womb and was even filled with the spirit while inside his mother. His calling was to be the man sent from God to announce Jesus' arrival.

God has also called you from your mother's womb. Did you know that you were sent from God as John was? But sent where... to do what? How do you find out what God wants you to do? First, accept Jesus as your Lord and savior. He will then make your individual calling clear in His way and in perfect timing. You must seize your destiny even though God planned it for you. You will not receive it passively. I found out the greatest satisfaction came when I submitted to God and fulfilled the purpose I was created for. God is awesome each and every day.

Tapping into my inner me lessened my pain, so I let it all go. Promise yourself to be strong that nothing can disturb your peace of mind. Look at the sunny side of everything and make your optimism come true. Think only of the best, work only for the best, and expect only the best. When we let go of fears, only then can we gracefully move from what was, into the miracle of what can be? I'm blessed and so are you!

"Faith takes patience!" I'm just a vessel; it's the Lord who's making all of this possible.

CYNTHIA O'DELL SPANN AND WILLIE SPANN
WHEN THEY FIRST FELL IN LOVE

MATTIE A. WILSON AND CLARENCE WILSON,
MY GRANDPARENTS

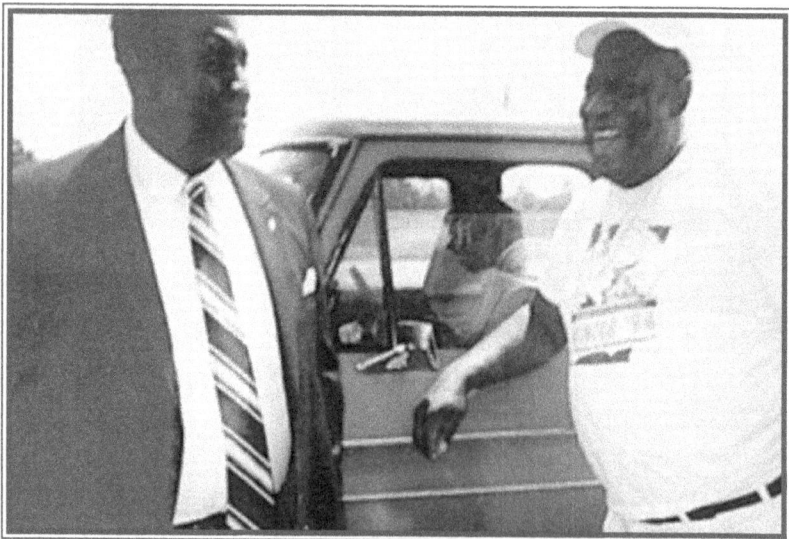

IN LOVING MEMORY OF MY GRANDFATHER CLARENCE WILSON "MY
BIG GENTLE GIANT" (ON THE RIGHT) AND
MY UNCLE CHARLES LEE WILSON

AUNT MARTHA AND MY GRANDMOTHER MATTIE WILSON (ON THE RIGHT)

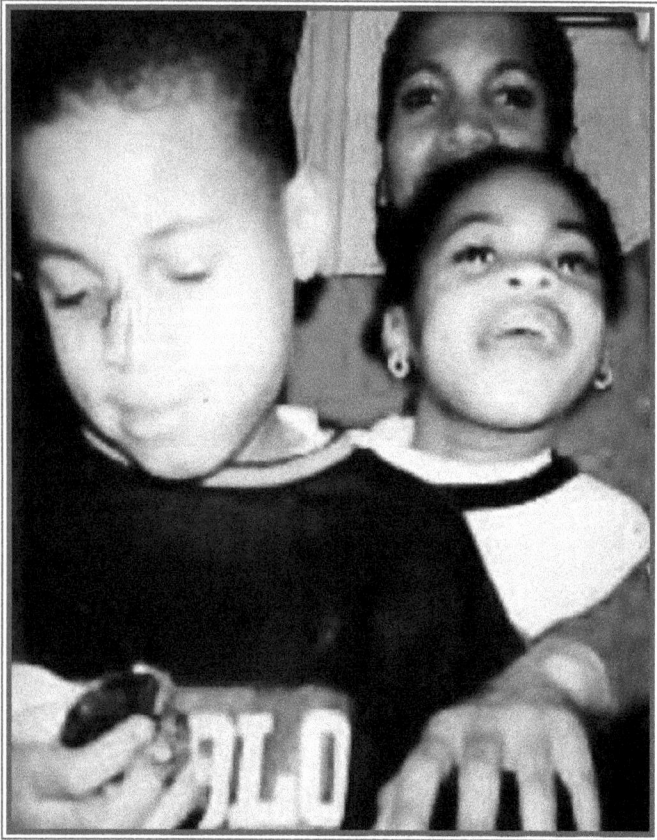

MY CHILDREN
TORSHIAN AND ZHANE' SPANN

ZHANE' SPANN'S WORLD

"THE JOYS OF MY LIFE" ZHANE', TORSHIAN, AKIRA MY
GRANDDAUGTHER FROM MY SON TORSHIAN

ACKNOWLEDGEMENTS

LA SHANA SPANN

I want to give honor and praise to my Heavenly Father for giving me the Blessings, Devine Health & Strength to make all this possible....I dedicate this book to my late mother Cynthia O'Dell Wilson, my Uncle Douglas E. Wilson, my Grandfather Clarence Wilson, I love and miss you so much!

I truly want to thank my parents Willie & Cynthia Spann for giving me life because without them I wouldn't be here. Through all that I've endured throughout your separation, has made me a stronger person and I love you still. The heartfelt love that I have for my Grandparents Clarence & Mattie Wilson for their unconditional love and support all these years!

I want to thank my young adults (my babies) Tor Shian & Zhane' Spann for their strong love and support along this journey when we had our many days, nights and hours apart, putting God first, He got us through it all. I'm so humble and grateful for His love and grace. The strength and love we have for one another no one will ever break! I love you very much for believing in me when others didn't!

I want to thank God for sending a special person in our lives who believes, cares and loves for so many, McKinley Horton, even when I didn't want to believe in myself after all the turmoil in my life, you encouraged me that GOD doesn't make any mistakes. I went through all I've experienced for a greater reason. Just BELIEVE! God may not come when you want HIM to, but He's ALWAYS on time. HE'S an on-time GOD! McKinley, you are truly always there for me and my family and that means the world to us, *(~_~)* Angel face is Smiling down!

McKinley James Horton Jr.

I want to thank our agent Bill Gladstone for believing in "The Third Shift" and giving us such a great opportunity as our publisher and friend at Waterside we thank you. Also, Mieke Roovers, thank you for your introduction to Waterside we are truly grateful and blessed. Also, James Shapiro for being the best partner anyone could have. God is the reason why we are here and James Shapiro was a blessing of God to keep us here, thank you man, and I won't forget our favorite word. ShaMack for life!!! Greg Garner our graphic designer who created our cover for the book. Thank you, man. And to my friend Beryl Wolk who gave a Wharton education. Thank you!

And to my parents McKinley and Edna Horton who introduced me to my Rabbi, Jesus the Christ and his Father who has the whole world in his hands. And my people who help me understand that everyone has the Third Shift. My children Christian, Dominique, Julian, Isaiah, Olivia and if I left anyone out please email at scootymack2004@aol.com and let me know who you are. By the way, without God and my brother Lorenzo Horton I would not have understood "The Third Shift". Meaning, that he loved me through my shifts of life and I miss him. We dedicate this book to the parents of Trayvon Martin and Hadiya Pendleton who lost their children. And to millions around the world searching for harmony and joy. Never stop to seek God's wisdom because some souls will never see their third shift because of senseless violence! "And to all of God's babies all over the world who have faced some form of abuse we lift your names to the heavens and through the communities to never forget!"

L a Shana Spann was born in Reading, Pennsylvania in 1973 to Willie Spann and Cynthia Spann. Early years of her life was based on moving from home to home, but her dreams and energy made her stronger in having to endure the unfair turn of events that would shape her life. Not having a father to grow and love, she turned to her Grandfather and Grandmother for moral and spiritual love and help.

La Shana was violated by a family member early years of her life, which led her to experience emptiness and trust. She recovered it in finding her Lord and Savior Jesus Christ at the St James church in Reading Pa. This is where her life got put back together for her to strive and to go forth. She had a passion for helping others and being a nurse, but motherhood would step in and place another challenge in her path. Most people would have let that stop them at such an early age of peer pressure. But La Shana, she would quote, "I refuse to let having a child at an early age get in the way of pursuing my dreams, I shall be a woman and honor my God" in that time period it was much tougher than it is today to have a baby.

No MTV shows to rock people about children. The choice was hers to have a baby or abort, she chose life. And in life, we learn that La Shana could accomplish her dream and beyond! Even though life can be hard, she made her mark for a better world. "The Third Shift", an autobiography by former nurse La Shana Spann depicting one woman's lifelong journey against the odds.

Beginning his professional music career as a teen, McKinley Horton first played keyboards and toured for several years with Harold Melvin and his legendary group The Blue Notes. Now, a veteran music producer and songwriter, McKinley has created such hits as Vanessa Williams' smash "Dreamin" and "Gotta' Get You Home Tonight." He is a collaborator of legendary music producers Jimmy Jam, Terry Lewis, Organized Noise, Sleepy Brown & Outkast, TLC, Foxy Brown, Cee-Lo Green and countless other industry giants. His talents have also contributed to hit film soundtracks for such features as "Shaft2000," "Snakes On The Plane," "Miami Vice" for Michael Mann and "Money Train."

Today, McKinley is benchmarking his success in the music world to expand more creatively into Television and Film, Music Licensing, and Book publishing. He most recently co-authored a book "The Third Shift" with La Shana Spann and continues to build successful brands. He also is Chief Operating Officer for Shamack Pictures which is currently in pre-production for the upcoming movie The GhostDancer. The legendary director Penny Marshall and McKinley Horton, as well as the talented Benny Boom, are working together on this project.